JOHN P. HALE

AND THE POLITICS OF
ABOLITION

JOHN P. HALE
AND THE POLITICS OF
ABOLITION

Richard H. Sewell

HARVARD UNIVERSITY PRESS

Cambridge, Massachusetts

~ 1965 ~

Distributed in Great Britain by Oxford University Press, London

Publication of this book has been aided by a grant from the Ford Foundation

Printed in the United States of America

Library of Congress Catalog Card Number 65-13849

TO MY
MOTHER AND FATHER

Preface

THE antislavery crusade brought John P. Hale both triumph and tragedy. Although conviction, not self-interest, carried him into the abolitionist camp, without the national crisis over slavery Hale would doubtless have passed his life as a lackluster politician from New Hampshire. His special talents perfectly suited the needs of political antislavery in its early phase; moderate yet firm in his abolitionism, he battled with skill, wit, and determination against great odds. In so doing, he heartened antislavery advocates and won a respected place at their head.

Yet, ironically, as the antislavery movement grew stronger, Hale's position in it weakened. The very qualities which made him an admirable minority spokesman prevented his giving constructive leadership to a party in power. Ever distrustful of partisanship and compromise, schooled in the arts of opposition, Hale inevitably lost prominence to more malleable, politically ambitious men. Well before the war against slavery had been won, therefore, Hale found himself shouldered aside, left to brood over disappointments and defeats. At the time of his death in 1873 he had already passed from the public's eye, and by the close of the century Thomas Wentworth Higginson (concerned, no doubt, with the permanence of his own fame as an abolitionist) regretted that "there is scarcely an American under thirty who is familiar with the name of John P. Hale, whom Garrison called 'the Abdiel of New Hampshire.'"

Historians have acquiesced in Hale's eclipse. Until now there has been no more complete biography of this once-influential senator than William A. Robinson's brief sketch in the *Dictionary of American Biography*. If they mention him at all, textbooks and monographs seldom say more of Hale than that he was the woefully unsuccessful Free Democratic candidate for President in 1852 or that he once so enraged Senator Henry S. Foote that the excitable Mississippian promised him a lynching if ever he came to the South.

While recognizing the exaggeration in Garrison's appellation (Garrison himself often applied less flattering parallels), I have tried to restore Hale to his proper standing among nineteenth-century politicians and reformers. In many ways he is *sui generis*. His political independence, his seeming indifference to social status, his broad wit—even his indolence—set him apart from most other antislavery politicians. Yet for all his uniqueness, Hale is representative of those abolitionists who sought to destroy slavery with political weapons, without doing violence to the Constitution. As such, his life assumes a larger dimension.

Since political abolitionism meant attacking a fundamentally moral issue with legalistic weapons, its advocates drew fire not only from Southerners and their "doughfaced" Northern allies, but also from within the antislavery movement itself. During the 1840's and 1850's abolitionists of the Garrisonian stripe often denounced antislavery congressmen for their moderation and accused them of compromising with the devil slavery. Free Soil and Republican politicians insisted, however, that they had compromised only to the extent of accepting the work of the Founding Fathers and of maintaining the dialogue with the Slave Power. Only the South's refusal to do as much—to work within the Constitution for redress of grievances, to accept the decision of the ballot-box—disrupted the dialogue and brought Civil War.

Such was Hale's position. Less vitriolic than Garrison, less brilliant than Sumner, less astute than Lincoln, he nonetheless distinguished himself as a pioneer abolitionist whose reasonableness and good humor tempered but did not blunt his attacks on slavery.

Ann Arbor, Michigan　　　　　　　　　　　　　　　　*Richard H. Sewell*
October 29, 1964

Acknowledgments

This book would never have been written without the encouragement and assistance of many persons. It is a pleasure to acknowledge my debt to some of them here.

Three busy historians generously took time from their own studies to read and criticize my entire manuscript: Frank Freidel, Harvard University, shared with me his special knowledge of political biography and gave encouragement when it meant most; Frank O. Gatell, University of Maryland, a model critic, improved this book in many ways; and Richard H. Brown, Northern Illinois University, labored (I hope with some success) to enlarge my point of view. For the errors and short-comings that remain, I have only myself to blame.

I am grateful as well to William R. Taylor, University of Wisconsin; Thomas Stirton, Long Island University; Tilden Edelstein, Simmons College; and Arthur Kaledin, Massachusetts Institute of Technology; all of whom read parts of the manuscript and offered helpful criticism.

Special thanks go to Philip N. Guyol, formerly director of the New Hampshire Historical Society, and to his assistant, Marcel L. Pittet, who did everything within their power to make my research trips to Concord pleasant and profitable. Rodney Armstrong, librarian of Phillips Exeter Academy, graciously helped me to reconstruct the Exeter of Hale's day.

I am indebted to John Parker Hale Chandler, Jr. of Warner, New Hampshire, for permission to quote from his great-grandfather's letters. Finally, I thank the Adams Manuscript Trust for allowing me to quote from the Diary and Papers of Charles Francis Adams, and the editor of *The New England Quarterly* for permission to reproduce material in Chapter VI which originally appeared in that journal.

R. H. S.

CONTENTS

Chapter   I ~ Beginnings   1

Chapter   II ~ Political Apprenticeship   13

Chapter   III ~ Democratic Congressman   36

Chapter   IV ~ The "Hale Storm"   52

Chapter   V ~ Fruits of Coalition   68

Chapter   VI ~ A Reluctant Candidate   86

Chapter   VII ~ "The Place of an Ishmaelite"   105

Chapter VIII ~ Crisis and Compromise   123

Chapter   IX ~ Law, Lyceums, and Free Soil   144

Chapter   X ~ The Coming of the Civil War   163

Chapter   XI ~ Radical Republican   191

Chapter   XII ~ An American in Spain   224

              A Note on Sources   237

              Manuscripts Cited   240

              Notes   243

              Index   283

JOHN P. HALE

AND THE POLITICS OF
ABOLITION

CHAPTER I

Beginnings

O N the afternoon of May 5, 1853, nearly 1500 men and women crowded into Boston's cavernous Fitchburg Railroad depot to pay tribute to John Parker Hale, lately United States senator from New Hampshire and Free Democratic candidate for President. Promptly at 2:15 the portly and jocular guest of honor entered and, as the band struck up a rousing tune, mounted a raised platform in company with the master of ceremonies, John G. Palfrey. Among those on hand on this festive occasion were distinguished representatives of nearly every shade of antislavery belief: William Lloyd Garrison, Ralph Waldo Emerson, Theodore Parker, Thomas Wentworth Higginson, Charles Sumner, Richard Henry Dana, Jr., Samuel Gridley Howe, Joshua Leavitt, Henry Wilson, and Charles Francis Adams.

After a short prayer, Francis Underwood presented the first of many ice-water toasts:

Our Guest, John P. Hale—In the House of Representatives, party could not command his allegiance in the commission of national iniquity. In the Senate, the insolence of majorities could never awe him to silence. As an advocate, he has added to the jurist the merit of successful resistance to executive and judicial tyranny. As the champion of the principles of the Free Democracy—

"Our hearts leap forth to answer
And echo back his words,
As leaps the warrior's when he sees
the flash of kindred swords."

Hale's modest denigration of his own "poor efforts" in no way stemmed the flood of praise which followed. Cassius M. Clay, the colorful Kentucky abolitionist, spoke of Hale as "the great leader" of the antislavery crusade, and Horace Mann pointed approvingly to his humanitarian reform of naval punishments. Even Garrison, warmed by this grand display of antislavery feeling, unbent enough to declare that whatever "may be our peculiar views as to the best measures to be adopted . . . [to free the slave] one thing is true here— we are all 'Hale fellows!'" It was 9 o'clock before the last of the cheers died away and the guests stepped into the soft spring night.[1]

The celebration at Boston marked the high point of Hale's career as an antislavery advocate, a career which took its color and flavor from family influences as well as from the course of events in antebellum America. Like so many other abolitionists, Hale came from old New England stock. Robert Hale, an intelligent and public-spirited blacksmith who crossed the Atlantic in 1632 as part of the Great Migration, was the first to bear the family name to the New World. Settling initially in Boston, he soon moved to Charlestown. His eldest son, John, graduated in 1657 from Harvard College, entered the ministry soon after, and went to Beverly, Massachusetts, as minister of the new First Church. Later John Hale won modest fame as chaplain in Sir William Phips' expedition against Canada (for which his heirs received 300 acres in Methuen) and as an instigator of the witch trials of 1692.[2]

Subsequent generations moved first to Newburyport; then to Portsmouth, New Hampshire; and finally back to Gloucester, Massachusetts, where John P. Hale's grandfather Samuel was born in 1745, the eldest of six children. Like his great-grandfather, Samuel had the advantage of a Harvard education, but unlike him he chose to enter the law rather than the ministry. After his graduation from Harvard in 1766, Samuel Hale moved to Portsmouth, New Hampshire, where he began practicing a few years later. He sat for many years in the colonial assembly, and in 1772 the Crown appointed him to the Superior Court of New Hampshire. An outspoken defender of royal authority in America, he watched with alarm the colonists' bold defiance of king and Parliament. Once hostilities broke out, Samuel left his home in Portsmouth and sought British protection. Soon thereafter he returned to England, leaving behind his wife and only son, John Parker Hale, father of the future United States senator. At the end of the Revolution, Samuel Hale received an appointment as consul in one of the American ports, but died during the Atlantic voyage.[3]

John P. Hale, Sr. grew up in Portsmouth where his uncle, "Sheriff" John Parker, looked after him and his mother Lydia. As soon as he was old enough, he entered the office of another uncle, John Hale, to prepare for a legal career. By the time he was twenty-one he was ready to begin practice on his own. After brief residence in Portsmouth and Barrington, he established himself in nearby Rochester and married Lydia O'Brien of Machias, Maine. There, on March 31, 1806, the second John Parker Hale was born.

The two were to have more than just a name in common. John P. Hale, Sr. was a hearty, stocky, good-natured man, popular with all who knew him. Possessed of a quick and ready wit, a sonorous voice, and a pleasing manner, he was an effective if sometimes slapdash lawyer. The story is told that on more than one occasion "Jack" Hale entered court totally unprepared, learned the names of the parties and the nature of the action from the recital of the writ, the facts from the opening statement to the jury, and then extemporaneously spun an argument so beguiling that the jury returned a verdict in favor of his client! In religion the senior Hale was a devout Congregationalist; in politics he was a confirmed Federalist. He liked nothing better than to join his Rochester cronies and, over glasses of ale, curse the "dambargo" or "Mr. Madison's war." He looked to men like Jeremiah Mason and Daniel Webster to protect the settled world of seaboard New England from Western mobs and Southern "infidels." But the world of the father was already in flux. The new order—or disorder—would differ markedly from the old. So too would the life of the second John P. Hale differ from that of the first.[4]

John's youth was much like that of most New Hampshire boys. At first his playmates were the boisterous brothers and sisters whom Lydia Hale delivered with remarkable regularity. Later his circle widened to include other youngsters in his neighborhood. When he was five or six his father, a member of Rochester's first superintending school committee, enrolled him in grammar school. Active and fond of sport, John was highly popular with his schoolmates. His teachers found him courteous, alert, quick to learn.[5] At home young Hale, his brothers and sisters (there was an even dozen by 1819) lived free from care under the benevolent rule of a father who, despite irregular earnings and free-spending ways, proved a good provider.[6]

All this changed abruptly when, in 1819, John P. Hale, Sr. suddenly died, leaving his widow and thirteen young children to shift for themselves. Without savings to fall back on, the Hales turned to relatives for support. Mrs. Hale sold their house in Rochester, packed the family belongings, and moved to Eastport, Maine, to be nearer her own kin. In 1822 she set up a home for boarders on nearby Moose Island, keeping some of the younger children with her, and sending the others to live with the O'Briens in Machias. In the meantime she had determined that despite the sacrifice it would entail, her oldest son should receive a first-rate education, and in 1820 she enrolled fourteen-year-old John in Phillips Exeter Academy.[7]

Exeter, founded in 1781, had since 1788 been directed by its capable headmaster, Benjamin Abbot, a benign if rather stiff old man who held the respect of all and the love of many of his students. Assisting him in the demanding task of schooling and disciplining the seventy-odd boys and young men annually enrolled in the Academy were two professors and one instructor. In 1820 all classes still met in the squarish Georgian building on Front Street constructed in 1794. Students boarded in homes nearby. There were altogether thirty-seven students who entered Exeter for the first time in 1820. Of them, some, like Hale, took courses in the classics department preparatory to college; others undertook an established course of English study. In his three years at Exeter, Hale received a solid classical education: Latin, geography, and arithmetic in his first year; Latin, Greek, Roman history, English grammar and declamation in the second; algebra, Latin, Greek, and English studies in the third.[8]

He was a competent though not brilliant scholar, much liked by his fellows. One student remembered him as "a droll, good-natured wit, full of fun and mischief."[9]

When, in 1823, Hale graduated from Exeter, he had already made up his mind to enter Bowdoin College. Though Exeter sent more of its graduates to Harvard than to any other college, for a New Hampshire youth of limited means, the choice quickly narrowed to Dartmouth or Bowdoin. The enthusiastic reports of his cousin William Hale, in 1823 a sophomore at Bowdoin, may have colored Hale's choice, or he may simply have wanted to be closer to his family. At any rate, after an uneventful summer he boarded a stage for Brunswick, Maine, where, after having presented certificates of his "good moral character," and having satisfied college officers of his proficiency in Latin, Greek, geography, and arithmetic, he was officially admitted to the class of 1827.[10]

Less than a quarter century before, strong men with sharp axes had cleared a few acres in the thick pine forest which covered the plain south of Brunswick. On the ground thus cleared they erected two Georgian brick buildings. Massachusetts Hall, nearly square and three stories high, which dominated the north end of the campus, doubled as laboratory and art museum. Maine Hall, built in 1807, provided rooms for students and space for recitation. There was, in addition, a small, unpainted and unheated wooden chapel, and by the time of Hale's arrival in 1823 there had been added a two-story wooden-frame library and New College, another red-brick dormitory, completed only the year before. An easy walk from the campus, nearer the rushing Androscoggin River, lay Brunswick, then a prosperous lumbering town.[11]

Amid these strange surroundings, Hale found some familiar faces. Of the thirty-one other entering freshmen, five had been his classmates at Exeter. Earlier Exeter graduates, now Bowdoin upperclassmen (his cousin William among them) also stopped by his room at 8 Maine Hall to say hello and, no doubt, to offer that friendly if gratuitous advice which freshmen soon learn to accept in good grace. Hale quickly expanded his friendships beyond this nucleus of Exeter chums. In February he moved to New College to be with John Hodgdon, a talented and well-to-do Quaker, but during that first term in Maine Hall he must have met a slender, open-faced youth from Hillsborough, New Hampshire, then in his last year at Bowdoin—Franklin Pierce. A close friend of Pierce and a frequent visitor to his room, a few doors from Hale's, was the shy and sensitive Nathaniel Hawthorne. Hale also came to know Hawthorne's classmate, Henry Wadsworth Longfellow, already giving flashes of poetical brilliance, who lived next door in New College during the spring of 1825.

At Bowdoin, as at Exeter, Hale's academic performance was competent if undistinguished. Dr. Abbot had done his job well at Exeter; Hale's sound preparation in the classics permitted him to acquit himself creditably despite an inclination toward dissipation. A quick mind and an excellent memory enabled him to get by with a minimum of preparation, a course he all too often took. In recitation he sometimes amused his fellows and distressed his instructors, as when in Professor Alpheus Spring Packard's Latin class he translated *dimidium facti, qui coepit habet* (well begun is half done) as "well lathered is half shaved." [12] Hale was, a classmate recalled many years later, "by far our most prompt and fertile debater. He had a passion for mock law cases and for making speeches, but he was no student; and his habits were so careless and indolent that I think his classmates did not anticipate for him the distinction he has gained." [13] Student debates were, indeed, events perfectly suited to Hale's special talents. Possessing a strong, pleasing voice, a facile mind which functioned well under pressure, and a keen dramatic sense, he delighted in all forms of public speaking. His greatest satisfaction, a schoolmate shrewdly noted in 1825, was "to *spout* before an awe struck assembly." [14]

This fondness for debate largely explains Hale's active role in the Athenaean Society, a society "formed for private and social intercourse; for forensic and extemporary disputation; and for literary and scientific improvement." [15] The Athenaean was the younger of two such societies at Bowdoin in the 1820's. The other, Peucinian, was more "aristocratic" in its membership and was favored by the professors. The Athenaean, said Hawthorne, was more "progressive or democratic," and under the lead of Franklin Pierce showed strong Jacksonian preferences. Still following in the path of his cousin William, Hale overcame his Federalist predilections and while a freshman accepted election to the Athenaean Society. He at once immersed himself in the society's affairs. Other members found him a cheerful, sympathetic, able companion, and chose him as their president during his junior year.[16]

Between meetings of the Athenaean Society, Hale, like other Bowdoin undergraduates, savored the pleasures of secret, informal fellowship. Ward's Tavern, a short walk from the college grounds, was the scene of many a raucous student party, and Hale joined the others in wine, cards, and loud song. Nearby general stores also sold "wet" as well as dry-goods which Hale and his companions smuggled into their rooms in "lamp-fillers" that had never known oil. "Hale was brim full of fire & liquor and afforded us much amusement—his wit was broad & coarse—almost buffoonery," one comrade reminisced many years later. "It was impossible to offend him so easy & happy was his temper." Clearly at this period of his life Hale and Demon Rum were anything but the resolute enemies they later became. Other, more innocent, pleasures might be easily had. For the patient angler, nearby brooks and the Androscoggin itself yielded up trout, salmon, and perch. On three sides of Bowdoin's campus stretched the beautiful pine forest where students might take quiet walks, flush squirrels and rabbits, and, in the summer, feast on the bountiful blueberries.[17]

These were happy years for Hale. Commencement came all too soon. And with it came the need to find a job. For a time he toyed with the idea of going to the West to seek his fortune.[18] Later he considered teaching school in New England.[19] But by July 1827 Hale had, for one reason or another, decided to join the profession of his father and his grandfather. He applied at first to read law with David Barker, Jr., who had once studied with his father, but when he found that another student had already been promised the sole vacancy, Hale gratefully accepted an offer to clerk for Jeremiah Hall Woodman. An old friend of Hale's father, Woodman was one of Rochester's staunchest foes of Jeffersonianism.[20]

After about a year with Woodman, Hale moved to neighboring Dover to continue his legal training in the office of Daniel M. Christie. Whatever prompted him to make this change, he had no cause to regret it. Dover, the Strafford County seat, was a bustling, burgeoning town whose population nearly doubled between 1820 and 1830, making it twice as large as Rochester. Numerous textile mills, already beginning to cluster on the banks of the swift-moving Cocheco River, which cut through the center of town, would soon bring Dover unprecedented prosperity. As shire town, Dover was the center of judicial activity for all of Strafford County. From faraway Chatham, Conway, and Albany; from Tamworth, Effingham, and Ossipee; from Farmington, Strafford, and Rochester came jurists to Dover's historic red-brick courthouse to argue their cases. There Daniel Webster, Jeremiah Mason, Ichabod Bartlett, and other titans of the New Hampshire bar had matched grandiloquent rhetoric and haggled over points of law. Few other New Hampshire towns offered an ambitious young attorney such opportunities for professional and political advancement.

Perhaps most influential in Hale's decision to remove to Dover was his desire to study under Christie. Then in his late thirties, Christie had for ten years been practicing in Dover and had already laid the foundations of a legal reputation unsurpassed in New Hampshire. Honest and hardworking like so many of his Scotch-Irish ancestors, Daniel Christie was thoroughly grounded in the law as were few other men of his day. He was as adept in the courtroom as he was in the preparation of briefs. For Christie law was very nearly life itself. "His work and his play were both found in the law," recalled a fellow barrister. "He indulged in no sports and in no idleness; he read little, if anything, unconnected with his profession; he had no fancy for society; he never speculated; he had no 'fads.'" Though never covetous of political office, Christie had in 1826 represented Dover in the state legislature, and about the time Hale entered his office, President John Quincy Adams rewarded his outspoken support with the district attorneyship for New Hampshire. During the months in which Hale completed his study of law under Christie's close supervision the two men established a friendship which lasted throughout Hale's lifetime, although in later years they often fought on opposite sides in legal and political battles.[21]

In August 1830 Hale passed the New Hampshire bar examination and entered on a practice of his own. His many years in Strafford County, his valuable associations with Woodman and Christie, had given local currency to Hale's name, and he soon had a thriving practice, not only in Strafford, but in neighboring counties as well. As a lawyer, Hale was more like his father than like either of his mentors. Despite the attentions of Woodman and Christie, he was never especially learned in the law, and though he never entered court with as little advance preparation as the senior John P. Hale often had, he was not at his best when it came to legal research and the drafting of briefs. What made him successful before the bar—and he was successful—was that he possessed a natural courtroom sense, a tact, self-control, and eloquence which juries found most persuasive. Hale's was a straightforward, commonsense approach that jurors understood. Masterfully he mixed humor and wit with pathos and righteous indignation, playing skillfully upon the emotions of those who sat in judgment. He carried in his mind a seemingly bottomless bag of anecdotes and homey aphorisms with which he gave point to his arguments. In all, he relied more on rhetoric than on close legal reasoning. Not that Christie's lessons had all been lost. Hale could, when necessary, do legal spade work, marshal common-law precedents to support his case; but this was not his forte and he did not enjoy it. When a case turned upon some tricky point of law, he often preferred to pick the brains of recognized legal authorities like Ichabod Bartlett rather than sift out the pertinent precedents for himself. It was when he stood before juries—before men—that Hale shone, not when he sat down with a sheaf of legal notepaper and some dusty treatise on the common law.[22]

This ability to sway the minds of men, eloquently to articulate what others felt but found hard to express, opened to Hale a career in politics. New Hampshire in 1830 offered ample opportunity for such a spellbinder. The men who had directed the state's political fortunes since the Revolution—the Langdons, the Gilmans, the Plumers—had died or were stepping down from public life. Younger men were rising to take their places—Levi Woodbury, Isaac Hill, Franklin Pierce. For Hale the rub was that by 1830 control of most state offices was firmly in Democratic hands, while his own loyalty lay with the opposition.[23]

Ever since the misguided Hartford Convention of 1815 the political heirs of Thomas Jefferson had had the field to themselves in New Hampshire. "Politics, at present, afford but a sterile field for speculation," observed a Concord editor in 1821. "It is only here and there—in the remoter corners of the great expanse of republicanism, that we can discern the foot of an intruder." [24] Yet though everyone called himself a Republican in this so-called "Era of Good Feelings," traces of old party alignments remained and beneath the surface factionalism flourished. Occasionally such factionalism broke into the open. In 1823 an uprising of Republican malcontents, aided by former Federalists, momentarily shattered party unity by electing Levi Woodbury governor in place of Samuel Dinsmoor, the regularly nominated candidate and the choice of Isaac Hill's powerful *New Hampshire Patriot*.[25] But in 1824 Republican stalwarts rallied sufficiently to seal party rifts and unseat Woodbury. That same year, New Hampshire voted with virtual unanimity in the national election for John Quincy Adams. Hill had tried to promote a William H. Crawford boom, but when early soundings revealed the futility of this enterprise, he too had reluctantly swung behind Adams.[26] New Hampshire's ranks remained outwardly unbroken.

By 1826, however, Granite State Republicans had split into two hostile camps. Never happy with Adams' brand of Republicanism, Isaac Hill soon broke with those who were and built a rival organization designed both to make Andrew Jackson President and to win political control in New Hampshire. In directing his Democratic machine, the hard-driving Hill exploited long-standing local antagonisms, particularly the distrust of the interior agricultural regions for the economic and political predominance of the coastal commercial centers.[27] Through his own *Patriot* and satellite journals, he brought the luster of Jackson's name to the service of the Democratic party in New Hampshire; the Hero of New Orleans was made to do battle against the Bells and Plumers and others whom Hill linked to the "monarchical" Adams. Hill's skill and Jackson's fame made a powerful combination; it was not long before the Democrats dominated New Hampshire. Adams men fought back hard, and at times won notable successes. In the spring of 1828 their gubernatorial nominee, John Bell, upset the Democratic incumbent, Benjamin Pierce, and that fall Adams carried the state against Jackson. Yet such triumphs were brief; Pierce returned to office the following year and Jackson, though he had lost New Hampshire, now ruled from the White House. To a young man who saw which way the political breezes were blowing, it was clear that the quickest and safest way to preferment was in the good bark *Andrew Jackson.*

Hale calculated long and hard before making his political plunge; for many reasons he found it hard to align himself with the Democrats. Since college, those who most influenced his thinking, notably Christie and Woodman, had been cordial haters of Hill. His friend and adviser David Barker, Jr., a pro-Adams member of Congress, wrote from Washington deprecating the "bucktail Jacksonians" and gloating over the success of New Hampshire Adams men in the March 1828 elections.[28] Many, if not most, of Hale's close friends loathed Democrats in general and Jackson in particular—a "demon who without remorse will cut our throats from ear to ear," "a man of neither talents nor knowledge, not having the fear of God before his eyes, but instigated by the devil to follow the dictates of his own diabolical passions."[29] Hale himself had backed Adams in 1828, declaring Jackson an "unqualified" candidate.[30]

Why then did he decide to switch his allegiance? It was not that like some Federalists who became Jacksonians he hated Adams as an apostate to Federalism. Nor does it appear that like another Federalist son, James Fenimore Cooper, he turned to Democracy as the best bulwark against commercialism and social disorder.[31] A better guess, perhaps, is that Hale perceived certain similarities between latter-day Federalism and Jacksonianism—particularly the stress each placed on strict construction and states' rights. He may well have found the constitutional conservatism of Democrats more congenial than the broad nationalism preached by Adams men.

Personal pressures and considerations go still farther toward explaining Hale's belated conversion. Democratic spirit had been strong at Bowdoin, especially among the Athenaeans, and it may have been there that the seeds of apostasy were sown. His friend from Exeter days and one-time Bowdoin roommate, John Hodgdon, was an ardent Democrat and a delegate to the Baltimore convention which renominated Jackson in 1832.[32] Frank Pierce himself may have had a hand in exposing Hale to the principles of the Democracy and the practice of extolling Old Hickory. And, most important of all, political expediency dictated a switch.

Whatever his reasons, Hale had, by 1831, broken the last of his Adams party ties. The announcement of his "somerset" took many friends by surprise. How, asked one astonished acquaintance, could he "now approve of the course of Jackson & Hill when 'till their measures had attained the climax of political dishonesty, intrigue, & even fraud" he was prominent in the opposition's ranks?[33] If he shocked Strafford county National Republicans, he delighted the local Democrats who welcomed him with open arms. Dover had long been a Federalist and National Republican stronghold, and the beleaguered Jacksonians were happy to obtain the services of the popular and capable young attorney. As if to burn his bridges behind him, they promptly nominated Hale for a seat in the New Hampshire House of Representatives as a candidate of a hastily organized Workingmen's party. Dover Democrats decided not to run a regular ticket for state representatives or town moderator in 1832. Instead, as the Dover *Enquirer* sourly reported after the March election, "Conscious that their case as *Jackson men,* was a hopeless one, the party abandoned that ground," and by uniting with disgruntled National Republicans, placed a handful of Dover Democrats in office. Not only was Hale elected to the state legislature, but he won a close contest for town moderator, defeating Samuel W. Carr by forty-one votes. It was an auspicious beginning.[34]

CHAPTER II

Political Apprenticeship

THE next decade was for Hale a period of political apprentice-ship. Between his initiation as a state legislator in 1832 and election to Congress early in 1843, he learned the ins and outs of New Hampshire politics, enlarged his influence within the Democratic party, and polished his political skills in a variety of public offices. An independent if not original thinker, Hale also developed during these years antislavery convictions which later precipitated a break with his party and shaped his future career.

It was also at this time that Hale took a wife and began to raise a family. His marriage to Lucy Lambert of Berwick, Maine, in September 1834 not only enriched his private life but fanned his worldly ambition. (Many years later he admitted to a friend that he had wasted his youth but had been "saved by an excellent wife.")[1] In June 1835 Lucy gave birth to a girl whom they christened Elizabeth. "Lizzie," as the family always called her, thoroughly charmed her father who fondly noted every step by which she became acquainted with the world around her. When she was old enough, he enrolled her in a day school, where, he reported with delight, "She has made some important discoveries lately. She says Miss Whidden told her that the world turned round and that when it comes up it is morning & when it goes down it is evening. She took a ball & explained it to me. Another discovery is that people when they go to sea in ships stay in the ships all night & eat their victuals there."[2] Six years later a second daughter (named Lucy after her mother) was born. By then Hale had the added cost of a handsome new home on Pleasant Street to pay for—as well as indigent brothers and sisters to rescue—and to cut expenditures "bought one half of a new milch cow," which contentedly provided each of her two owners with milk. He also kept a few pigs, fattening them on meal and apples from his own trees, and grew vegetables for his table in a lot behind the house. He was especially proud of his flower garden where in summer verbena, geranium, and oleander blossomed in riotous color.[3]

Hale's political education began early in June 1832 when he took his seat in the State House at Concord. Then as now a quiet town, Concord had since 1807 been the seat of New Hampshire's government. Each year in the first week of June (and in November in presidential years) representatives from all parts of the state descended upon it to pass laws, appropriate funds, and play politics. Legislative sessions seldom lasted more than a month, so that by mid-July Concord could again resume its normally tranquil routine. But during that month the town hummed with political excitement.

The legislature that met on June 6, 1832 was decidedly Democratic. Of the 223 members of the House of Representatives, well over half were Democrats; in the Senate only one of twelve was a National Republican.[4] State and local issues—militia and licensing laws, acts incorporating banks and turnpikes—were the most important determinants of party alignment, though increasingly since 1828 national measures exerted a shaping influence on New Hampshire politics. Jacksonian strength was greatest in the northernmost counties where the soil was rocky and the farms poor. From the forests of Coos County came ten representatives to the General Court—all Democrats. Grafton County, south of Coos and nearly as mountainous, sent only seven National Republicans as opposed to twenty-seven Democrats, and thirty-six of forty-five Strafford County representatives were of the Jacksonian persuasion. National Republicans were most numerous in the rich agricultural counties in the south where ties with Connecticut and Massachusetts were close and the influence of established commercial interests still strong. Representatives from the three southernmost counties—Cheshire, Hillsborough, and Rockingham—accounted for more than half the

National Republicans in the 1832 legislature. Yet everywhere except Cheshire, Democrats were heavily in the majority.[5]

Of the three issues which were to preoccupy New Hampshire politicians in the 1840's—temperance, railroads, and slavery—only the first was important in 1832. Since Governor Samuel Bell had first called attention to the growing problem of intemperance in his annual message of 1820, legislative attempts to control the sale of liquor had stirred heated debate both within and without the State House walls. To this debate Hale contributed his bit. Though at Bowdoin he had raised the cup as often as his companions, he began soon after graduation to shun hard liquor himself and to show concern for intemperance in others. His own newly awakened interest in temperance coincided with the first well-organized attempts to check the use of alcohol. The American Society for the Promotion of Temperance, founded in February 1826, soon spawned scores of local auxiliaries, one of them in Hale's home town. Early in 1828, then only twenty-one years old, Hale joined the Rochester Society for the Suppression of Intemperance, and like other members pledged not to use "ardent spirits," a pledge he never broke.[6]

In 1827 temperance reformers were sufficiently powerful to force through the legislature a stringent "Act Regulating Licensed Houses," imposing a fine on anyone selling spirits in quantities less than a gallon without license from town selectmen. Two years later, again in response to the pressures of local temperance societies, the legislature amended the 1827 act so as to prohibit the sale of liquor by all except retailers selling measures of a pint or greater, and then only on condition that nothing be drunk on the premises.[7] In some ways less harsh (it was now possible for workingmen of moderate means, unable to afford gallon jugs, to buy and carry off pints), the 1829 law was in other ways more rigid: it made drinking in pubs or taverns illegal and banned sales of less than a pint, license or no license. At a time when heavy drinking was more the rule than the exception, such severity courted evasion. Events soon proved that it was openly and widely violated. Men drank as they had before: at home and at work; at weddings and funerals; in public, in private; in sickness and in health. Officials often winked or looked the other way rather than make arrests for illegal sales, and when they did enforce the act, caught only the little fish—the pubkeepers who sold in small measure—letting the big ones swim freely. For Hale this was simply further evidence in support of a thesis he had come to accept, namely that temperance reform could be achieved only by moral persuasion, not by prescriptive ordinances.[8]

When, on June 8, Hale addressed the House for the first time, he took for his text the failings of the existing licensing law. The subject was, he began, one he approached "with extreme diffidence." He was aware of its highly controversial nature, and in no way wished to disparage the "strenuous exertions" which high-minded people had made and were making to suppress intemperance—that "great and crying evil." But experience seemed to suggest that legislative interference was ill-advised. Surely it was a "monstrous anomaly" that despite severe penalties enacted against breaches of the licensing law, it was "openly and unblushingly violated." Such being the state of affairs, Hale proposed the appointment of a select committee to inquire into the efficacy of changes in the present law. His own opinion was that legislative enactments would not of themselves check intemperance, and that laws which public opinion would not enforce were worse than useless and should be repealed. The House thought well enough of Hale's remarks to approve the committee of inquiry which he proposed, and Speaker Franklin Pierce appointed him one of its three members.[9]

On June 15 the committee made its report, accompanied by a bill to modify the existing act. Feeling that neither went far enough, Hale offered a resolution of his own calling for an end to "unequal and burdensome taxes on any branch of business," whether in spirits or otherwise. Speaking, he said, as a representative of the working class, he denounced the preferential treatment accorded distillers— "probably . . . ably represented in this very Hall"—at the expense of "the humble dealer in the smaller measure." Again he lashed out at the existing law. "Why, the grog shops are brought upon wheels, to the very gates of the State house, even now, in spite of your enactments," he declared. "If you repeal the laws upon this subject, do you believe they will enter the portals of the capital, and jingle their glasses in your Hall?" No, he concluded, "You cannot legislate men into Christianity or temperance." Sound policy and public opinion, not "well meaning, but ill judging" temperance associations, should guide the drafting of a new licensing law.[10]

Hale's vigorous speeches on temperance and the licensing of pubs marked him as an orator of ability, a young man of promise. Heavily-built and nearly six feet tall, with straight black hair and soft blue eyes, his appearance was dignified but neither more nor less impressive than that of most public figures. What gave him distinction as a freshman representative was his strong, resonant voice that carried clearly to all corners of the hall. Likewise, the moral earnestness which colored his remarks attracted interest and respect. Yet these speeches offended many who concluded that Hale's message was anti-temperance, if not in intent, then certainly in effect. His repeated expressions of sympathy for the temperance movement, as well as his own pledge of abstinence, were largely ignored or discounted. (Recalling Hale's bacchanalian days at Bowdoin, Hawthorne saw his present course as "quite . . . characteristic and consistent," adding in a letter to Pierce: "I presume he gives the retail dealers as much of his personal patronage as ever.") At any event, the House easily tabled both Hale's resolution and the bill of amendment.[11]

In fact, neither the June nor November sessions of 1832 produced much legislation of any kind. A good many social problems were debated—relief for debtors and the care of the insane, the poor, and the deaf and dumb—but cautious representatives postponed final consideration of most proposed statutes. Acts of incorporation—banks, turnpikes, bridge and canal companies—fared better. The Democratic legislature passed twenty acts of incorporation in the June session and eighteen in November. Hale spoke often, but to little effect. Only his proposal that the governor be authorized to advance funds to the state prison received the concurrence of the House. If nothing else, the months in Concord schooled Hale in the frustrations of democracy.

After the November session, Hale returned to Dover. Legal business and his duties as town moderator kept him busy, but he found time to campaign quietly for reelection. The March elections blasted his hopes. Dover National Republicans, regaining their old supremacy, swept back into office. In the contest for town moderator, George W. Kittredge won handily and Hale failed by fifty-five votes of reelection to the House. Yet he took his double defeat in stride. The year which followed Hale spent practicing law as well as keeping political friendships alive. In March 1834 he again stood for election as town moderator, but again the National Republican machine in Dover proved too strong and he lost. By then, however, he had his hook baited for a more important and more lucrative office.[12]

For some time political leaders in New Hampshire had been surveying the field of respectable Jacksonian lawyers for someone to fill the post of United States district attorney. At a meeting of prominent Democrats at Concord in February 1834 Hale's friend and political confidant, Henry Y. Simpson, recommended Hale. "I found it took well," he confided. Among those present was Nathaniel G. Upham, the year before appointed a justice of the Superior Court. "He entertains a very favorable opinion of you," Simpson reported, and urged Hale to ask Upham to write in his behalf to Isaac Hill, then in the United States Senate, the man whose word controlled all major political appointments in New Hampshire. Upham's recommendation would carry great weight, said Simpson, since Hill considered Judge Upham "one of the strongest men in the State" and relied heavily on his judgment. Apparently Hale followed Simpson's advice, for on April 8, 1834, President Andrew Jackson appointed him Attorney of the United States for the District of New Hampshire.[13]

The appointment was welcome. For one thing it was proof to Hale of the trust in which Democratic chiefs held him. It kept him politically alive. More immediately important, it assured him the financial security which his fees as federal prosecutor would bring. His own practice had been growing—"I for the first time made the largest number of entries & had also much the largest number of defences," he wrote after the April session of the Court of Common Pleas—but a larger and more secure income better prepared him for the imminent responsibilities of husband and father.[14]

Yet Hale's new office was no sinecure and proved an imperfect blessing. It required that he travel widely, and he was frequently away from home for weeks at a time—no mean sacrifice for a man who loved his family as much as did Hale. Trial work took him not only to all corners of New Hampshire, but to Maine and Massachusetts as well. Whenever possible he combined private practice with his travels as district attorney. His law partner during these years, Charles W. Woodman, tended affairs in Dover while Hale argued before courts from Lancaster to Boston. The trips to Boston, Hale found the least onerous. There, at least, he might mix a little pleasure with his business, attend a recital or see a play. (In 1837 he saw Edwin Forrest, then at the top of his powers and fresh from a triumphal London engagement, in a memorable performance of *Richard III*.) At all events his travels made possible a broadening of his circle of acquaintances which later proved useful. Little known beyond Strafford County in 1834, Hale was by 1841 a figure of some prominence, one who was on close terms with leading politicians of both parties throughout the state.[15]

The gauges of Hale's rise to prominence are many. Candidates for public office began to seek his endorsement. Democratic Associations in New Hampshire, Maine, and Massachusetts, cognizant of his stature within the party and impressed with his power and eloquence as a public speaker, begged him to address mass meetings. In 1836 Hale attended the Dartmouth commencement as the special guest of President Nathan Lord, and Governor Hill appointed him a commissioner to investigate British charges of aggression by New Hampshire settlers in the disputed Indian Stream Territory.[16]

Yet though during his years as district attorney he was able to advance both his political and professional interests, Hale's climb to prominence and preferment was not without setbacks. There were still defeats and disappointments. In every year between 1834 and 1843, except for 1839, Hale ran for town moderator of Dover. Only once, in 1837, was he successful. That he *ever* won in such a Whig bailiwick was remarkable, yet the repeated defeats stung him deeply. More disspiriting still was an abortive bid for appointment to the Superior Court in 1838. Hale still enjoyed his district attorneyship (Van Buren had renewed his commission), but he fretted over the future. It especially alarmed him that having hitched his wagon to the Democratic star, the heavens seemed increasingly bright with Whigs. "Many of our friends," he confided gloomily to one associate, "think the indications for the future are not so decidedly favorable as to render it absolutely certain that the Democratic party will be in the ascendancy in the State & Nation in two years from this time." [17]

Eighteen-forty brought with it twin dangers for New Hampshire Democrats, and these dangers in turn snapped Hale out of his doldrums. The first and most obvious threat came from a resurgent Whiggery. Excluded for years from the spoils of office, Granite State Whigs, sensing victory (especially after the nomination of Harrison and Tyler in December 1839), worked like men possessed to break the Democratic hammerlock on New Hampshire. Threatened from without by the Whigs, New Hampshire Democrats had also to contend with a serious rift within their ranks, engendered by disputes over the terms of railroad charters. [18]

Hale was in the thick of it all. In May 1840 at Baltimore the nation's Democrats renominated Martin Van Buren for President. New Hampshire Jacksonians were quick to swing behind him. As president of the State Democratic Convention held at Concord in June, Hale oversaw arrangements designed to insure a party sweep in November. Nothing was to be left to chance. Plans were laid for an organization "so perfect that not a single Democrat in any Township in the State, who can be *carried* to the polls . . ." would fail to vote. [19] At mass meetings throughout the state, Hale and other party orators railed at Federalism and Hard Cider. Franklin Pierce, then United States senator, was seemingly ubiquitous, reminding voters of the fearful consequences of a Whig victory: "aristocracy" would reign and turn the powers of government to its own diabolical ends;

New Hampshire would be saddled with a million dollars of states' debts; an ignorant and incompetent President would unhesitatingly do the bidding of Webster, Clay, Biddle, and other Tory Federalists.[20] On October 14 Hale and Pierce crossed paths at Concord where Hale addressed the town's Democratic Association, an address "which my friend Col Pierce did me [the honor] to pronounce as good as any one he ever heard," Hale proudly confided to his wife.[21] In November such hard work paid off: though he lost to Harrison, Van Buren carried New Hampshire by more than six thousand votes. It was the only New England state not to succumb to the blandishments of Hard Cider.

Having at least temporarily disposed of the Whig menace to their hegemony, New Hampshire Democrats next set about to put their own house in order. Already by the end of 1840 there were signs of serious intra-party dissension.

In 1835, the New Hampshire legislature had granted articles of incorporation to the Nashua and Lowell Railroad. Three years later the first locomotive, belching clouds of black smoke and showering sparks in its wake, chugged north from Lowell, through Chelmsford and Tyngsboro, then across the border and into New Hampshire where, after a run of little more than five miles, it rattled to a stop at a temporary station in Nashua. The railroad had come to New Hampshire, bringing with it new headaches for harried politicians.[22]

It was the railroads' need for right of way that stirred the controversy which threatened Democratic unity. In 1836 and 1837 interests friendly to the railroads had pushed through laws granting broad rights of condemnation, permitting expropriation of lands without the consent of the owners. In a state as solidly rural as New Hampshire this was bound to cause trouble. Angry farmers rose in arms against corporations which they distrusted and which now threatened to encroach upon the land which was theirs and their grandfathers' before them. Feeling the full force of the farmers' protest, the legislature reversed itself in June 1840, repealing all laws permitting "any corporation to take, use, or occupy any lands" without the owner's consent, except where construction had already started. In December the legislature took most of the bite out of this act by extending the exception to any road that had been surveyed. This solution satisfied neither the farmers nor the railroads, and with an eye to more complete triumph, each side sought allies among the state's most powerful and influential political leaders and girded itself for future battles.[23]

Within the Democratic party the controversy resolved itself more and more into a power struggle between the "Radical" faction which sided with the farmers, led by Franklin Pierce, and the "Conservatives" who championed the cause of the railroads, whose foremost spokesman was the vitriolic Isaac Hill. Hill brought to his cause great political acumen, bitter determination, and an impressive reputation. Long the editor and publisher of the influential *New Hampshire Patriot,* Hill had by 1840 held most of the important offices his state could bestow: state representative and senator, governor, United States senator. A close political friend of Andrew Jackson, he had been as responsible as anyone for shaping the Democratic creed in New Hampshire. His opposition to the Radicals was understandable enough. In the first place, his relations with Pierce had been souring for some years, and he resented the threat to his leadership which young and self-assertive politicians of Pierce's stripe represented. Moreover, as a banker and businessman, he found obnoxious a Democracy that checked economic growth in the name of individual liberty. Especially important, Hill had a personal interest in the welfare of at least one railroad: he was a director of the Concord Railroad which in 1841 began laying track between Nashua and Concord—the very monster at which the Radicals directed their fire.[24]

From the start, Hale, like most young Democrats, cast his lot with the Radicals. Principle, expediency, and friendship all shaped his decision. Genuinely sympathetic to the farmer, he denounced the subterfuge by which the General Court permitted the use of eminent domain in getting land for the railroads. At the same time, he recognized that the Conservatives were in the minority and that to join their secession would be to invite an early political death. Finally, and perhaps most decisive, Pierce was a much better friend than Hill.

At first, Democrats managed to conceal their family feud, but sharp observers detected signs of trouble. After a futile attempt to buy back the *Patriot* (which he had earlier sold and which was then under Radical editorship) Hill published in August 1840 the first edition of a rival paper—*Hill's New Hampshire Patriot*. Not even its conciliatory motto—"We come not to destroy, but to fulfill"—could hide its belligerency. During 1841 relations between Radicals and Conservatives steadily worsened. The two *Patriots* gently jabbed at one another in print, and only grudgingly did Hill and his followers accept in July the nomination of Radical Henry Hubbard for governor. Early in 1842 the Conservatives stepped up their attacks on the Radicals. In an editorial on January 7, *Hill's Patriot* hit out against "the Democratic young lawyers . . . who joined the democracy to destroy it by advocating ridiculous doctrines—that canals, turnpikes and railroads all stand upon the same footing, and that either may be arrested by any owner of land standing out against them." Equally pernicious was the Radical demand that stockholder liability ought to be unlimited. With some cause the Conservatives saw their enemies as willful obstructors of economic progress and prosperity.[25]

The Radical-Conservative breach became complete in February 1842 when, after a tempestuous meeting of Concord Democrats, the Radicals stormed out of the town hall, leaving the Conservatives to organize themselves and to nominate separate candidates for governor and councillor. For the next two years the Democratic split threw New Hampshire politics into a turmoil. Though the Radicals administered resounding defeats to the Hill faction at the polls, Conservative Democrats refused to knuckle under. With three parties now in the field, often no candidate for the state legislature received a majority, so that more towns went unrepresented at the capital than ever before.[26]

The rift within the New Hampshire Democracy, although provoked by a special issue, reflected similar splits in other states. The disparate forces that had rallied behind Andrew Jackson in search of political power and plunder fell to quarreling among themselves once the Bank War ended and the Hero retired to the Hermitage. Such quarrels surfaced in the late 1830's and 1840's. As in New Hampshire, they usually developed over secondary issues—canals, banks, tariffs—but everywhere the real fight was for political control. After 1841, plotting Presidential aspirants—especially Tyler and John C. Calhoun—both aggravated and exploited Democratic factionalism.

The Radicals' attack was to brand the Conservatives as schismatics who were playing more or less willingly into the hands of the Whigs. The *Patriot* repeatedly accused Hill and his minions of alliance with Tyler in an attempt to destroy the Democracy in state and nation. Edmund Burke, editor of the Newport *Argus & Spectator* and a New Hampshire congressman, confided to Hale his fears that such charges were only too true. Calhoun might also have a hand in the Conservative revolt, Burke suggested, a surmise which took on the ring of truth when, beginning with its February 28, 1843, issue, the Conservative *New Hampshire Gazette* carried the South Carolinian's name at the top of its columns.[27]

To these charges Conservatives replied that *they* were the true guardians of the Jacksonian heritage, that the "old" Democratic party had been subverted by "a few federal lawyers, such as Henry Hubbard, Charles F. Gove, John P. Hale, Lyman B. Walker, *et id omne genus.*" Such men, they said, were greedy for office, "generally vacillating in their course and always too democratic for the democratic party." From start to finish, Hale was a prime target of the Conservatives. Hill, ignoring Lyman Walker's warning "that John Parker Hale has grown too hard, of late, for even yourself to bite, with any reasonable hope of saving your teeth," pitched into Hale at every opportunity. Whether bad blood existed between the two men prior to the Conservative break is uncertain. There is some evidence that when in 1830 the United States Senate refused to confirm Hill's appointment as Second Comptroller of the Treasury, Hale was among the "largest and loudest in his rejoicings." If true, and if Hill knew it, it accounts for some of the ferocity of the editor's later attacks. Certainly Hale's eleventh-hour leap to the Democratic bandwagon had done little to win Hill's trust. Then, too, there is little to show that Hill, jealous of his position as king of the Democratic mountain, showed affection for any young, ambitious politicians. He had a way of patronizing younger members of the party which Pierce, for one—and no doubt Hale—found annoying.[28]

Whatever their relation before Hill's secession, after it they battled constantly. There were weak spots in Hale's armor, and at them Hill aimed his thrusts. One was Hale's stand on temperance reform, a question of great importance in the 1830's and 1840's and one never more hotly debated than during these years of political schism. Few men worked harder than Hale in the temperance crusade. He spoke repeatedly and in all corners of the state on the need for moderation in the use of spirits. He was himself shunning hard liquor. Yet because he persisted in his belief that it was "absurd and ridiculous" to attempt reform "by penal statutes and criminal prosecutions," because he preferred instead to enforce "the truths of soberness & temperance by appeals to the hearts & understandings of men," he was often maligned, even by temperance advocates themselves. In addition, Hale's work as defense counsel for violators of the license law seemed to some further evidence of the insincerity of his reform sentiments.[29]

His Federalist antecedents provided still more ammunition for Conservative broadsides. If only because so few Radicals were vulnerable in this way, Hill and his associates took special pains to impugn Hale's Democracy. Not content merely to exhume his one-time objection to Jackson, Conservatives reminded voters that Hale's father had died a Federalist and his grandfather a Tory. No more than a leopard could he change his spots.[30]

As if purposely to infuriate Hill, as well as to reward Hale for his allegiance and hard work, the Radical Democrats at their state convention in November 1842, chose Hale as a candidate for United States representative. The nomination delighted Hale. In 1840 and again in 1842 he had received votes in party caucuses for nomination as United States senator, though not nearly enough to edge the successful candidates, Levi Woodbury and Charles G. Atherton. In the former year he had written his brother Augustus that there was a "probability" of his being elected, only to lose on the sixth ballot to Woodbury. Tyler's appointment of a Whig to succeed him as district attorney made the prospect of a term in Congress all the more pleasing. There had been some objection to Hale's nomination, a fact which Whigs and Conservatives took pains to point out. The other Radical candidates—Edmund Burke, Moses Norris, Jr., and John R. Reding—were picked on the first ballot, Hale on the second. "The objection to Jack," it seemed to the Dover *Enquirer,* "was, that his 'democracy' was of too late a date—rather musty." [31]

While Radicals applauded Hale's nomination, Hill was preparing a thunderbolt designed to consign Hale to political oblivion. A month before the election, on February 9, 1843, *Hill's Patriot* promised its readers: "We have the documents which will exhibit John P. Hale in that light as a public officer which will make every fair minded man in the State ashamed to own him as a citizen of the State." The following week Hill made public his charges under headlines that screamed:

THE TREASURY PLUNDERS!

JOHN P. HALE'S SUITS FOR THE GENERAL POST OFFICE

He accused Hale and Federal Marshal Charles Lane of "unjust and extravagant" claims for services as district attorney and marshal, publishing those claims he thought most excessive. He also printed correspondence between Hale and C. K. Gardner, a postal auditor, by which he sought to show that Gardner thought that fees asked by Hale in 1837 for civil suits against New Hampshire postmasters and their sureties were excessive, and that they had been belatedly paid in 1839 only after Senator Pierce interceded in Hale's behalf. Not only had Hale enriched himself at public expense, contended Hill, but his success had opened the way for other gougers. [32]

Hale was attending a session of the Court of Common Pleas at Gilford when a friend informed him of Hill's most recent indictment. He had ignored previous accusations—accusations which if true would have "rendered me a more fit candidate for a convict's cell, than a seat in Congress," Hale remarked—but he could no longer keep still. In a letter to editor John T. Gibbs, which appeared in the Dover *Gazette* on February 25, he came out swinging: "I directly charge Isaac Hill, or anybody else who furnishes what Mr. Hill says he transcribed as claims preferred and allowed by me, with FORGERY of the public records." Hill's article had misstated both facts and figures. "I have never received one dollar from the public treasury," Hale insisted, "except for services performed, and at such compensation as the law allowed." In a final rhetorical flourish, which he would repeat on more than one subsequent occasion, he announced: "I court the investigation of friends and defy the malice of enemies."[33]

If Hale hoped to spike all Hill's guns he was disappointed. Election eve brought new disclosures by the Conservative chieftain. Still billed as "The Treasury Plunderer," Hale was said this time not only to have demanded inordinate compensation for his services while district attorney, but also to have falsified expense accounts. Hale had not time before the election on March 14 to answer Hill's final salvo, but there was no need, so groundless were these new accusations. As the clerk of the House of Representatives noted shortly after the election: "though uncontradicted except in a general manner, [they] passed you by like the idle wind that you heed not."[34]

Election results offered ample evidence that few New Hampshire voters had swallowed Hill's charges. Everywhere Hale ran neck-and-neck with the rest of the regular Democratic ticket which scored a nearly two-to-one victory over Whig candidates for governor and federal representative. In most counties the Conservatives finished a bad third. In Dover Hale received more votes than any other candidate for Congress and fifteen more than Governor Hubbard.[35]

Perhaps the most remarkable aspect of these elections was not the size of the Democratic victory, or even that John P. Hale came through Isaac Hill's heavy shelling unscathed, but rather the marked rise in antislavery sentiment, measured by the showing of Daniel Hoit, Liberty party candidate for governor. In January 1841 a handful of antislavery advocates had met in the anteroom of Concord's courthouse to nominate Hoit. At the March election that year 1,273 voters had supported him. Two years later he nearly tripled his vote, in Strafford and Hillsborough counties outpolling the Conservative nominee. Another index of the growth of antislavery sentiment during these years is the vote cast for James G. Birney in the Presidential elections of 1840 and 1844. In 1840 New Hampshire gave Birney only 126 votes in a total of nearly 60,000; by 1844 he had climbed to over 4,000.[36] Hale must have noted this upward swing of political abolitionism with interest, for, though he kept it a well-guarded secret, he had himself by 1843 traveled far along the road to antislavery.

Just when or why Hale joined the crusade against slavery is unknown. He probably did not know himself. For Hale, as for many others who, in one way or another, took up the cause of the slave in the years before the Civil War, conversion was a product of subtle pressures, persistent introspection, and the force of events. The path of Right and Duty became clear, not in a blinding flash, but slowly, gradually, often after years of searching. Still, it is possible to sketch roughly the influences most responsible for Hale's transformation from a baiter of abolitionists to a leading spokesman for the antislavery cause in America, and to outline the steps by which that transformation was made. A brief discussion of New Hampshire's attitude toward slavery will place this change in perspective.

The 1830's were hard times for avowed abolitionists, in New Hampshire as well as in the rest of the nation. Their ranks were thin, their organization weak, and their principles intensely unpopular. Founded in November 1834, the New Hampshire Anti-Slavery Society exerted only the loosest control over its membership and reached by no means all who sympathized with its aims. There was little if any coordination of its activities and those of local associations. The moving spirit during these years was not, in fact, the state antislavery society, but a handful of devoted, zealous individualists who, working against incredible handicaps, set out to arouse popular opinion against the sin of slavery.[37]

One such voice in the wilderness was Nathaniel P. Rogers. Lawyer, editor, "moral gadfly," he had in 1838 assumed charge of the *Herald of Freedom,* nominally the organ of the New Hampshire Anti-Slavery Society, but in fact the weekly expression of Rogers' own mind. A moral reformer in the strictest sense, a man who at times out-Garrisoned Garrison, he eschewed political action. Another New Hampshire abolitionist of the Garrison school was Parker Pillsbury. Ordained a Congregationalist minister, Pillsbury, by his heretical views on slavery brought down upon his head the wrath of church authorities who in 1841 revoked his license to preach. Thereafter he toiled selflessly as an antislavery lecturer. Stephen S. Foster, carpenter turned minister, was a third antislavery apostle. Like Rogers and Pillsbury, Foster preferred nonpolitical tactics in his campaign against the "peculiar institution." His technique, first conceived in 1841 and first practiced in Concord's Old North Church, was a novel one. Entering a church on the Sabbath, he would wait patiently until the time of the sermon. Then, rising in his pew, speaking in respectful but earnest tones, Foster would interrupt, demanding consideration of the church's obligation to blacks in bondage.[38]

The common reward of such men as Rogers, Pillsbury, and Foster, was imprisonment, social ostracism, personal indignities, and violence. When he tried to speak in the slave's behalf, Foster was hauled from a house of God, beaten, kicked, and flung down a flight of steps. Time and again unruly mobs broke up peaceful antislavery lectures, often held in churches because other meeting places were closed to anyone arguing for emancipation. In Concord in September 1835 a mob hurled brickbats at the Quaker poet and abolitionist John Greenleaf Whittier and the great British friend of the slave, George Thompson—an experience Whittier did not soon forget.[39] To understand why all this should have been so, one must examine the attitudes toward slavery and its abolition most prevalent in New Hampshire during the 1830's and 1840's.

There were, to begin with, few if any who felt anything but sympathy for the slave and repugnance for the system that bound him, though some like Isaac Hill could speak of the "mutual relations existing between the master and his slave which often endear one to the other," and could argue the superior moral condition of slaves to free Negroes.[40] Slavery never had more than a toehold in New Hampshire, and the constitutional interpretation of 1783 which legally abolished it was superfluous. But while there were few who would condone chattel slavery, there were not many more who were willing to take action, however mild or indirect, to abolish it in the South.

Only a slave state might constitutionally legislate on that institution, it was commonly held. Southern citizens had a constitutional right to the protection of their property, and Congress should neither stop the interstate slave trade nor abolish slavery in the District of Columbia. Certainly it was the duty of all Northern legislatures to scotch abolitionist attempts "to excite revolt among the present servile race." Likewise, talk of "immediate emancipation" should be exposed for the madness it was. Abolitionist caveats to the contrary notwithstanding, hard-headed New Hampshiremen saw in these words just that—immediate emancipation. And it conjured up in their minds all sorts of dark and disturbing consequences. Always there ran just below the surface a strong current of anti-Negro feeling. Emancipation would lead either to racial war or Negro domination of the South. Both were unthinkable. "Shall the land of Washington and Jefferson be surrendered to a race of slaves, without capacity, brutal, cowardly, grovelling in their dispositions, upon whom nature has fixed the seal of perpetual inferiority? It is not to be believed." So spoke a select committee of the New Hampshire House of Representatives in 1839. Removal of American Negroes to some colony abroad might be the best solution. Surely emancipation without colonization "would be productive of calamities, moral and political, such as should be deprecated by every friend of humanity."[41]

It followed that "incendiaries" who preached immediate emancipation (even when it meant gradual emancipation immediately begun) must be resisted at all costs. In Congress this meant "gag rules," which prohibited the discussion of petitions dealing with the touchy problems of slavery and the slave trade. In the states and towns it meant legalistic harrassing of antislavery organizations, and, though the more responsible citizens were quick to decry it, vigilantism. And all this might be done with the clearest of consciences, for, as men were fond of telling each other, the abusive language and wild schemes of Garrison's band of fanatics (in New Hampshire all outspoken critics of slavery were automatically identified with Garrison) would only postpone the day when slaveholders would of their own accord emancipate the blacks.[42]

None were more decided in their condemnation of abolitionist zeal than New Hampshire churchmen. With few exceptions (most notably the Free Will Baptist preachers) they rebuked those who placed personal liberty and natural rights above social order. In 1841, for example, the Church Committee of Dartmouth College threatened Stephen S. Foster with excommunication for having "lost sight of social distinctions, the necessity & lawfulness of rule & restraint, & the wholesome regulation of the word & Providence of God by which alone society is preserved." His singleminded crusade against slavery, the committee warned Foster, had blinded him to the beneficence of God-appointed "gradations of society" and made him "a disorganizer & a leveller." [43] Better to leave the slave in chains than to upset the established order.

Politicians too, especially Hale's Democratic associates, worked to stifle abolitionism. Steeped in states' rights and anxious to retain the good will of their Southern allies—on whom the gold of patronage depended—New Hampshire Democrats regularly took the side of the slaveholder. "Doughfaces," critics called them—Northern men with Southern principles. Their votes upheld the gag rule and slavery in the District, their resolutions decried "inflammatory appeals" and counseled "moderation."

Given the state of the antislavery movement in the 1830's and early 1840's and the strength and prestige of its opponents, it is not surprising that at the beginning of his political career Hale should have denounced abolitionist agitators. Garrisonian assaults on the Constitution must have been particularly repugnant to Hale's legalistic, essentially conservative mind. His first and last public clash with abolitionists occurred in the summer of 1835. At the time it earned him a certain local renown; in later years the incident would be recalled by angry Southerners bent on discrediting the purity of his antislavery beliefs.

In August 1835 the Rev. George Storrs, an agent for the New Hampshire Anti-Slavery Society, arrived to deliver a series of four abolitionist lectures in Dover's Methodist Meeting House. The first two talks ("Bible and Slavery" and "Fruits of Slavery") provoked no disturbances. On Tuesday, August 18, however, Dover citizens found posted about town broadsides announcing: "All those who are in favor of *disunion* are requested to meet this evening at the Methodist meeting-house precisely at 8 o'clock." Accordingly, when Storrs began his lecture that evening he found facing him an unexpectedly large and hostile audience, Hale in its midst. Twice as he spoke he was interrupted by the shuffling of feet. At the close of the lecture, Hale rose and "with manifest warmth" demanded "liberty of *discussion*" for those who held different beliefs. To hecklers' cries of "Go ahead, Jack!" he proceeded, in a "short but animated address," to expose "some of the fallacies of the doctrines of the abolitionists, and briefly stated a few of the evils to which a success of the abolition plans would expose the citizens of the Southern States." The abolitionists' course he labelled insurrectionary, and, if Storrs' subsequent account is reliable, dismissed the slaves as "BEASTS IN HUMAN SHAPE AND NOT FIT TO LIVE," adding in a barely audible voice: "free." So violent was the demonstration which followed Hale's rejoinder that Storrs prudently cancelled his concluding lecture. Gleefully the Dover *Gazette* boasted: "The deluded fanatics of hypocritical philanthropy have been taught that in Dover there is no resting place for their emissaries —no abiding place for their doctrines." [44]

In later years, Hale freely admitted his part in the Storrs incident. But, he said, when the light shone upon him, when he saw that abolitionists "were not insurrectionary in their movements, and that they sought by force of reason, and argument, and persuasion" to achieve their aims, he had altered his views. Conviction, he claimed, not expediency, dictated this change of opinion. [45]

What caused this light to shine? What forces so profoundly altered his convictions regarding slavery? Certainly religious conviction was among the most powerful: Judgment Day was never far from Hale's thoughts. Early in life he became a compulsive churchgoer, and although a Unitarian, and a warden of that church in Dover, he attended other services as well—Baptist, Congregational, even Catholic—in search of a spiritually satisfying sermon. For Hale religion was an intensely personal affair. "The kingdom of Heaven is to be built up within us," he believed, and one should constantly and energetically be striving after "higher degrees of Christian excellence." In Jesus man had not only a model of abstract virtue, but a standard for everyday conduct. "I am persuaded," he told his wife, "that we lose much of the force and effect of Christ's teaching by not reflecting that he is to be our example. We look upon him as so exalted that we seem to think the virtues he exhibited are to be admired & venerated rather than imitated. This is surely a great & ruinous error." When faced with temptation, he added, "let us honestly ask ourselves what would Jesus have done in precisely similar situations." [46]

The weakness of such a philosophy was, of course, that it was not always easy to know just what Jesus *would* have done. But in this Hale could count on the friendly advice of John Parkman, from 1840 to 1849 minister of Dover's First Unitarian Society. A graduate of Harvard College, Parkman detested slavery. Immediately before coming to Dover, he had served as a vice-president of the Massachusetts Anti-Slavery Society. At first Hale sharply disagreed with Parkman's abolitionist views. Yet from the beginning he defended the new minister's right to air his beliefs freely. When in 1842 Parkman threatened to resign because of grumbling over his antislavery sermons, it was Hale who drafted and secured passage of resolutions upholding the minister's "right and duty" to preach freely on "the moral questions of the day"—slavery included. Before long the two men established a warm and confidential relation. By pointing up the un-Christian character of slavery in weekday chats as well as in Sunday sermons, Parkman helped gradually to convince Hale of the need for some form of antislavery action. Powerful abolitionist sermons which Hale heard at the Free Will Baptist services he occasionally attended augmented Parkman's preachings. And after 1844 the influence of his law partner, John H. Wiggins, who had published an abolitionist pamphlet in New York before coming to Dover, bolstered his recently acquired convictions.[47]

In addition to these personal influences which inclined him toward an antislavery position, there was the pressure of events.

One distinguished historian has shown that "the abolition movement became inextricably bound up with the preservation of civil liberties, and that the relationship strengthened it and helped to insure its final victory by mobilizing Northern public opinion on its side."[48] Something of the sort happened in New Hampshire, and helps to account for Hale's change of heart on the slavery issue. In the suppression of free speech and right of assembly, mob action was most dramatic. But in different, less obvious ways, these freedoms were also abridged, and in ways no less distasteful to responsible citizens conscious of the heritage of Stark and Langdon. Although it unhesitatingly gave permission to literary associations, the Colonization Society, and the New Hampshire Temperance Society to use the Representatives' Hall for evening meetings, the state legislature by overwhelming votes regularly refused such permission to antislavery groups. Similarly, the House voted 184 to 34 against incorporating a Free Will Baptist printing establishment because that sect was ardently opposed to slavery and apt to flood the state with "incendiary" literature if given a chance.[49]

Such arbitrary restrictions on free expression aroused many who had little sympathy for the abolitionists' belief in equal rights for blacks, but who believed fervently in equal rights for whites. As one man wrote in denouncing the legislature's denial of a charter to the Free Will Baptist press and its refusal to let its hall be used for a lecture on slavery: "We do not advocate the principles, but the rights of the Abolitionists on which are staked the rights of every citizen."[50] Once one advocated the *rights* of the abolitionists, however, it was often but a short step to the advocacy of their *principles* as well. Perhaps Hale's mind moved in such a channel.

In one other way the force of events made it easier for Hale to slough off his early anti-abolitionism. This was the rise of political antislavery. The leaders of New Hampshire's abolition movement in the 1830's—men like Rogers, Pillsbury, and Foster—had all rejected political action in favor of moral reform. But in the 1840's, with the emergence of the Liberty party and its state and local affiliates, the lead passed into the hands of antislavery politicians. Working within constitutional limits, they sought to foster and to capitalize upon a rising tide of antislavery sentiment which one day would place the powers of the federal government within their hands. Armed with these powers the forces of Right would surely prevail.

But although the Liberty party in New Hampshire showed signs of potential strength by 1843, and though Hale found its methods more congenial than those of the Garrisonians, he was still more Democrat than Liberty man. On all major issues save slavery he saw eye to eye with his Jacksonian brothers. Among them he had formed many personal as well as political friendships, and from them gained public office. As for the Liberty party, its "one-idea" platform seemed to him unduly restrictive, and he still had grave doubts about the constitutionality of some measures demanded by most of its members— abolition of the interstate slave trade and slavery in the District of Columbia, for example.[51] At the same time, although giving promise of future vitality, the Liberty party was still very much in the minority. For these reasons, it seems, Hale decided to attempt a reconciliation of ambition and principle, to work within the Democratic party, to make it if possible the party of freedom. As a Democrat with latent antislavery sympathies, he went to Congress.

CHAPTER III

Democratic Congressman

THE Twenty-Eighth Congress was scheduled to convene early in December 1843, and as the day of his departure from Dover approached, Hale made the necessary preparations. His partner, John H. Wiggins, was to conduct the affairs of their law office and keep him advised of local political affairs. Mrs. Hale would remain at home with Lucy and Lizzie until he was firmly settled in Washington. To help her with work around the house during his absence, Hale hired a colored girl named Fanny who came "well recommended" at a dollar a week.[1]

It was with mixed emotions that his thoughts turned toward the national capital that fall. Once before, on the occasion of Van Buren's inauguration in 1837, Hale had gone to Washington. Then he had seen much that pleased him—the Capitol building ("It exceeds my expectations entirely"), the White House, "Ladies of the most perfect beauty . . . dressed with a richness & splendor which we do not see in our cold regions of the North"—but much also that repelled him. "I must confess," he had written home, "that my ideas of the dignity of the American Congress have not been elevated by what I have seen & heard here." There were too many representatives like Henry Wise of Virginia, "a miserable, brawling Blackguard" for whom Hale felt "utter loathing." And, indeed, "Universal, wide-spread, unblushing licentiousness . . . may with confidence be said to characterize the morals of this City." Most unappealing of all was the thought of so long a separation from family and friends. Yet even so, he must have had feelings of excitement and anticipation as he prepared to take his seat in the national Congress.[2]

Hale left Dover in the last week of November 1843, and arrived in

Washington early on the morning of the 29th, having stopped in Boston and Philadelphia to visit friends and relatives. From the railroad station he went directly to Mrs. Hamilton's boardinghouse on Capitol Hill, where he engaged a comfortable room on the top floor. Among the other roomers, who took their meals in Mrs. Hamilton's diningroom, were several congressmen, the most important of whom was Senator Levi Woodbury of New Hampshire. Woodbury and his wife had rooms immediately below Hale's, and he saw a good deal of them, especially during his first days in Washington. They went out of their way to help him get settled and become acquainted with other legislators, and he was happy to discover them "pleasant & social." Privately he wrote off Woodbury as a man whose "ambition & policy make him subservient to the South." The representatives at Mrs. Hamilton's he found politically more sound. "These gentlemen are all Democrats, all married men & all sympathize with my notions about slavery & the right of petition," he reported. Robert McClelland of Michigan he liked best of all, for his frank and cordial manner pleased him, and the two men, each in his first term, struck up a warm friendship.[3]

Hale arrived in Washington nearly a week before Congress convened, and he spent a good deal of it strolling about the capital, much like any sightseer. As on his earlier visit, he still found the Capitol itself the greatest wonder of all. Its sheer size he found overwhelming ("unused as I am to such masses") and its labyrinthine recesses still "impossible for a stranger to find his way about in." As if to balance the grandeur of the Capitol, there was Greenough's toga-clad statue of George Washington: "a most miserable affair," Hale concluded, "got up in exceedingly bad taste, nay in shocking and monstrous taste." In this first week he also paid social calls on other members of the New Hampshire delegation and their wives, and on December 6 he accompanied Senators Woodbury and Atherton to the White House where he met President Tyler.[4]

Always regular in his habits, Hale soon established a schedule for himself which he adhered to closely throughout his initial months in Washington. Rising at daybreak, he washed in cold water, shaved, and dressed. He then took a short walk and read newspapers until breakfast at 8:30 or 9. After a light breakfast of buckwheat cakes or bread and butter, he usually made a few calls, read, or, when the weather was good, took another walk, arriving at the Capitol shortly before noon. In the evening he returned to Mrs. Hamilton's, joining the other guests in a substantial dinner by candlelight. Dinner-table banter often continued afterwards in the parlor, where one might also read the day's papers or the latest Dickens novel. Frequently Hale retired to his room early, to answer letters, prepare speeches, or to chat in greater privacy with McClelland or some other political associate. In his early letters home, Hale noted with interest but no sign of repugnance that Mrs. Hamilton owned or hired slaves, one of whom acted as his *valet de chambre*. Each morning before Hale awoke, the slave kindled a fire. After breakfast he returned to black Hale's boots, brush his clothes, and do "any other little job of that sort." [5]

On weekends and at other times when Congress was not in session, Hale amused himself with steamboat rides on the Potomac, Washington fairs, or social calls. In Mrs. Atherton he found an unexpected friend (she was "really quite a social New England sort of a body," he informed his wife), and he spoke with her at length about what dresses Mrs. Hale should bring when she came to Washington in the spring, and traded small talk about common and uncommon acquaintances. He also found time to hear his first Italian opera, an experience he did not altogether enjoy. In February 1844, Lucy Hale, leaving the children with relatives in New Hampshire, joined her husband in Washington. Together they took boat trips, rented horse and chaise and rode across the Potomac into the rolling countryside of Virginia, and traveled to Mount Vernon to see Washington's tomb. Caught in the mainstream of capital society, the Hales swept from party to party, joined other members of Congress and their wives on sightseeing excursions, and entertained friends in the house Hale had rented upon his wife's arrival. John Hale's open and easygoing manner and Lucy's beauty and charm made them welcome wherever they went. Southern slaveholders and Northern abolitionists alike opened their doors to them, and the Hales reciprocated cordiality wherever they found it.[6]

But parties and balls, however pleasant, were merely incidental diversions. In Congress there was work to be done, and Hale spent the better part of his days at it.

The House of Representatives which convened on December 4, 1843, included a galaxy of illustrious politicians. Some, like ex-President John Quincy Adams, and Joshua Giddings, the antislavery voice of Ohio's Western Reserve, had already won national prominence. Many more—Hannibal Hamlin, Hamilton Fish, Stephen A. Douglas, Andrew Johnson, Alexander H. Stephens, and Howell Cobb—were like Hale newly elected, men whose hour of fame was yet to come. In the organization of the House, Hale was appointed to the Committee on Commerce—"an honorable place," he felt—along with Robert C. Winthrop, Preston King, Alcee LaBranche, and five others. LaBranche, a mild and pleasant Louisiana Democrat, was a curiosity to Hale: he had killed a man in a duel. At the second session of the Twenty-Eighth Congress, Hale served on the Committee for the District of Columbia where he got to know well a more distinguished defender of Southern rights—Alexander H. Stephens of Georgia.[7]

When Hale entered Congress, he recalled many years later, "I was as good a Democrat . . . as there was in the world." [8] In most respects his political behavior during his single term in the House bears this out. Together with other Jacksonians he supported resolutions declaring that a Bank of the United States "is hostile to the spirit of our institutions, and that its establishment would be destructive to the interests and dangerous to the liberties of the people," and voted for an Independent Treasury Bill which passed the House in December 1844. He regularly opposed federal appropriations for internal improvements. He favored a tariff for revenue only. He spoke out against imprisonment for debt, and in demagogic language championed lower postal rates in behalf of "the humble poor, whom necessity drives from the parental roof and the domestic fireside," and warned of the monopolistic character of the Post Office. He joined the successful fight to refund to Andrew Jackson the $1,000 Jackson had been fined in 1815 for contempt of a New Orleans court. And like every good Democrat he called for a strict construction of the Constitution, which was, he said, a "sacred" document, not "a plastic instrument to be shaped to suit every man's purpose." He hewed to this line even when it meant upholding the sanctity of the "federal ratio" which gave the slave states an estimated twenty-five additional seats in the House of Representatives and which John Quincy Adams proposed abolishing.[9]

In his dedication to another article of the Democratic faith, economy in government, Hale surpassed all but the most zealous Jacksonians. Tightfisted himself (a reaction, one suspects, to his father's free-spending ways), Hale demanded as much of Congress. Strict economy was a necessary condition for tariff reduction and abolition of the national debt—both desirable objects in Hale's eyes—and he was constantly on guard lest some extravagance pass unnoticed. No proposed expenditure was too small to escape his scrutiny. During debates on a general appropriations bill, he sought to reduce the salary of the Treasurer of the United States. He voted against a resolution that House and Senate funds be used to pay the funeral expenses of victims of the *Princeton* explosion, and he vigorously opposed a bill which would have provided a gratuity of six months' pay to widows and orphans of sailors who went to the bottom in the *U.S.S. Grampus*.[10]

The biggest piece of appropriations pie went to the army and the navy, and in their expenditures Hale saw the greatest possibility for retrenchment and reform. With stinging sarcasm he damned the army's practice of carrying supernumerary officers on its payrolls. "It was said these officers were employed; but employed in what?" Hale wanted to know. "It was said they were employed in bureaus; but if they were, they were ladies' bureaus, decorating their persons. Many of these officers were allowed forage and horses—to do what? To ride from one bureau to the other?"[11] Another proposal for cutting military spending, recommended by the New Hampshire legislature and forcefully advocated in Congress by Hale, was that of abolishing the United States Military Academy at West Point. Not only was the Academy too costly, Hale contended (its annual budget was about $200,000 a year), but "it failed to furnish officers for defense of the country, except in times of peace"; the capability of its graduates was open to serious question; and the number of officers was already disproportionally large. Even worse, West Point was "aristocratic in its tendency" and "utterly at variance with our democratic institutions." In this he was ostensibly referring to the element of favoritism in the appointment of cadets, but may well have been reflecting John Hodgdon's opinion that West Pointers "mostly have an arrogant, supercilious air . . . and are whigs in politics." [12]

The Navy Department seemed to offer even greater opportunities for economy. Three weeks after Congress assembled, Hale presented a resolution calling upon the Secretary of the Navy to report to the House current and anticipated expenditures for the home squadron. His object in asking for this information, he explained, was to show how, by abolishing the home squadron (which cruised the Atlantic coast from Newfoundland to the Amazon), Congress might at a stroke substantially reduce the government's $4.5 million deficit. He saw no reason why the Secretary's request for $9 million might not be cut in half. The home squadron served no real purpose, he argued, certainly none important enough to justify its staggering expense. He had no desire to destroy the navy, Hale protested. On the contrary, he was most friendly to it and wished only to reform its abuses. But, he charged, "the navy has been the pet child of the nation, and, like all other pet children, has run away with the whole patrimonial estate." It was foolish for the United States "to endeavor to contend with monarchies in keeping up the pageantry of a naval establishment." Retrenchment was called for and the home squadron was the place to begin. Hale's arguments proved unavailing, however, for although the decommissioning of the sloop *Vincennes* and the loss at sea of the schooner *Grampus* temporarily reduced the strength of the home squadron from nine vessels to seven, by 1845 eleven sail patrolled the waters off America's eastern coast. [13]

On all these issues, then—the Bank, internal improvements, the tariff, imprisonment for debt, Jackson's fine, strict construction, and economy in government—Hale took an orthodox Democratic stand. To be sure, his proposed military and naval reforms were unpopular with most Jacksonians (especially his Portsmouth constituents), but even here he was responding to recognizable Democratic prompt-ings. The rhetoric, too, of most of his early speeches was Demo-cratic, if not, as John Quincy Adams said, demagogical. Time and again Hale inveighed against "class aristocracies" while defending the interests of those of "humble station." [14]

Yet while the spectre of the "monster" Bank still disturbed the sleep of loyal Jacksonians, and while tariff reform and hostility to federal support for roads and canals still belonged to the Democratic creed, such issues had already lost much of their explosive power. New questions of disruptive force were fast rising to replace them, questions made the more violent by their relation to slavery. Freedom of petition and the annexation of Texas touched off the most heated debates in the Twenty-Eighth Congress, and on those issues Hale, revealing his antislavery leanings, took what many party leaders called an un-Democratic position.

In the House, controversy over the right of petition centered on House rule 21, the so-called "gag" rule. Behind it lay half a century of congressional experience in the receipt of antislavery petitions. The first petitions to Congress relating to slavery were those ad-dressed in 1790 by Pennsylvania Quakers and the Pennsylvania Society for the Abolition of Slavery, protesting against the slave trade. For forty years thereafter memorials and petitions trickled into Congress praying for the abolition of slavery in the District of Columbia, an end to the interstate and foreign slave trade, and gradual emancipation. Quietly received, they were referred to select committees and seldom heard of again. In these early decades of the nineteenth century, petitions touching on slavery, in one way or another, arrived from the South as well as the North. But after about 1830, with the rise of organized abolitionism, petitions of protest came increasingly from the North, and Southern opposition to them increased. In their demands for checks on antislavery petitions, slave state representatives received support from many Northern Democrats who looked upon the swelling stream of such petitions as a Whig tactic designed to obstruct Democratic programs by clogging legislative machinery and also to keep in the public eye a question embarrassing to Democrats. On May 26, 1836, therefore, the House approved the Pinkney gag rule, providing that

all petitions, memorials, resolutions, propositions, or papers relating in any way or to any extent whatever to the subject of slavery shall, without being printed or referred, be laid upon the table and that no further action whatever be taken thereon.

It was thereafter renewed at each session until 1840 when, in a somewhat more severe form, it became standing rule 21.[15]

From the beginning there had been strong opposition to the gag rule, and by the time Hale entered Congress the forces favoring its repeal were aggressive and well-organized. Leading the fight in the House was the flinty ex-President, John Quincy Adams. Receiving able support from antislavery Whigs like Giddings of Ohio, William Slade of Vermont, Nathaniel Borden of Massachusetts, Seth Gates of New York, and Francis James of Pennsylvania, and astutely advised by Theodore Weld and Joshua Leavitt, Adams pressed for repeal with such vigor that angry Southern representatives had in 1842 tried formally to censure him. Unsuccessful in this attempt, the House did censure Giddings shortly after for his introduction of the antislavery *Creole* resolutions. But Giddings dramatically established his right to discuss slavery in the House of Representatives when, after resigning his seat, he returned with a clear-cut mandate from the Western Reserve. By 1843 the days of the gag rule seemed numbered.[16]

Hale came to Washington prepared to assist in its demise. Other New Hampshire congressmen, he knew, would not be likely to vote with him. For one thing, most still believed that if all abolitionist petitions were read their "senseless ravings" and "dull homilies" would obstruct the proper deliberations of Congress. The right to *assemble* and *present* a petition had not been abridged, they said, nor had Congress passed any *law* abridging such a right—merely a House *rule*. Furthermore, Senator Atherton himself, when a member of the House in 1838, had given his name to a gag rule, and New Hampshiremen were naturally reluctant to oppose what he so publicly had advocated. In any event, party discipline could be expected to keep most Granite State Democrats in line. But Hale's mind had been made up for some time. Sounding out his messmates at Mrs. Hamilton's before Congress convened, he was pleased to find "the prospect of a respectable Democratic vote in favor of the right of petition" stronger than he had anticipated.[17]

His own objections to the 21st rule were two: it was an unconstitutional abridgment of the right of petition, and it gave unwarranted aid to the slaveholders. The gag benefited the slaveholders, he explained, by avoiding direct votes on the receipt of abolitionist petitions (which made it easy for those "who have not courage enough to vote as their conscience dictates") and by stifling debate on slavery. While admitting that the federal government might not rightfully interfere with slavery in states where it existed, Hale was unwilling that Congress should in any way assist in its perpetuation or extension.[18]

On the opening day of the first session of the Twenty-Eighth Congress, Adams moved to amend the House rules by excepting the 21st rule. The division which followed showed ninety-one in favor of repeal, ninety-five opposed. Of the New Hampshire delegation, only Hale voted for repeal; Burke, Norris, and Reding responded "nay." Hale's vote came as a pleasant surprise to most congressional defenders of the right of petition, the more so because of what Adams called "New Hampshire sycophancy to the South." Giddings heard Hale's resonant "aye" and said to himself, "There's a man the slaveholders can't use."[19]

At home, the response to Hale's independent stand, though mixed, was generally favorable. Many had freely predicted that Hale would put himself into the party traces as readily as Burke or Atherton, reported John Parkman. "These men now give you credit for more moral [fiber] than they thought you had." From Exeter, Amos Tuck, recently a Democratic representative to the General Court, wrote warmly praising Hale's stand on principle. There was grumbling among party chiefs, he disclosed, but many Democrats openly approved of his vote. "No 21st Rule will prevent our speaking plainly," he promised. Many others wrote telling of wide popular approval of Hale's course.[20]

The Democratic press, more accurately reflecting the views of the party bosses, reacted less warmly, yet even in the fourth estate Hale had his champions. The Dover *Gazette,* the Exeter *News-Letter,* and the Manchester *Democrat* all upheld Hale's vote on the gag. "Instead of regarding his vote on the gag rule as any dereliction of duty," said the Dover *Gazette,* "we think he did his duty . . . to his God and his constituents, and that both approve of it." The *New Hampshire Patriot,* not wishing to wash dirty linen in public, at first passed over Hale's defection in silence. Not until December 28, in an editorial entitled "Union our Strength," did it mention the right-of-petition controversy, and then its rebuke to Hale was gentle—not even mentioning him by name. By far the most critical, understandably enough, was Congressman Burke's Newport *Argus & Spectator.*[21]

Hale had plenty of time to ponder the probable effect his vote would have on his political career because, as he wrote his law partner on December 14, Congress spent several days "doing just exactly nothing" because of adjournments honoring recently deceased members. In a way, he seemed a little surprised to have caused such a stir, since, as he correctly pointed out, "every other member from the New England States except my colleagues voted as I did." His motives, he insisted, were pure and simple. Conscience and principle had dictated his votes against the gag and in favor of receiving antislavery petitions, not, as *Hill's Patriot* contended, hopes of making "political capital" out of "Northern Abolitionism." He was pleased with the many letters of approval received from constituents and others, "but still if it were otherwise," he told his wife, "I would infinitely prefer resigning & going home to staying here in the receipt of all the honors & emoluments which the Government can offer" if it meant retracting from his position. "I want the record which is made up of my votes on this subject to stand right for time & for Eternity." [22]

Still, while keeping an eye on Eternity, Hale was not without temporal ambition and did what he could to protect his interests. When early in January 1844 he got wind of attempts to censure him at various county and district Democratic conventions soon to be held, he at once wrote to political friends asking that they use their influence to quash any such resolutions in their part of New Hampshire. It seemed to Hale that the campaign of censure directed against him was mainly the work of a handful of Democratic leaders whose devotion to party unity blinded them to popular opinion. His own mail indicated strong public support for his actions. "If this be so," he asked, "why cannot the people speak out their true sentiments boldly & not leave a few managers to manufacture a spurious public opinion for them." [23]

Just how favorable New Hampshire voters in fact were toward Hale's vote on the gag rule is not easily answered. His backing was strongest in the eastern portion of the state, especially in Strafford, Rockingham, Carroll, and Merrimack Counties. There all political conventions taking stands on the right-of-petition controversy "heartily approved" Hale's "manly and independent" stand.[24] Not even Frank Pierce, since 1842 state Democratic chairman, could prevent the Concord town meeting from passing by large majorities resolutions upholding the right of petition and upbraiding Reding, Burke, and Norris for supporting the gag. In the West, pro-Hale sentiment was decidedly weaker, particularly in Burke's barony, Sullivan County, where Democrats censured Hale's vote, "in regard to the reception of incendiary petitions." [25]

On the whole, Hale found that his stand against the 21st rule had done him no harm. The Democratic leadership frowned but dared not treat him harshly because of his sizable following among the rank and file. Right of petition had proven a surprisingly popular issue—even men like Pierce objected less to Hale's views than to the open display of party disunity which they occasioned. " 'Gags,' " Moses Cartland wrote to John G. Whittier, "are getting to be unpopular.

The old 'Empire' presents a better front than she is wont,—and our comical Jack Hale will be, on the whole, more popular for his upright vote on the 21st Rule." [26]

In December 1844 the House, with Hale's support, at last rescinded the gag rule. For old John Quincy Adams it was a glorious end to a long and hard-fought battle. "Blessed, forever blessed, be the name of God!" he exulted. But already the forces of antislavery were rallying to meet a new and graver threat: the annexation of Texas and the extension of slavery.[27]

Sentiment favorable to the annexation of Texas was nothing new. Only with reluctance had the United States yielded its claims to that region in the Adams-Onís Treaty of 1821, and repeatedly thereafter American presidents had negotiated for its purchase. Yet once the Lone Star Republic had won its independence and offered itself for annexation, first Jackson and then Van Buren demurred, each afraid to raise the volatile question of slavery expansion.

At the time, most New Hampshiremen likewise were content to let the matter lie. In 1838 Governor Hill declared: "I consider the present territory of the United States to be sufficiently extensive, and would not, on that account, favor the annexation of Texas or any other country to the United States." The state legislature declined to consider resolutions either for or against annexation. Leading newspapers, Democratic as well as Whig, damned the Texas question as a "firebrand," and denounced proposals for annexation as "BLACK AS INK—AS BITTER AS HELL!" Such was the state of popular opinion when Hale left for Washington in November 1843.[28]

Soon after the Twenty-Eighth Congress convened, President John Tyler made it clear that he planned to renew attempts to add Texas to the Union. The resignation of Secretary of State Daniel Webster in the summer of 1843 had given Tyler free rein, and in his annual address to Congress in December he plumped unmistakably for annexation. Democratic Senator Robert J. Walker of Mississippi followed with a long article printed in the Washington *Globe* on February 3, 1844, strongly advocating immediate annexation. When Walker then published in the Richmond *Enquirer* a letter of Andrew

Jackson's which stressed the strategic importance of Texas, the case for its acquisition was fully stated and could no longer be ignored.

Hale found this turn of events distressing. Though his fears were less elaborate than those of Adams, who saw the annexation of Texas as "the first step to the conquest of all Mexico, of the West India islands, of a maritime, colonizing, slave-tainted monarchy, and of extinguishing freedom," he objected strongly to what he conceived as a Southern scheme to extend its peculiar institution. He watched with alarm as John C. Calhoun carried forward annexation negotiations begun by the unfortunate Abel P. Upshur, killed in February by the explosion aboard the *Princeton*. "The annexation of Texas is an engrossing subject of conversation," Hale wrote to a friend on March 25, adding glumly: "I fear the danger of such a measure is more threatening & immediate than is generally supposed." [29] Yet in the House debates on Texas during the spring of 1844, he gave small support to the foes of annexation, limiting himself to one brief speech in which he ridiculed "that spirit which was so courageous to Mexico, and yet sat tamely still and listened to the roar of the British lion in Oregon." [30] One reason for this reticence was his awareness of growing pro-Texas feeling in New Hampshire.

Between November 1843 and April 1844 a number of leading New Hampshire Democrats, previously lukewarm or hostile to Texas, came out for annexation. The party press reflected this transformation of sentiment. In March both the Dover *Gazette* and the *New Hampshire Patriot,* previously cold toward annexation, became more sympathetic. In April *Hill's Patriot* urged adding Texas to the Union.[31] Whatever the reasons for this shift of opinion (Jackson's letter and mounting fears of British designs on Texas were two of the more important), by the time of the national convention in May 1844 annexation sentiment was widespread among New Hampshire Democrats. Few of them objected when despite pledges their delegates deserted Martin Van Buren, an opponent of immediate annexation, and backed the dark-horse James K. Polk on a pro-Texas platform.[32]

In mid-June, after Congress adjourned, Hale returned to New

Hampshire. He found his party already at work with an eye to the Presidential election in November. Unhesitatingly he gave his support to Polk. He made no secret of his disagreement with the Tennesseean on the subject of Texas. But, as he explained later, "Disagreeing with Mr. Polk on this single point, I did not deem it a matter to justify my desertion of the party with which I had acted," and he therefore campaigned vigorously for Polk's election.[33] Democrats from all parts of New England and beyond sought Hale as a speaker of proven effectiveness. Much of October and November he spent on the stump. Thanks in part to Hale's efforts, Polk carried New Hampshire and Maine by comfortable margins, although other New England states fell to his Whig opponent, Henry Clay.

From the moment Congress reconvened in December 1844 it was apparent that Texas would be its major concern. In June 1844 the Senate had rejected Secretary of State Calhoun's treaty of annexation by a vote of 35 to 16. Two days later, Tyler, with a view to annexation by joint resolution, sent the rejected treaty and related documents to the House. Now, in December, interpreting Polk's victory as a national mandate for annexation, he recommended effecting union with the Lone Star Republic by "joint resolution, or act, to be perfected and made binding on the two countries, when adopted in like manner by the government of Texas." [34]

During December and early January Hale watched in silence as Charles J. Ingersoll, Stephen A. Douglas, and others introduced joint resolutions for annexing Texas. These resolutions either made no specific mention of slavery or proposed its exclusion north of the Missouri Compromise line—a barren concession to those who demanded free soil.[35] Ingersoll, as chairman of the Committee on Foreign Affairs, was leader of the pro-annexation forces in the House. A self-styled "constant and unhesitating advocate of getting back Texas," Ingersoll insisted that the will of the people was clearly for annexation, that it was the duty of Congress to act upon that will. Apprehensions of the spread of slavery he dismissed as "unfounded." "Slavery cannot increase by the annexation of Texas," he asserted, "probably the contrary." [36] Robert Charles Winthrop, a Massachusetts

Whig and a descendant of the Puritan governor, most eloquently argued the case against annexation, mainly on constitutional grounds. Quoting Calhoun's doctrine "that Congress cannot make a contract with a foreign nation," he warned that though the people of Massachusetts loved the Union, if "there was any act which would absolve them from their allegiance to ... the constitution, it was the proposed act for the annexation of Texas." [37]

Winthrop had the advantage of speaking for a state which sheltered a large and influential anti-Texas faction and which had backed Clay in the November election. Hale's position was a good deal more difficult. Not only had New Hampshire voted solidly for the annexationist Polk, but on December 27, 1844, the state legislature had overwhelmingly passed a series of nine joint resolutions supporting the "reannexation" of Texas and calling on the state's representatives in Congress to work for that end. Hale had no wish to disobey the legislature's instructions, nor did he wish to support annexation. The eighth of the legislature's resolutions seemed to offer the only way out of this dilemma. That resolve declared:

> That we believe with Mr. Clay, "that the reannexation of Texas will add more free than slave States to the Union, and that it would be unwise to refuse a permanent acquisition . . . on account of a temporary institution."

Accordingly, after presenting New Hampshire's resolutions to Congress on January 7, 1845, Hale announced his intention, when he got the opportunity, to propose "an amendment calculated to test the accuracy" of the eighth resolution.[38]

On January 10 he moved for suspension of the House rules in order to introduce his proviso regarding Texas, that it might be referred to the Committee of the Whole on the state of the Union, and printed. As read by a clerk, Hale's proviso would, once the boundary dispute between Mexico and the United States had been settled, have divided Texas into equal parts by a line running northwest from "a point on the Gulf of Mexico midway between the northern and southern boundaries thereof on the coast." In the territory lying southwest of that line, slavery was to be forever excluded. The vote in favor of suspending the rules at Hale's request was 92 to 82, far short of the required two-thirds. Reding, alone of the New Hampshire representatives, supported the introduction of Hale's proviso; Burke and Norris both helped kill it.[39]

Hale's whole intent had been to point up the pro-slavery character of annexation, and, if worst came to worst, to make annexation as unexceptionable as possible. "I should have voted against the measure, even if my amendment were adopted," he claimed in later years. To Hale's mind, the House's refusal to consider his proviso gave lie to the eighth New Hampshire resolution and freed his hands. His course seemed clear. On January 11 he mailed to his constituents copies of a letter explaining why he could not support the annexation of Texas. Its receipt in New Hampshire seeded a political storm the marks of which remained until the Civil War.[40]

CHAPTER IV

The "Hale Storm"

HALE'S letter "To the Democratic Republican Electors of New Hampshire," printed by Blair and Rives, bore the date January 7, 1845. Probably he wrote it soon after learning of the state legislature's pro-Texas resolves, and sent it to press early in January. He kept its existence a carefully guarded secret until he released it on January 11. In June 1844 New Hampshire Democrats had renominated Hale for Congress. Now, with the election but two months away and the national House of Representatives rapidly moving toward a vote on Texas, he felt bound to explain "that course of action which an imperious sense of duty impels me to pursue." This his letter to his constituents set out to do.[1]

"I desire to refer this matter [of Texas] to you, a committee of the whole people of the State," Hale began, "that you may decide the whole question and announce that decision at the polls. I might have taken a different course; I might have asked the advice and counsel of those who, by their place and station, may be considered as authorized and legitimate exponents of the popular will; but I prefer to go directly to the people. They constitute the only true fountain of power; they are best qualified to declare truly their own opinions." This flattering preface out of the way, he launched first into a brief discussion of the constitutionality of incorporating Texas into the Union. Like a good lawyer with a bad case, Hale took his precedents where he could find them. In this instance, he exhumed the constitutional arguments of Van Buren and Levi Woodbury against United States participation in a Pan-American mutual-defense pact (made at the time of the abortive Panama conference in 1826), and with a straight face passed them off as "impregnable" arguments against the annexation of Texas. It was an unconvincing effort.[2]

Hale was on stronger ground when he spoke of the proslavery character of schemes for annexation. The South wanted Texas "as the sure and effectual means of sustaining slavery," and it was a "fond delusion" for Northerners to pretend that annexation would facilitate its gradual extermination. As for the belief that Texas would yield more free than slave states, if there were any substance in it, Hale said, he would cheerfully support annexation by constitutional measures. But such a belief was illusory. He quoted remarks of Secretaries of State Upshur and Calhoun and United States Representatives Ingersoll and James E. Belser to show the implacable determination of leading public officials to keep Texas free of abolition. The proslavery Texas constitution indicated clearly enough the impossibility of any free state being formed out of that territory, unless abolition were made a legal condition of annexation. Otherwise, annexation would extend the area of bondage, not the area of freedom.

This, at any rate, was Hale's opinion. He could only hope that his constituents agreed. "Should what I have here expressed meet your approbation, and that approbation expressed at the polls," he said in conclusion, "I shall be most happy . . . But if, on the other hand, you shall think differently from me on this subject; and should, therefore, deem it expedient to select another person to effectuate your purposes in Congress, no citizen of the State will bow more submissively to your will than myself." [3]

Surely Hale must have realized that a direct appeal to the people on this issue would anger party leaders, all more or less committed to annexation, and thus jeopardize his political career. Why then did he write his letter? At least two answers suggest themselves. Convinced that slavery was a sin, and equally convinced that annexation would extend and help perpetuate that sin (beliefs daily strengthened by the impassioned arguments of other anti-Texas congressmen), he apparently decided that the time had come to speak out. Christian duty as well as political honesty seemed to demand as much. To make his views known in New Hampshire before the March election required a public statement. Secondly, with the success of his independent stand on the gag rule still fresh in his memory, he likely felt that once again the rank and file would sustain him and protect him from reprisals from the Democratic bosses. There was ample reason to believe that it might. Shortly after Polk's nomination, Amos Tuck had promised Hale strong Democratic support if he openly declared his anti-Texas convictions, and on January 4, 1845, William Claggett, a Portsmouth Democrat of some influence, penned a note saying that those in New Hampshire who supported annexation did so only because they had been deceived into believing that the object was to extend the bounds of freedom. Once enlightened, he was sure, they would oppose annexation, and *"Dough Faces* will not much longer flourish hereabouts." Hale likely viewed his letter as an instrument of such enlightenment, as an important step toward bringing his constituents right on antislavery. Whatever his motives, one thing seems clear: he had no intention of splintering the Democratic party in New Hampshire.[4]

Yet his actions had precisely that effect. Hale's New Hampshire colleagues in Washington received his letter on January 11. All were quick to see the threat it posed for party unity. That same day Burke and Woodbury denounced Hale's insubordination to State Central Committee Chairman Pierce and suggested a special Democratic convention "to decide whether they agree with the Legislature or Mr. Hale & if not with him—whether they think best to present & support a new nomination?" Two days later, on the 13th, Senator Atherton sounded a calmer note. Hale's letter he called "ill-judged & ill-timed," but he cautioned Pierce against taking any hasty steps. He feared that a new convention and nomination, as Woodbury and Burke proposed, would be to play into Hale's hands. "Would it not," asked Atherton, "be raising the very issue he desires, for ulterior purposes, & would it not probably, at this late period before election, afford him a triumph which then would seem to be a triumph over the Democratic party?" Better, he felt, to pay as little attention as possible to Hale's letter, and to rebuke him, if deemed necessary, by having "his vote (imperceptibly as to reasons) dwindle below that of his fellows on the Ticket, without any organized opposition on the

part of the Democratic party or any concerted public movements."
On the 15th Atherton wrote again, informing Pierce that Woodbury
and Moses Norris, Jr., both now agreed with him on the inexpediency
of assembling a special convention. But by then Pierce had already
set party machinery in motion against Hale.[5]

Franklin Pierce first learned of Hale's "insubordination" in the
letters he received from Burke and Woodbury on the afternoon of
the 15th.[6] Despite his friendship for Hale, which dated from Bowdoin
days and which survived differences on the gag rule,[7] Pierce acted
with vigor to punish Hale's "deliberate betrayal of the party which
had so long supported him."[8] It was one thing for Hale to oppose
established Democratic policy by his votes and speeches in Congress;
it was quite a different thing to appeal for support over the heads
of the party chieftains, especially when such support, if forthcoming,
would stand as an implied rebuke to all those who advocated the
annexation of Texas.[9] Hale, Pierce concluded, had grown ambitious
and was seeking to exploit the slavery issue to further his own ends.
"Self alone is apparently in his mind—his party & his friends have no
place there," he remarked bitterly. Not if Pierce could help it would
Hale's "miserable, double dealing scheme" succeed. Party regularity
must be preserved at all costs, particularly if New Hampshire hoped
to get its share of patronage from the incoming, pro-Texas Polk
administration.[10]

Pierce moved swiftly to ostracize Hale. He opened with an article
in the *New Hampshire Patriot* which expressed "unqualified condemnation" of Hale's "factious, selfish and disorganizing" actions. In
this same article he also first leveled the charge, so often repeated in
subsequent months, that Hale had acted in collusion with Rufus
Choate in drafting the letter to his constituents.[11] Next, Pierce sum-
moned all state committeemen to Concord on January 20 to make
plans for a special convention sometime in February. Having for the
time being done all he could from his office in the capital, Pierce set
out on a rapid swing through Strafford, Rockingham, and Hillsborough Counties to gauge at first hand the amount of pro-Hale
sentiment and to make clear to party regulars the path of duty.[12]

His first stop was Dover. There he discovered most Democrats "surprised greived [*sic*] & vexed" at Hale's anti-Texas stand, and willing to scratch his name from the ticket.[13] To be sure, John T. Gibbs, long a friend of Hale and editor of the Dover *Gazette,* had already set in type the text of Hale's letter together with a hearty commendation of its contents; but Gibbs was no match for the Democratic chairman, and before Pierce left town Gibbs had changed his stand. The Whig *Enquirer* hinted that Pierce's threat to establish a rival Democratic paper in Dover had brought Gibbs back into line.[14] Dover apparently secure, Pierce moved next to Portsmouth where he received assurances of fealty from all Democrats save John Lord Hayes. Hayes, then clerk of the federal court and chairman of the town's Young Men's Democratic Association, gloomily warned Hale the next day: "It is evident that the whole of the party discipline is against you and you must rely upon the people." From Portsmouth Pierce traveled first to Exeter (where Amos Tuck, David A. Gregg, and Henry F. French alone among prominent Democrats, stood up for Hale), then on to Nashua, Manchester, and back to Concord.[15]

Everywhere Pierce hammered away at the same theme: had Hale been content to vote or speak against annexation, New Hampshire Democrats could not have objected. But Hale had not been so content. He had publicly asked the Democratic voters to endorse his anti-Texas views, knowing full well that such endorsement would tacitly condemn the other Granite State congressmen and state legislators who approved the pro-annexation resolutions. Hale was being wilfully factious and must be thrown overboard.

Pierce was pleased that so many seemed willing to make a new nomination. "You can hardly conceive the decided condemnation with which Hale's appeal is received by our people," he gleefully informed Woodbury upon his return to Concord. "There is but one voice upon the subject & that voice demands a new State Convention." On January 20 the central committee issued a call for such a convention to meet at Concord on February 12. By then even the cautious Atherton was willing that Hale be formally deposed.[16]

The Democratic press, Pierce had assured Woodbury, would "be perfectly united." [17] He knew whereof he spoke. Not only did all Radical papers roast Hale for his "ambitious" and "double-dealing" conduct, but Conservative journals as well sharply criticized his "treachery." Early in 1844 there had been signs that the Conservatives were "fast crawling back" to the fold. [18] Hale's presence as a common enemy as well as agreement on the paramount question of expansionism facilitated reconciliation, and by February 6, 1845, the two chief Conservative organs had declared for Governor John Steele and the regular Democratic candidates for Congress: Norris, Mace Moulton, and James H. Johnson. As if to assure the Radicals of their renewed loyalty, the Conservative press abused Hale at every chance. His "somerset," said *Hill's Patriot,* was really no more than a predictable return to Federalism; it was no coincidence that Hale's arguments against the annexation of Texas smacked of those used by Jefferson's opponents against the acquisition of Louisiana in 1803. Together with the Radical *Patriot,* the *New Hampshire Gazette* attacked Hale's "skulking attempt" to buttress his anti-Texas position with the opinions of Woodbury and Van Buren on the Panama mission, unscrupulously "lugged in head and shoulders." [19]

With Democratic leadership and party press solidly against Hale, the outcome of the special nominating convention was a foregone conclusion. Under Pierce's watchful eye the delegates wasted little time in condemning Hale. His letter they labeled "insidious in character, and deceptive in its presentation of the question of annexation," and with near unanimity chose John Woodbury, a lackluster party hack from Salem, to replace him on the Democratic ticket. All proceeded smoothly, as Pierce had planned. Only Stephen S. Foster, an uninvited looker-on, sounded a discordant note—demanding the right to refute some of Pierce's remarks. But the chairman promptly ruled that only delegates had a right to the floor, Foster grudgingly gave way, and the convention finished its business in good order. [20]

In deciding to jettison Hale, the delegates to the special convention seem to have given little if any attention to the merits or demerits of his views on Texas. Instead they conceived of their duty in terms of party loyalty, not party policy. "The argument of the convention, that appeared to have the most influence in setting aside the regular nomination," a delegate from Candia noted, "was that J. P. Hale . . . has sold himself, soul and body to Mr. Choate, and the Massachusetts whigs." [21]

If Hale was surprised at the speed and decisiveness with which his party moved against him, he nonetheless reacted calmly. In his letter to his constituents he had promised to "bow submissively" should they select another candidate in his place, and he showed no inclination to renege, despite pleas from friends in New Hampshire that he return home and fight for reelection. Still, Democratic misrepresentations and innuendoes disturbed him, and on January 18 he wrote a long letter to Pierce designed to set the record straight.

"I want to write one word to you as a friend, not a solitary one as a Politician," Hale began. Whether or not his views on the Texas question were correct, he would not say. But they were his honest convictions, he insisted, and he had done no more than act upon them. When the state legislature had requested him to pursue a course which his conscience told him was wrong, he had felt bound "plainly, distinctly and unequivocally" to lay open his "whole mind to the people." Should this "result in defeating my re-election," Hale continued, "I do not ask any friend of mine to feel the least aggrieved on my account." And however much those convictions might differ from others', there was surely "no occasion or necessity for angry denunciation or crimination growing out of this." "I will say to you what I would not say to the Public lest it might seem like affectation and hypocrisy," Hale wrote in closing. "That is that I believe in conscience, in duty, in right and wrong & above all in God who is over all. I have acted in obedience to my convictions of what is due to all the impulses proceeding from those sources. I would not retract what I have done for the most brilliant political career that ever flattered the hopes of the most ambitious political aspirant, though political oblivion were to be the result of my present position. I do not ask any friend to justify, excuse or palliate what I have done in a political point, unless his own convictions approve it." But he did ask that they do him the credit of believing that he had acted with honest motives.[22] If Pierce's reply (which began with a chilly "my dear Sir" and which termed Hale's circular "cruel and unjust") ever reached Hale, it simply confirmed the outcast's jaundiced view of New Hampshire politics.[23]

Although keeping an eye on developments in the Granite State, Hale gave most of his attention between mid-January and March to Congressional affairs. On January 25, the annexation of Texas by joint resolution came to a vote in the House. True to his word, Hale joined Whigs and a handful of Democrats (including, surprisingly enough, John Reding) in the minority opposition.[24] Yet on most rollcalls, such as on appropriations for the Cumberland Road, he voted with his party. So pessimistic was Hale about his political future, he later recalled, that when he left Washington early in March he "had no more idea of being returned to Congress again from New Hampshire than ... of succeeding to the vacant throne of China." In fact, he had already made tentative plans to enter a law partnership with Theodore Sedgwick in New York City.[25]

But while Hale prepared for his political demise, others were hard at work to avert it. From the beginning there had been signs that a fair number of Democrats (not to mention Whigs and abolitionists) approved his stand on the Texas issue, and that only the strong action of Franklin Pierce had headed off public displays of support. Scores wrote to Hale in Washington, pledging their allegiance and urging that he return to New Hampshire to plead his case in person.[26] Many towns instructed their delegates to the February 12 nominating convention to uphold Hale's renomination, and on February 4 Democrats of northern Coos County adopted an address to their fellow citizens of New Hampshire praising Hale for his "correct and manly course," and scoring the "driving, blustering clique of party leaders" who had forfeited "confidence by their subserviency to the interest of the southern slaveholders." [27] But the Democratic press, loyal to Pierce's bidding, uniformly ignored such expressions of approval of Hale's stand, while apathy and heavy snows kept the special convention from accurately representing the opinions of party members. Only one of Coos County's forty-five towns was represented at the meeting that "decapitated" Hale, only two of Carroll's fourteen, ten of Cheshire's twenty-two, twenty of Grafton's thirty-eight. Pierce, playing heavily on feelings of party loyalty, led the rump convention where he wanted.[28]

Those Democrats who came to Hale's defense did so far a variety of reasons. Some, like James Peverly, a Concord dry-goods merchant, strongly opposed the admission of Texas, denied that Polk's election was a mandate for annexation, and felt compelled to back a man who dared to speak against it. A follower of Isaac Hill, Peverly had in 1843 voted against Hale. "But now," he wrote in January 1845, "whatever our views may be on State policy & State matters, on this question of annexation I am with you, and if an attempt is made to impeach your democracy for expressing sentiments which every freeman ought to approve, my humble aid shall cheerfully be given in your behalf."[29] Never before had a national issue so affected state politics. Many others sided with Hale because they disapproved of the high-handed, imperious way Pierce had punished Hale's nonconformity. Pierce, like Isaac Hill before him, had kept party control firmly in the hands of himself and a small group of Democratic leaders, known to their enemies as "the Clique," or "the Concord Regency." This group, controlling and working through the state central committee, set policy, disbursed patronage, made and unmade political careers—in short, managed the Democratic party in New Hampshire. With so few men exerting so much power, it was inevitable that their actions should breed discontent. Such discontent, coming to a head in 1845, worked strongly to Hale's advantage.

To many, Hale seemed an innocent victim of political despotism, a man whose only crime had been to "refuse to follow in the wake of certain would be *dictators* of the Democratic party, however zig zag their course may be."[30] To be so victimized for expressing sentiments entertained by many if not most Democrats, "could they be allowed to express them independently," was especially galling.[31] For men like Amos Tuck, the time had come for action. "The state

has been cursed with dictation of small men for years," Tuck told
Hale, "and I am willing for a division; if that becomes inevitable
in consequence of your doing your duty." [32] That Tuck himself was
then in the Clique's doghouse no doubt contributed to the equanimity with which he viewed such a political schism. The same might be
said for N. Porter Cram, another early defender of Hale. In 1844
Cram had run unsuccessfully for state senator, so unsuccessfully in
fact that the Democratic machine dropped him in 1845 in favor of a
more promising candidate, much to Cram's disgruntlement. It was
only natural that Tuck, Cram, and others like them, nursing grudges
against "self-constituted party leaders," should throw their support
to Hale. [33]

Another source of discontent among Radical Democrats which
benefited Hale was the backsliding of Pierce, Hibbard, and other
party leaders on the railroad issue. At its November session in 1844,
the legislature had passed, and Governor Steele had signed, a new
railroad act. In a roundabout way, this act approached Conservative
ground by providing for the establishment of a state railroad commission with powers, under certain conditions, to assess damages and
force unwilling farmers to sell lands along the surveyed route of
chartered railroads. In giving its blessing to this new law, the Clique
apparently hoped to pave the way for a reconciliation with the Hill
faction. In this their hopes were to a large extent realized, but only
at the expense of alienating many Radicals, particularly farmers, to
whom the railroad seemed a menace. "The *real* Radicals are dis-
affected at the Gen Railroad Law," observed Jacob Ela. Even Governor Steele "admitted that abandoning the radical ground was
working badly." [34] Steele himself, whose eccentric religious views had
recently drawn him into a public controversy with an orthodox
clergyman, was yet another millstone about the Democracy's neck.

Prior to the Concord convention which dropped Hale, his champions acted for the most part individually. Without an organization
to direct and coordinate their efforts, without a friendly press to
publicize their speeches and resolves, without even active aid and
encouragement from the man whose actions they were defending, the

friends of Hale were no match for the Clique's well-oiled machine. Typical of the difficulties they faced during the first months after Hale's Texas letter reached New Hampshire, was the experience of John L. Hayes. At a Democratic caucus held in Portsmouth on February 7 to choose delegates to the Concord convention, Hayes attempted to deliver a carefully prepared pro-Hale address. He had hardly begun to speak before "outbursts of condemnation prompted by the party leaders" forced him to stop. The next day, at his own expense, Hayes had his speech printed and circulated it in pamphlet form.[35]

The ease with which the regular Democrats dropped Hale from the ticket was convincing proof to his backers that to defeat Woodbury in March, some sort of statewide organization was essential. Not long after the Concord convention, Tuck and Hayes took the first step toward such an organization. Meeting in the jury room of Exeter's Old Court House, the two lawyers drafted a call, soon signed by 263 Rockingham Democrats (mainly farmers, merchants, and mechanics), asking that all Hale's political friends meet in the vestry of the First Church of Exeter on February 22, "to make a full declaration of their sentiments, and take into consideration the present position of our party."[36]

Despite bad weather and all but impassable roads, a sizable number of Independent Democrats (as Tuck and Hayes christened the pro-Hale forces) turned out for the meeting on Washington's birthday. At the morning session conferees elected Professor Joseph G. Hoyt presiding officer and rocked the vestry with cheers and applause as he, Tuck, Hayes, and others praised Hale and lambasted the Concord Clique. In the afternoon Hayes presented and the convention endorsed resolutions calling for a rededication of the Democratic party to "the principles of human equality and universal justice," denouncing slavery as an institution disgracing America in the eyes of the world, opposing the admission of Texas, and lauding Hale, the "fearless advocate of human rights." Before adjourning, the convention also adopted an address to the Democrats of New Hampshire and established an Independent Democratic organization to work for Hale's reelection to Congress. "There was a good deal of deep feeling manifested, and not a little native eloquence," reported the Exeter *News-Letter*. Fairer than most, the *News-Letter* described the convention as "respectable in numbers, respectable in talents, respectable in the character of those who composed it." It seemed that William Claggett had been right. "The Democracy is in commotion," he had written Hale two days before the Exeter meeting. "The Concord dictators may begin to shake—they put too much fire under the pot, causing it to boil over & put it out." [37]

The most immediately noticeable effect of the convention was the lift it gave to Independent Democratic spirits. Their labors seemed more purposeful and prospects less bleak. Pulling in harness along a clearly marked path, they might yet carry Hale to victory. Following the gathering at Exeter, organizational meetings throughout the eastern counties further stimulated pro-Hale feeling. Committees of publication and correspondence broadcast long lists of resolves denouncing the Clique's "tyranny" and condemning the annexation of Texas. Independent Democrats combed the countryside for contributions of money and talent, circulated anti-Texas literature, and explained to wavering voters why Hale should be sustained. In the first place, they argued, Hale had voted according to his convictions on annexation. Secondly, he was the regularly nominated candidate. And, finally, he had represented his constituents with honor and independence in Congress and had displayed "the talent and moral courage to combat and withstand the *wicked influences of a corrupt, slave representation in Congress*." [38]

But although Hale's supporters benefited from high morale and improved organization, many difficulties remained: the "chains of party," a shortage of funds, and, most important, a hostile press. As one Independent Democrat complained to Hale, "if we do get up a Democratic meeting to approve your course and pass resolutions we cannot get them published except in Whig prints and they do not get to the Democrats." From all parts of New Hampshire political friends implored Hale to return home before the March election and stump the state. But Hale refused to alter his determination passively to await the people's choice. [39]

One obvious source of strength that few Independent Democrats boasted about was the aid of Whigs and abolitionists. The Pierce forces were alive to this danger and strove to damn his backers as an unholy band of "Federal whigs, Abolitionists, and a few deluded individuals still believing themselves democrats, but who are travelling directly . . . on the high road to political treason!" [40] For their own part, the Independents welcomed votes from Whigs and Liberty men, but did so quietly and without tarnishing their image as the true defenders of the Democratic faith.

More Liberty men than Whigs were willing to give Hale their votes, although they kept a candidate of their own in the field until March. In January 1845 William Claggett, an antislavery Democrat, confidently predicted that he could deliver "the whole liberty party vote," and N. F. Barnes assured Hale that he could count on "the whole of the abolitionists." [41] Antislavery men from all the Northern states had applauded Hale's Texas stand and now watched with sympathetic interest the struggle of the Independent Democrats to secure his reelection. Nowhere did Hale's course win more joyful approval than among New England abolitionists. Garrison's *Liberator* printed Hale's letter in full, calling it "a miracle of political independence and uprightness," and at a board meeting of the Massachusetts Anti-Slavery Society on January 25, Garrison announced that he "was *very* anxious to do something that should secure John P. Hale's election." Despite its avowed aversion to political action, therefore, the Society decided to send four of its agents into New Hampshire to plug for the Independent candidate. [42]

Perhaps as effective as the Garrisonians in swinging Granite State abolitionists to Hale's side, was antislavery's poet laureate, John Greenleaf Whittier. Ever since the day in 1835 when he and George Thompson had had to flee before a hostile mob in Concord, New Hampshire, Whittier had taken a special interest in the "redemption" of that state. Hale's bold stand on Texas delighted him, and he was among the first to congratulate the New Hampshire representative for his letter to his constituents: "I would rather be the author of that letter than the President of the United States. Under all circumstances, it is one of the boldest and noblest words ever spoken for Liberty."[43] To "the noblest combat ever waged with Tyranny," Whittier contributed a poem:

> God bless New Hampshire! from her granite peaks
> Once more the voice of Stark and Langdon speaks.
> The long-bound vassal of the exulting South
> For very shame her self-forged chain has broken,—
> Torn the black seal of slavery from her mouth,
> And in the clear tones of her old time spoken!
> Oh, all undreamed-of, all unhoped for changes!
> The tyrant's ally proves his sternest foe;
> To all his biddings, from her mountain ranges,
> New Hampshire thunders an indignant No![44]

And among the abolitionists of New Hampshire and Massachusetts he drummed up support for Hale.[45]

The Whigs were also pleased with Hale's break with his party, though for somewhat different reasons. And, understandably, they were more guarded in expressing that pleasure. Publicly, while agreeing that Hale's position regarding Texas entitled him "to the respect of men of all parties," New Hampshire Whigs told one another that Hale was "as much a locofoco as ever" and that "no whig with any consistency or self respect" could vote for him.[46] But in private correspondence and conversations, many Whig leaders freely admitted that it might be profitable to throw a little support Hale's way. Whig editor and state committeeman Asa McFarland, for one, was of the opinion that "The treatment of Hale, if properly handled by us . . . is a good lever by which to pry." The Democrats, he was convinced, were in deep trouble. If the Whigs worked hard, there was no reason why they could not prevent the election of at least one Democratic candidate for Congress. In this a vote for Hale would be as good as a vote for a Whig.[47]

Some Whigs wished not only to block the election of a Democrat, but to secure Hale's return to Congress. Two weeks before the March election, Salma Hale, a former United States representative and one of the most influential Whigs in New Hampshire, confidentially urged upon the editor of the Portsmouth *Journal* the importance of a Hale victory at the polls. If it appeared that Hale could win without open aid from the Whigs, Salma Hale thought it best not to interfere. But if such assistance became necessary, it should unhesitatingly be given. He reported that George W. Nesmith, a Whig candidate for Congress, had offered to withdraw in favor of Hale if that were required to elect the maverick Democrat. Salma thought it a good idea. Sustaining Hale, he believed, "would have the effect of encouraging independence of thought & action in the democratic party." There is also evidence that Independent Democrats secretly pressed the Whigs to back their candidate, offering as a *quid pro quo* support of Whig nominees for state and local offices. "I tell some of the [Whig] leaders, confidentially, that they need not expect to carry their ticket, and that they cannot, unless they unite also for you," Claggett informed Hale, adding "I cannot but think that they will ultimately." [48]

As election day approached, the Clique intensified its attack on Hale. Other Democrats were reminded that he was an ambitious traitor, "The Benedict Arnold of New-Hampshire Democracy," "one who but a few years [ago] emerged from the ranks of federalism, in which he had been a loud and boisterous vituperator of Democracy, and a vilifier of that old Patriot of the Hermitage." To sustain Hale, they were warned, would be to rebuke all those with whom he disagreed, and "*necessarily throw the state* in opposition to the new administration"—a potent argument to anyone considering the realities of patronage. Hale's backers, the Clique insisted, were Democratic johnny-come-latelys, "aristocratical federalists," and abolitionists. At the same time, regular Democrats sought to discredit Hale among antislavery men by calling attention to his vote in the House in favor of admitting Florida as a slave state, and by claiming that in his proviso to divide Texas half slave, half free he had "offered a bargain recognizing and sanctioning the principle and the institution of slavery." [49]

The Independents did their best to counter these charges. The lack of a newspaper of their own made it difficult to get their arguments before the people, but they did what they could through

Whig weeklies and the Granite *Freeman,* a Liberty paper. Carefully they concealed all signs of an alliance with Whigs and abolitionists, and publicly ignored Democratic references to Hale's proviso and his Florida vote. Secretly, Tuck believed that the Texas proviso had done more harm than good, by weakening Hale's moral position regarding slavery and confusing New Hampshire voters. Unsuccessfully he pleaded with Hale to take the stump to explain himself, or, failing that, to write a second open letter. Likewise Jacob Ela admonished Hale for "trusting too much to the goodness of your course, and making no effort to meet the black-hearted opposition." If nothing else, said Ela, this gave his opponents the argument that had he been honest he would have appeared before the people. But Hale chose to remain in Washington, contenting himself with discreet inquiries about the state of affairs in New Hampshire, mailing home "documents tending to sustain himself," and awaiting the decision of his constituents.[50]

On March 11 Granite State voters decided. The result was unmistakably a defeat for the Clique. In what proved to be New Hampshire's last congressional election on the general ticket system, three of the Democratic candidates for Congress—Norris, Moulton, and Johnson—won handily, as had been expected. But Hale stole enough votes from Woodbury (who needed a majority over the high men on other tickets) to prevent his election.[51] A run-off election would have to be held in September between Woodbury, Hale, and Ichabod Goodwin, the top Whig candidate. Democrats angrily blamed Woodbury's defeat on "The spurious, counterfeit and cheating tickets, got up by our unscrupulous opponents," and confidently predicted victory in September. But disappointment showed through their bravado. "Disguise it as they may," crowed Ela, "the Dictators have received a lesson they will not soon forget." There had been, as Tuck exultantly reported, "a *terrible Hale* storm" in New Hampshire.[52]

CHAPTER V

Fruits of Coalition

THE March election was a victory for the Independent Democrats, but a narrow and incomplete victory. Woodbury's 21,719 votes were three times the number Hale received, and only 841 short of the combined total of Hale and Goodwin. Only in Rockingham, Strafford, and Carroll counties had Hale shown real strength; only in Strafford and Carroll had his vote exceeded Woodbury's. All signs pointed to a stiff fight for the Hale forces if they were to stop Woodbury again in September, let alone return Hale to office. And that fight would be all the more uphill if, as the Radicals alleged, "spurious ballots," seemingly identical to the Democratic ballot but which substituted Hale's name for Woodbury's, had padded Hale's total in March. In September when each party had but one name on its ticket there would be little chance for such shenanigans.[1]

Yet there was good reason for optimism in the Independent Democratic camp. Even Henry F. French, who had with misgivings voted for Woodbury, admitted after the March election: "Considering that every democratic press was muzzled, & not a word suffered to appear in Hale's favor & that his friends had no organization, it shows a very strong feeling in his favor, or rather against the State Convention, that Woodbury is defeated." Now, with six months in which to organize and proselytize more effectively than had been possible in the confused weeks before March 11, Hale's backers had cause for cheer. Also, many Democrats who had stuck by Pierce's side in hopes of receiving patronage plums once Polk took office, came unstuck when these hopes were not realized. "The distribution of offices will help you again," Hayes informed Hale at the end of March. "Men openly declaim for you who would do nothing before the Election." Even more important in infusing new spirit into the Independents and in steeling them for the campaign ahead, was the decision of their candidate to return to New Hampshire and lead the battle against the Clique.[2]

The Twenty-Eighth Congress adjourned on March 3, 1845. Two days earlier Tyler had signed the joint resolution for the annexation of Texas, and on the 4th James K. Polk was inaugurated as President. Not long thereafter Hale left the capital and traveled to New York, presumably to make further arrangements regarding the establishment of a law office there. While in New York, a former Capitol Hill messmate advised him "to go home and fight the rascals."[3] Others no doubt had told him the same thing before he left Washington. But such advice counted for less in making up his mind than Woodbury's defeat at the March election, which Hale heard about shortly before leaving New York. To his mind it released him from his pledge of inactivity, and when at last he arrived home on March 21 or 22, he felt both free and willing "to take the stump in the Western fashion."[4]

Heartened by Hale's determination to take his case directly to the people, and eager that his cause be fully and forcefully presented, leading Independent Democrats decided that the time had come to establish a party newspaper. During the campaign just past this lack had sorely handicapped them. Now, with their leader, candidate, and most effective orator about to stump the state, it was more important than ever to have a journal that would sympathetically report his words and actions and answer the attacks of his enemies. In March 1845 Nathaniel D. Wetmore, a well-to-do Rochester manufacturer, answered the prayers of Hale's lieutenants by offering to put up most of the money. Robert C. Wetmore became editor, less for his abilities than for his brother's financial generosity, and on April 1 he issued a prospectus for a new weekly journal—the *Independent Democrat*—to be published in Manchester beginning in May.[5] As its name implied, said Wetmore, the new paper would be both independent and democratic. It would seek to expose slavery as "a moral, social and political evil," but one to be met only by constitutional means. "For the present," Wetmore proclaimed, "this paper will advocate the election of Hon. JOHN P. HALE, as a member of the next Congress," a man he described as "a Democrat of the Jefferson school." [6]

The first issue appeared as scheduled on May 1. From the start it was, like nearly all other New Hampshire journals of the day, violently partisan. Conceived as an instrument of political warfare, the *Independent Democrat* was neither more nor less addicted to the truth than its competitors, and often grossly misrepresented its enemies. Still, it did assist the rude working of the democratic process by giving voice for the first time to a significant minority party. The Radical press, recognizing the threat it posed, greeted the birth of the *Independent Democrat* with silence or scorn. "Democrats, touch not the accursed thing," warned the Dover *Gazette*. "Its sole object is to destroy the Democratic party in this state." [7]

Hale's followers cheered the new paper, but soon doubted the wisdom of publishing it in Manchester. Even before the first issue went to press, James Peverly had detailed his arguments against establishing it there. In a long letter to Hale in April, Peverly pointed out that communications from Manchester to other parts of New Hampshire were poor, that enemy plots were most often hatched in Concord and might best be scotched there, that subscriptions would be easier to raise in Concord since many persons placed them with their representatives to the legislature, and that a newspaper at Manchester would appear local, while with offices at the state capital it would be more truly a state journal. Jacob Ela agreed. In fact, he felt so strongly the need for a campaign paper in Concord that he issued a prospectus for *The Hale-Storm,* soliciting editorials from Whittier's friend Moses Cartland and others. Before this scheme got off the ground, however, Wetmore had moved the *Independent Democrat* to Concord, and Ela dropped his plans for *The Hale-Storm*. Beginning July 3, 1845, the *Independent Democrat* issued weekly from offices in the state capital. [8]

Peverly's theory that subscriptions might more readily be obtained in Concord than in Manchester was probably most influential in the decision to shift bases. Publishing a newspaper is a risky business under the best of circumstances, and these were hardly the best. Wetmore complained that he had one subscription agent, Ela, and that Independent Democrats were slow to subscribe. By the end of July, four months after circulating his prospectus, Wetmore had only 633 regular subscribers to the *Independent Democrat*. Of these, nearly half came from seven towns in southeastern New Hampshire: Dover, Rochester, Exeter, Ossipee, Manchester, Deerfield, and Concord.[9] With so few subscribers, not all of whom paid in advance, the new paper had rocky going during its early months but somehow managed to survive. Hale himself loaned Wetmore $300 to help him meet initial expenses, and others gave freely of their money or talent. Tuck and Joseph G. Hoyt, Professor of Greek and Mathematics at Exeter Academy, wrote most of the editorials during 1845. It may also be, as Democratic papers hinted, that the *Independent Democrat* received financial as well as moral support from Boston.[10]

Hale did not wait until he had the *Independent Democrat* behind him before taking his case to the voters. Beginning in mid-April he set out systematically to stump the state "from the Cocheco to the Connecticut, and from Coos to Strawberry Bank."[11] On April 21 he touched off his campaign with a two-hour speech at Exeter. At great length he reviewed all the arguments against (and ignored those for) the acquisition of Texas, stressing, as Tuck had suggested, "the moral aspects of the question." He had not wished to break with his party, Hale insisted, but a time had come when a politician had to ask himself "whether he should obey God or Man." It was all well and good to talk about party discipline, but any man with a conscience could see that annexation was "purely a naked question of slavery," and "for so long as God occupied the throne of eternity" He would look upon human bondage as a sin.[12]

By May, Hale was in full swing, speaking in all corners of the state to audiences large and small, indoors and out, seeking by eloquence and force of argument to win converts to his cause. "Eloquence," says Santayana, "is a republican art." Among politicians, Hale was one of the most outstanding practitioners of that art. He was a stump speaker *par excellence,* a master orator with a common touch. He spoke in a language that even the humblest New Hampshire farmer or mechanic could understand, but with force and polish few could match and in a voice whose resonance and power was truly extraordinary. In Congress he had frequently been congratulated on his "splendid voice," and he boasted that although the acoustics of the Hall of Representatives made it an orator's nightmare, "I think I can fill it better than any man here although there are some members who have been constantly accustomed to speak in it for ten years or more." He stood straight when he spoke, shoulders back, his 220 pounds balanced evenly on both feet. His gestures were free and graceful. "He was a natural orator," a friend later recalled, "and had the easy and commanding pose of an orator—not the more limited and restricted style of a reasoner, a philosopher, or a conversationalist." This gift of oratory Hale now brought to bear in his own behalf.[13]

The Radicals deprecatingly referred to Hale's stumping tour of New Hamphire as a "course of abolition lectures," but were clearly worried about the effect it might have on Democratic voters. So when Hale accepted the invitation of Peverly, George G. Fogg, Jefferson Noyes, and others to speak in Concord on Election Day, June 5, 1845, the Clique decided that he should not go unanswered. Pierce himself agreed to be on hand to counter Hale's charges, thus setting the stage for the most celebrated debate in New Hampshire's history.[14]

Hale's backers had shrewdly scheduled his address for a time when Concord would be bursting with men from all parts of the state, for not only did "election week" mark the opening of the legislative session, but it was also a time when many religious and charitable associations held annual meetings in the capital. On the appointed day, Hale, in company with Fogg, Peverly, and Noyes set out on foot for the meeting at Old North Church. As they walked along, the streets seemed nearly deserted, and though he kept his thoughts to himself, Hale felt "gloomy and despondent." But as they turned the last corner, he "looked up and saw the crowd at the doors of the old church surging to get in, the people above and below hanging out of the windows." Reassured, he entered the building and, from a platform recently used by a Whig convention, began his speech.[15]

He introduced himself as "a doomed man—a decapitated man," one upon whose head had been poured "the vials of wrath" by "*the great* men—those who assume to exercise *all power*." From time to time he referred to newspaper clippings and public documents which he had brought wrapped in a red silk handkerchief, and for the most part cleaved to the arguments of his printed letter to his constituents in defending his opposition to Texas. To Radical accusations that his stand against annexation marked a return to federalism, Hale gave special attention. He insisted that he had merely done, and was doing, his duty as he saw it in a "great moral conflict," and he denounced as false the oft-repeated charge that in his course he had consulted with Rufus Choate. Finally, he counterattacked, accusing the delegates to the Baltimore convention of greater apostacy than his by abandoning Van Buren for Polk, despite pledges to back Old Kinderhook.[16]

When he finished, Hale took a seat in a pew at the front of the church and listened attentively as Pierce, "pale, excited, and passionate," answered him. At length Pierce berated his former friend, impugning his motives and accusing him of plotting an alliance with Whigs and abolitionists designed to destroy the Democratic party and send Hale to the United States Senate. But it was Hale's meeting, and to Hale went the last word. Once Pierce had concluded, Hale rose again and delivered a brief but effective rejoinder:

I expected to be called ambitious; to have my name cast out as evil. I have not been disappointed. But, if things have come to this condition, that conscience and a sacred regard for truth and duty are to be publicly held up to ridicule, and scouted at without rebuke, as has just been done here, it matters little whether we are annexed to Texas or Texas is annexed to us. I may be permitted to say that the measure of my ambition will be full, if, when my earthly career shall be finished and my bones be laid beneath the soil of New Hampshire, when my wife and children shall repair to my grave to drop a tear of affection to my memory, they may read on my tombstone, "He who lies beneath surrendered office, place, and power, rather than bow down and worship slavery." [17]

To an age more given to high rhetoric and sentimentality than our own, language such as this could be remarkably persuasive, and Hale's friends accounted his performance a huge success. "Your address has created a greater sensation in this place than anything that ever occured [sic] in Concord," exulted Peverly. "Gov. Hill himself," wrote Fogg, "told me that Pierce failed to touch your main positions, and that he thought your speech a *great rhetorical* effort . . . You have taught your enemies to respect you, you have converted many who were indifferent or hostile into warm friends." As if apprehensive of Hale's effectiveness in his exchange with Pierce, the Democratic press stepped up its vituperative attacks on him. Dusting off a favorite simile, the Dover *Gazette* sneered: "He is now heart and hand with his *old* federalist friends—having returned like the dog to his vomit, *and the sow to her wallowing in the mire*." [18]

The debate at Concord foreshadowed the disruptive effects which slavery was to have on political parties and, ultimately, the Union. Here in 1845 two former friends and political brothers publicly quarreled about the proper course for their party to pursue, one insisting that discussion of slavery be suppressed in the interest of party harmony, the other contending that no party (and by implication, no nation) was worth saving unless the issue were freely discussed and reform begun. In the years ahead other politicians in other states would take sides in this quarrel until the only solution was civil war.

Through the summer of 1845 the Independent Democratic candidate crisscrossed the state tirelessly, pleading his case wherever he got the chance. He seemed to those who saw him to be "in his usual good spirits," and even good Democrats admitted to one another that he "w[oul]d carry the day, were not party fetters too strong." [19] On the fourth of July Hale spoke for nearly three hours at Moultonborough, and by the end of August he was speaking at least once on every day except the Sabbath. Texan acceptance in July of the United

States' offer of annexation (although never in doubt once the offer was made) embarrassed Hale and his followers by reminding all that a prime issue had been lost. To steady the fainthearted, the *Independent Democrat* published in August a list of three reasons why its readers should stick by Hale: (1) that he might in the next Congress oppose "consummating the annexation of Texas," (2) that in Congress he might vote against the admission of *any* slave state into the Union, and (3) that as a United States representative he might investigate Congress' power to abolish slavery in the District of Columbia and to regulate the interstate slave trade. Besides, the success of the "foul scheme" in no way diminished the glory of Hale's fight against it. And, of course, the issue of dictation remained as much alive as ever. So wherever Hale spoke, crowds turned out to listen.[20]

The Radicals redoubled their attempts to defeat Hale. During the summer they organized special committees of vigilance in every school district to make sure that each anti-Hale man voted on September 23.[21] Senators Levi Woodbury and Charles G. Atherton canvassed the state for John Woodbury, damning Hale for "his treacherous & unprincipled course." [22] The Democratic press sniped at Hale's Federalist antecedents and explained his conversion to Democratic principles as simple thirst for office.[23] Yet despite their prodigious efforts in Woodbury's behalf, Democratic leaders secretly fretted over the widespread apathy they everywhere encountered, and feared that not enough voters would go to the polls to put him over. Election day bore out their apprehensions. Woodbury received 18,010 votes to Goodwin's 10,155 and Hale's 8,355, with 121 scattered among other candidates. He was still 521 votes short of a majority, and Governor Steele ordered a third trial for November 29.[24]

Nearly six thousand more voters appeared in November, but the outcome was the same. This time Woodbury lacked 2198 votes of election. Hale's total fell off somewhat in Whig towns, but picked up in Democratic strongholds, the result, apparently, of a renewed rift between Hill and Pierce.[25] Ever since the March 1845 election the Radicals and Conservatives had been drifting apart, and early in

November their feud once more erupted when the *New Hampshire Patriot* accused Hill of giving aid and comfort to Woodbury's enemies.[26]

By this time, it was becoming more and more clear that Woodbury's enemies were the Independent Democrats (including Liberty men who had dropped their own candidate and who regularly voted for Hale) *and* the Whigs, and that these "allies" were working in close if secret cooperation. Their plan, the details of which emerged slowly during the early months of 1846, was not only to block the election of Woodbury, but by coalition to win control of the legislature. If all went as expected, the legislature would have within its power the choice of a governor and a United States senator.[27] Hale's followers had long dreamed of sending him to the Senate to replace Atherton, and although their agreement with the Whigs was not to be clearly defined until after the March 1846 election, there was enough friendly understanding by January for the Dover *Gazette* to "expose" the "villainous plan" to put the Whig Anthony Colby in the governor's chair in return for Hale's election to the Senate.[28]

But before the Allies could put their plan into operation, they had to weather one more storm. They had to prevent the election of a Democratic governor and a Democratic legislature in March. To this task they bent their energies during the winter months of 1845–1846. Once more Hale struck out across the state, steadying the faithful and making converts where he could. Often he spoke two or three times a day, traveling in the dead of winter in an open sleigh or a drafty stagecoach from one meeting to another. A letter to his wife, written from Haverhill in February, describes the rigors of his campaign:

I went from Littleton after speaking there to Bethlehem the same evening & spoke there, & the next morning went down through Franconia Notch to Campton & from there to Plymouth, took the stage about 7 o'clock & reached this place at about two in the morning. I rode all night till 2 in the morning most of the time in an open sleigh & must have suffered much with the cold had it not been for an ingenious contrivance of Mr. Morse the stage proprietor, who kindly took a new Buffalo skin and wrapped me entirely up in it, cutting button holes in it with a knife

& fastening [it] around me, head & all, & then giving me a seat with my back to the wind.[29]

Through it all he retained his usual high spirits.

In February the Independent Democrats removed one source of intraparty friction by replacing Robert Wetmore with George G. Fogg as editor of the *Independent Democrat*. Hale and others had for some months been displeased with Wetmore and his management of the paper, as much for his attendance upon "haunts of dissipation" as for his differences of opinion with leading Independents. When in January Wetmore asked to be relieved, his request was speedily granted. Fogg assumed the editorship beginning with the February 5 issue, and thereafter—working closely with Tuck and Hale—made the *Independent Democrat* a more effective campaign weapon.[30]

The Whigs too worked diligently. In December 1845 the Whig state central committee drew up a list of all towns showing anti-Woodbury majorities in the previous elections and divided the list among its members. Each was charged with seeing that the towns for which he was responsible remained in the Allies' column.[31] In districts, counties, and towns, Whigs, Independent Democrats, and Liberty men bargained with one another about votes for minor officials. In Bath, Whigs and Independents united in supporting a state representative of one party and a town officer of another; in Concord, Independent Democrats put one Whig on their ticket and the Whigs put one Independent on theirs. The Allies did the same thing in other localities, trading a state senator for a councillor, a town moderator for a registrar of deeds. Insofar as possible the Allies kept their dealings a secret.[32]

But the Democrats, whatever their shortcomings, were not politically naïve. They were quick to discover the alliance against them and fought with all the methods at their disposal to destroy it. No one was more active than Franklin Pierce. Though he had resigned as Democratic chairman the previous fall, Pierce vigorously campaigned throughout the state against the apostate Hale, calling on party regulars to scotch the infamous Federalist coalition. Before the

election, Pierce returned to Concord to bear a hand. There, claimed
James Peverly,

The most potent agent that was used was rum. Every miserable rum
hole in Concord was combined against us. These places were open for
days before the election where all, who felt disposed, went and partook of
whatever they desired free, and also through the four days of election.
"*All Hell broke loose*" could not have belched up so miserable, so degraded a group of vagabonds as appeared at our election . . . And the
most disgusting scene of all was to see Hon. Franklin Pierce actively
engaged in loading these drunken devils up to the polls. It is notorious
that Pierce scoured round among these underground drunken holes and
led men to the Ballot Box so drunk they could not stand without his
aid . . . Wednesday night he took a man out of bed at 9 o'clock so drunk
that it took two to carry him to the polls. But suffice it to say that Frank.
Pierce was the most active man at our election in dragging miserable
drunken ragged loafers up to the ballot box.[33]

Roused by the exhortations of all parties, more New Hampshire
men trooped (or were carried) to the polls in March 1846 than had
gone to any election since 1840. Their votes proclaimed a triumph for
the Allies. Both Woodbury and Jared Williams, the Democratic
gubernatorial candidate, fell short of election, though each received
large pluralities. The seat Woodbury sought would remain unfilled
until after the next general election. Williams' fate—and that of his
chief rival Colby—would be determined by the legislature at its June
session. And it soon became apparent that in that legislature the
Allies would hold a narrow majority. On hand when the general
court convened would be John P. Hale who, with Whig support,
had been elected to New Hampshire's House of Representatives from
Dover.[34]

This was a victory the poet Whittier had long awaited. "New
Hampshire has done gloriously," he cheered. "I was half tempted
when I learned of her triumph to take off my Quaker hat, & 'Hurra
for Jack Hale!'"[35] Soon there appeared in the Boston *Chronotype*
and Garrison's *Liberator* an apocryphal and anonymous letter,
supposedly from Pierce to Moses Norris, Jr. at Washington, giving
news of the March election:

'Tis over, Moses! All is lost!
    I hear the bells a-ringing;
Of Pharaoh and his Red Sea host
    I hear the Free-Wills singing.
We're routed, Moses, horse and foot,
    If there be truth in figures,
With Federal Whigs in hot pursuit,
    And Hale, and all the "niggers."

Alack! alas! this month or more
    We've felt a sad foreboding;
Our very dreams the burden bore
    Of central cliques exploding;
Before our eyes a furnace shone,
    Where heads of dough were roasting,
And one we took to be your own
    The traitor Hale was toasting!
I dreamed that Charley took his bed,
    With Hale for his physician;
His daily dose an old "unread
    And unreferred" petition.
There Hayes and Tuck as muses sat,
    As near as near could be, man;
They leeched him with the "Democrat;"
    They blistered with the "Freeman."

                    .   .   .

The ides of June! Woe worth the day
    When, turning all things over,
The traitor Hale shall make his hay
    From Democratic clover!
Who then shall take him in the law,
    Who punish crime so flagrant?
Whose hand shall serve, whose pen shall draw,
    A writ against the "vagrant"?

Alas! no hope is left us here,
    And one can only pine for
The envied place of overseer
    Of slaves in Carolina!
Pray, Moses, give Calhoun the wink,
    And see what pay he's giving!

We've practiced long enough, we think,
    To know the art of driving.

And for the faithful rank and file,
    Who know their proper stations,
Perhaps it may be worth their while
    To try the rice plantations.
Let Hale exult, and Wilson scoff,
    To see us southward scamper;
The slaves, we know, are "better off
    Than laborers in New Hampshire!" [36]

While Hale's friends gloated, New Hampshire Democrats wasted little time sulking. Instead they set about to detach enough strength from the Allies to prevent Hale from becoming United States senator. Less than a week after the votes were in, Democrats made overtures to the Whigs—promising a more acceptable liability law, and abolition of the general ticket system together with the creation of congressional districts—their object being to keep the Independent Democrats from power.[37] Later there were more crude attempts at bribing state representatives-elect to vote against Hale come June.[38] "The Radical slave clique . . . are now making the most tremendous efforts which they have ever put forth to frustrate the already expressed sentiments of the Public," Hale noted in April. But, he added, "I have strong hopes and great confidence that they will not succeed. There are probably a few impracticable Whigs returned to the next legislature, but I hope not enough to defeat our movements." [39]

Between March and June the Allies refined their understanding. Just how direct a hand Hale took in final negotiations with the Whigs concerning the distribution of offices remains unclear. Presumably he left most of the bargaining to his lieutenants, Tuck, Hayes, and Fogg. Whatever the channels of this Allied diplomacy, not long after the March election the tacit agreement of several months standing hardened: the Whigs would support Hale's election to the Senate, if Independent Democrats agreed to make Colby governor. Nathaniel Berry, the Independent Democratic candidate, by finishing a poor third to Williams and Colby in March, had removed himself as a gubernatorial possibility, a fact which disappointed Liberty men and Independent Democrats, but which made it a great deal easier for them to go for Colby. As part of the bargain, Hale men pledged themselves to vote for the Whig candidates when the legislature met to elect state senators from the six districts that had made no choice in March. The Allies also agreed to cooperate in the election of other state officials annually chosen by the legislature.[40]

It was one thing for party sachems to strike such a bargain, but something else to convince their followers to aid in its execution. (Hale had this in mind when he wrote Giddings in April: "Our Legislature . . . meets in June. We shall wait till then with great anxiety.") Yet the advantages of cooperation were so obvious that, although diehards on each side accepted the arrangements with a certain lack of grace, they accepted nonetheless. By May 3 Tuck could confide to Fogg that though it was still necessary to be "continually on the *qui vive,*" lest the Democrats "prevail to bribe whigs enough to defeat our designs . . . I think the election of Mr. Hale to the Senate *cannot* be prevented." At the same time he wrote for the *Independent Democrat* an article designed to sugarcoat the bitter pill Hale Democrats and Liberty men were asked to swallow. Headlined "Bargains and Coalitions," Tuck's article argued that Independent Democrats had no alternative but to "bargain with the Whigs or Old Hunkers." It was a choice between two evils, and "in voting for men, as for measures," there could be "but one rule." That rule, said Tuck, was adherence to principle. So long as a man was "willing in good faith to help along the car of Liberty and Reform . . . we care not whether . . . [he] be called a Whig or a Democrat." Given a choice between Colby and Jared Williams ("whose whole life as a politician has been a series of the basest truckling to Southern slavery"), a virtuous man could make only one decision.[41]

The New Hampshire legislature assembled on Wednesday, June 3, 1846. If the Democrats still nursed hopes of upsetting the Allies' plans, they soon found them shattered. That same day the coalition forces filled all state Senate vacancies with loyal Whigs and elected

John P. Hale Speaker of the House. On Friday morning the House and Senate met in convention to choose a governor. Although the Hall of Representatives was jammed almost to suffocation, onlookers sat quietly as the count was taken. But when the speaker announced the result, a ripple of applause passed through the galleries: Colby had won with ten votes to spare.[42]

Hale's partisans had fulfilled their part of the bargain; it remained for the Whigs to deliver. There was little doubt that they would. Knowledge of the "deal" had for some time been widespread, and even persons outside New Hampshire were freely predicting Hale's election.[43] On the morning of June 3, Daniel Clark, an Independent Democrat whose duty it became to notify the governor that the House was organized, duly reported that the House was organized "by the election of John P. Hale as *Senator*." He corrected himself quickly, saying "Speaker," but the damage had been done. Governor Steele, relishing Clark's embarrassment, cheerfully remarked that "secrets would out," and that he expected soon to hear of the senatorial election which had been prematurely announced. That election eventually took place on June 9. Two days earlier, sensing victory, Hale had invited his wife to join him in Concord.[44]

She came in time to share in his triumph. With scarcely a single defection, Whigs joined with Independents and Liberty men to elect Hale to a six-year term in the United States Senate, beginning December, 1847. In the House, Hale received 139 votes to Democrat Harry Hibbard's 119, with three votes scattered; in the Senate eight of twelve marked their ballots for Hale, three voting for Hibbard and one for Benning W. Jenness, also a Democrat. From atop Sand Hill a cannon boomed the news of Hale's election, while an embittered Radical editor set in type a headline announcing: "THE TRAITOR REWARDED."[45]

When, three days later, the Allies elected Peverly state treasurer, Fogg secretary of state, Asa McFarland state printer, and chose Liberty man Joseph Cilley to fill out the remainder of Levi Woodbury's term in the Senate, the disbursement of offices was complete.[46] But the Alliance did not end here. While differing on such traditional determinants of party alignment as the tariff, Independent Democrats and Whigs nonetheless shared common views on slavery, and in 1846 slavery was *the* issue, preoccupying politicians North and South. First the annexation of Texas and then the war with Mexico, which began in the spring of 1846, seemed to threaten a large-scale expansion of slavery. Using their newly acquired control of the state government, the Allies were determined to place New Hampshire on record as unalterably opposed to any restriction in the area of freedom.

Governor Colby sounded the new note from New Hampshire in his annual address to the legislature, delivered June 5. "Texas," he said, "has been annexed to the United States for no higher object than to perpetuate an institution which degrades the human race, and dishonors the God of heaven." New Hampshire might in part atone for her complicity in this matter by now taking steps to protect the fundamental rights of all men. He suggested a personal liberty law to obstruct the return of fugitive slaves, and to Granite State congressmen he advised: "If Congress have not the constitutional right to abolish slavery in the District of Columbia, it would look better for them to remove the seat of government to some free state." [47]

Taking their lead from Governor Colby, Allied legislators sought as a first step to embody their antislavery sentiments in a joint resolution. On the afternoon of his election, Hale stepped down from the speaker's chair long enough to propose a resolution which vigorously denounced the annexation of Texas and the Mexican War, and pledged New Hampshire's "cordial sympathy" and active cooperation "in every just and well-directed effort for the suppression and extermination of that terrible scourge of our race, human slavery." [48] Defending his resolve against heavy Democratic attack, Hale delivered on June 25 a two-hour tirade which in the violence of its language far outstripped the resolution itself. The Texas scheme was dark and unholy, yet even darker was the war which it produced— a war, Hale thundered, *"unparalleled in infamy in modern history."* It was a war for slavery and against liberty, and only contemptible hypocrites could "come before the world to talk about '*extending the area of freedom*'" by means of such conquest.[49] In July, both houses approved Hale's resolution. Governor Colby concurred, and New Hampshire went firmly—if temporarily—on record against the "pro-slavery" course of the national government. To Hale, it was all "very gratifying."[50]

In other ways, too, the Allies expressed their antiwar, antislavery beliefs. Against strong Democratic opposition, they forced through the legislature a joint resolution requesting New Hampshire congressmen to press for abolition in the District of Columbia, exclusion of slavery from the territories, suppression of the domestic slave trade, and urging them to resist the admission of any new slave states.[51] At the same time, the Independent Democratic-Whig coalition beat down jingoistic resolves commending General Zachary Taylor and his men for their "distinguished and gallant conduct" in action with the Mexicans, and hailing Polk's vigorous prosecution of the war, his "wisdom, statesman-like forecast and patriotic energy."[52] Not content merely to wage a campaign of joint resolutions, the Allies followed Colby's recommendation by adding to the statute book "An Act for the Further Protection of Personal Liberty." This act, like those already in effect in many other Northern states, made it a crime (punishable by a heavy fine or six to twelve months in jail) for any citizen of the state, "not holding a commission from the government of the United States," to assist in the arrest, detention or imprisonment "of any person for the reason of his being claimed as, or suspected of, being a fugitive slave."[53]

The work of the 1846 legislature over, Hale could reflect on the previous year and a half with satisfaction. The success of the Independent Democratic movement had been especially important, he believed, not only because of what it meant for New Hampshire, but because its success would inevitably encourage similar experiments in other Northern states. He hoped that a series of such revolutions as the one he led in New Hampshire might "arouse the Democracy to a sense of their duty and their danger on the momentous question of Freedom & Slavery."[54]

His expectations were well founded. During the following three years not only did antislavery Democrats bestir themselves in New England, New York, and Ohio, at times winning noteworthy victories, but out of unregenerate Pennsylvania came David Wilmot, a Democratic congressman with impeccable credentials, demanding an end to slavery expansion.[55] To be sure, the anticipated consequences of the Mexican War did more to set the "forces of freedom" in motion than the triumph of New Hampshire's Allies. Yet Hale and his backers took pride in having pointed the way.

Certainly in New Hampshire the fruits of coalition had been as delicious as Hale could reasonably expect. The Democratic giant had for the time been rendered helpless, virtually the whole of the Allies' legislative program had passed unscathed, and Hale himself was now United States senator-elect. In the months following his break with the Democratic party he had risen from relative obscurity to a position of considerable eminence in Northern antislavery circles. Even in England, his name won a limited currency among reformers like Joseph Sturge, who viewed his "course with great satisfaction." Antislavery men of all parties shared the opinion of Charles Francis Adams that much now depended on Hale. "I do not know whether he will be equal to the crisis," mused Adams. "But I hope much from him."[56]

CHAPTER VI

A Reluctant Candidate

HOPING much from Hale, slavery's critics asked much and, since his Senate term did not begin until December 1847, he spent what time he could spare beating the drums for antislavery. In September 1846 he stumped across Maine in support of Hannibal Hamlin and other freesoil Democrats then in the process of shaping a coalition after the successful New Hampshire model.[1] Also that month he accepted the invitation of Ellis Gray Loring, Charles Sumner, Samuel Gridley Howe, and other Massachusetts Conscience Whigs to speak to the citizens of Boston in Faneuil Hall on September 18—a date purposely set shortly before the Whig state convention in hopes that Hale could "infuse among the rank & file a spirit" that would "manifest itself in high toned resolutions by the convention."[2] Boston friends greeted him enthusiastically upon his arrival; he dined with Theodore Parker, the great Unitarian preacher and abolitionist; and after his speech he was able to boast to Mrs. Hale: "My remarks were very well received indeed." Yet despite these personal tributes, his mission failed in its immediate purpose, for at the Whig convention five days later the Conscience Whigs failed to carry their antislavery resolutions.[3]

Hale labored even harder, but with as little success, on behalf of the New Hampshire Allies during the winter of 1846–1847. Once again he bundled himself up and stumped the state from Dover to the White Mountain country of Coos County, denouncing the injustice of the Mexican War and exhorting voters to support Independent Democratic candidates. Yet in spite of Hale's strenuous efforts, the Allies suffered a "truly mortifying" defeat at the March election. The unpopularity of their antiwar views had proven too heavy a load to carry, and the Democrats had stolen much of their campaign thunder by denouncing slavery extension. Both the executive and legislative branches reverted to Democratic control.[4]

Still, the Allies did not come up empty-handed. Voting for the first time by congressional districts instead of by general ticket, they had in March managed to block the election of the Democratic candidates for United States representative in two of four districts. Thanks in part to determined action by Hale and to the persuasive efforts of Joshua Giddings (then touring New England as a spokesman for free soil), Whigs and Independent Democrats succeeded at the second trial in July in electing Amos Tuck from the first district, and James Wilson, an antislavery Whig and a good friend of Hale, from the third. It meant that half of the New Hampshire delegation to the Thirtieth Congress would be firm foes of slavery.[5]

During the nearly three years between his break with the Democratic party and the day he took his seat in the United States Senate, Hale's antislavery convictions became stronger, more clearly defined, and more central to his political philosophy. All that was latent in his earlier hatred of slavery became overt, and while he still insisted that the crusade against human bondage be waged within the rules of the Constitution, more and more he sought guidance in the word of God, rather than in the word of Man. In part the greater intensity and singlemindedness with which he now campaigned against slavery was a reaction to the annexation of Texas and the Mexican War. As he saw it, the renewed aggressions of the Slave Power, which sought by bloody and unjust conquest to acquire fresh lands for its peculiar institution, demanded vigorous counteraction by the forces of freedom. Slavery had become beyond all doubt *the* issue. In part also, Hale's more forceful antislavery views derived from his New Hampshire experience. He owed his election to a motley coalition of Independent Democrats, Whigs, and Liberty men who shared little besides opposition to slavery expansion. Now free of party discipline, he was free to speak his mind on matters of importance and to ignore the rest.

Repeatedly in the months following his election to the Senate, Hale aired his opinions about the war with Mexico and about slavery in the territories the United States would in all likelihood acquire, and in a way which attracted the attention of men looking toward the formation of "one grand Northern party of Freedom." [6] The Mexican war was an "infamous" war, Hale charged again and again. It was folly to suppose that a nation could sow "the seeds of *war* and *slavery*" and reap "the fruits of peace & Liberty." [7] David Wilmot's proviso, which would have excluded slavery from all territory acquired from Mexico, was admirable as far as it went. But it did not go far enough. It did not, for example, challenge "the monstrous anomaly that man can hold property in man," nor did it in any way touch the slave trade in the District of Columbia, permitting "the Federal City to remain in infamous notoriety, the great market-place of souls in which men, women, and children are constantly exposed to sale as mere articles of merchandise." [8]

Nowhere did Hale find more general agreement with such beliefs than among members of the Liberty party. For years the followers of James G. Birney, twice Liberty candidate for President, had campaigned on a platform that called for the exclusion of slavery from free soil and an end to "the peculiar patronage and support hitherto extended to slavery and slaveholding by the general government." They rejoiced to hear Hale echo these sentiments. To be sure, Hale's moderation—his reluctance to affirm the constitutionality of abolition in the District and prohibition of the interstate slave trade—tainted him in the eyes of some Liberty men. But by the end of 1846 more and more of them believed that he was with them "in heart and hand, in purpose and action." [9] To many, who foresaw that the antislavery issue would bulk even larger in the 1848 Presidential campaign than it had in 1844, he seemed a desirable standard-bearer, one who belonged in spirit to the Liberty party but whose abolitionism was moderate enough to attract men of antislavery principles away from the major parties. Not only had Hale moved closer to the Liberty party's position, but Liberty men, believing with Gamaliel Bailey that "no new and small party can live simply by holding its

own," were by now willing to accept leadership from one not originally of their number. [10]

As early as the fall of 1846, therefore, Hale began to get inquiries
about the possibility of his accepting a Liberty nomination for
President. Despite the cold reception he gave to all such overtures,
antislavery newspapers in East and West increasingly advertised him
as the candidate most likely to rally Wilmot Proviso Democrats and
Whigs under the Liberty banner. It all made Hale uneasy. He
wanted no part of the nomination, and it piqued him that those who
knew his wishes best had been most responsible for advancing his
candidacy. Talk of nominations so long before the election seemed to
him premature, he had no illusions about chances of success in 1848
(or indeed soon thereafter), and to be so suddenly thrust into national prominence appeared a rather frightening prospect. Besides, he
preferred to enter the Senate as an unfettered independent, believing
that in such a role his political and moral influence would be most
broad. In all his political struggles, he insisted, "nothing has occurred
which I would more gladly have avoided . . . than this use of my
name in connection with this office." [11]

By the early summer of 1847 antislavery journals from Maine to
Illinois had come out in favor of a Liberty ticket headed by Hale.
Sam Lewis and Salmon P. Chase were most often mentioned as
Vice-Presidential possibilities. A number of local Liberty conventions
also suggested Hale as a strong candidate, and although Chase counselled delay, the Liberty National Committee issued a call for a
nominating convention to meet at Buffalo in October. [12]

Conscious of the "very strong desire among a great many leading
anti-slavery men" that Hale become the Liberty party nominee,
Henry B. Stanton, Joshua Leavitt, John G. Whittier and other
prominent Eastern Liberty men invited the Senator-elect from New
Hampshire to meet with them in Boston in July. [13] Since the meeting
offered Hale a chance to make clear his own wishes regarding the
much-talked-about nomination, he accepted the invitation. First,
however, he sought the counsel of three distinguished Conscience
Whigs: Charles Sumner, John G. Palfrey, and Charles Francis

Adams. Already looking toward "a more extended combination" of antislavery factions the next spring, and fearful that by accepting the Liberty nomination in October Hale might cripple his position in the Senate, these men advised him to decline all offers for the time being.[14] Yet their advice, though it fitted mainly with his own views, came to nothing. On July 24, together with his lieutenants, Tuck and Fogg, Hale conferred with leaders of the Massachusetts Liberty party and several from other states, including Lewis Tappan, eminent New York merchant, philanthropist, and abolitionist; Professor Charles D. Cleveland of Pennsylvania; and Austin Willey, editor of the *Maine Standard*. In conversations that day, Hale made it clear that he favored postponing the convention until spring, and once again declared that his personal preference was strongly against becoming the Liberty candidate. At the same time, he convinced those present that he was "with the Liberty party in principles, measures & feeling," and hinted that he would not refuse a draft nomination.[15]

By no means all of Hale's friends felt that he should accept the nomination if it came from the Buffalo convention. Amos Tuck cautioned him in August 1847 that many New Hampshiremen believed it would be a mistake to do so, since as Liberty candidate he would be identified "with a very small party, a faction," of no real consequence. Now that the Mexican War and the Wilmot Proviso had set in motion antislavery men of all parties, it would be foolish, they contended, for Hale to tie himself to a party which had all but outlived its usefulness. Tuck himself seems to have been hoping for some broadly-based Northern coalition united behind Silas Wright of New York. George G. Fogg warned Hale against committing himself too soon "in connection with this convention movement," and cautioned him to be chary of leaving his fate "unreservedly to Joshua Leavitt."[16]

Men from other Northern states also expressed doubts about the wisdom of Hale's pledging himself so early to carry the Liberty colors. Sumner wrote to Joshua Giddings of his efforts to dissuade Hale from accepting a Liberty nomination, and Charles Francis

Adams confided to his diary: "The more I meditate on it, the more am I doubtful as to the effect of the proceeding."[17] But it was Ohio's Salmon P. Chase who presented the most closely reasoned arguments in favor of Hale's standing aloof.

Himself a Liberty man for more than six years and now commonly mentioned as a likely runningmate for Hale, Chase had of late grown pessimistic about his party's chances of progress. "As fast as we can bring public sentiment right, the other parties will approach our ground, and keep sufficiently close to it to prevent any great accession to our numbers," he complained. This in fact had been the case in New Hampshire, where the Democrats had recently endorsed the Wilmot Proviso. What course, then, ought Liberty men to pursue? For a time it seemed to Chase that they should abandon independent action and instead organize a national "anti-slavery league," with local affiliates, which would support anti-extension men in the traditional parties. He had special hopes of regenerating the Democratic party, and like Tuck leaned toward Silas Wright as one well fitted to "rally the anti-slavery sentiment" in all quarters.[18] By September 1847, however, whether because of Wright's death in August or for other reasons, Chase was once again advocating the need for an independent organization, "not of a Liberty Party, exactly, but of an Independent Party, occupying Liberty & Liberal ground, making Slavery or Freedom its paramount issue." He hoped to see Hale head such a party, "composed of ALL honest opponents of slavery"—or so he told Hale.[19] But he stubbornly opposed a nomination in the fall of 1847, trusting that "the events of the winter" would make possible a more broadly based antislavery coalition. Meanwhile Hale might best serve as "an Independent Democratic Senator, occupying very nearly the same relation to the Democratic Party, on the Antislavery side of it, as Calhoun on the proslavery side," and not allied with the Liberty party, "compelled . . . to share the undeserved opprobrium" attached to it.[20]

Yet while some advised Hale to reject a Liberty nomination, others prodded him to accept. No one plugged more strongly for Hale's candidacy than did John Greenleaf Whittier. In letters and newspaper articles he sought to drum up support for Hale among Liberty men and to soothe that candidate's apprehensions. Tactfully he strove to draw from Hale written consent to have his name presented to the Buffalo convention. Armed with a favorable answer from Hale, Whittier explained, his backers hoped by circulating it "in manuscript to a few of our leading friends in other States" to secure an "entirely unanimous" nomination. There was no need to worry that acceptance would make his labors in the Senate more difficult. Far from it; "the nomination would give a much stronger position," and would set at rest fears of Independent Democrats that he was playing into the hands of the Whigs.[21]

Stanton, and apparently Lewis Tappan, also pressed Hale for some statement that while not actively seeking the Liberty nomination, he would, for the good of the cause, accept it if it were offered. But they pressed in vain. For the truth was that Hale, beset on all sides by urgent and conflicting advice, was utterly confused. Even if he ignored all personal preferences, it was by no means clear what duty demanded of him. In this irresolute state of mind he drifted through the summer and early autumn of 1847, neither affirming nor denying his readiness to take the Liberty nomination. Not even the enthusiasm of Amos Tuck, for whom the death of Silas Wright had swept away all doubts about Hale's candidacy, could make him lift a finger. He still found all talk of his nomination "very repugnant." If drafted, he hinted that he might accept out of obligation to his friends. But he was determined to do or say nothing "that malevolence even can construe into a solicitation of the nomination." Short of an outright refusal to run, Hale could scarcely have been more cool to those who sought to project his candidacy.[22]

Stanton, Leavitt, and Tappan decided nonetheless to go ahead with their plans to nominate the reluctant Hale, and they personally directed his fortunes at the national Liberty convention which convened at Buffalo, October 20, 1847. Present on that day were 140 regular delegates from all Northern states, together with a good many voluntary delegates and Liberty Leaguers—a group of antislavery extremists who in May had nominated Gerrit Smith for

President on a platform that abandoned the "one idea," adding to political abolitionism a broad assortment of reform proposals. Under a curious rule, all enjoyed equal privileges at the convention. Private conferences and caucuses met in Buffalo hotels; full sessions were held in a mammoth revival tent, brought from Ohio for the occasion.[23]

The first and sharpest fight of the convention came over the platform. The Liberty Leaguers, ably led by Smith and William Goodell, believed fervently in Lysander Spooner's doctrine that slavery was everywhere unconstitutional—in states as well as territories—and sought to force their views on the convention. Only with difficulty did the "expedient" faction beat down Liberty League amendments embodying Spooner's radical preachings, and pass instead more moderate resolutions calling for the exclusion of slavery from the territories, abolition in the District of Columbia, and repeal of the Fugitive Slave Act of 1793. It was an important victory for the Hale men, for their candidate would never have consented to run on so aggressive and "unconstitutional" a platform as Gerrit Smith proposed.[24]

Next day the convention turned to nominations. No sooner was the resolution to nominate offered than Chase was on his feet, moving that no choice be made until spring. Once again Leavitt, Tappan, and Stanton triumphed; although Chase's motion touched off a great deal of discussion, in the end it was overwhelmingly rejected.[25] Having failed to win the postponement he desired, the Ohioan bowed to those who advocated Hale's candidacy. Earlier in the convention there had seemed to be a great hesitancy on the part of Liberty men, particularly those of the East, to go for so recent a convert to their cause. Hale's constitutional scruples about interfering with the domestic slave trade disturbed many delegates,[26] while others, with less precise misgivings, also held back.[27] At the close of the first day, Leavitt reported, things had looked "somewhat dark & tangled." But on the second day, after Tappan and others had sung Hale's praises, "the clouds all rolled off, everything looked bright & hopeful, & a most cordial unanimity of feeling pervaded the whole convention." [28] Washed in this aura of good feeling, the delegates nominated Hale for President on the first ballot, giving him 103 votes to 44 for Gerrit Smith. After picking Leicester King of Ohio as its Vice-Presidential candidate, the convention adjourned.

Although Hale's nomination disturbed some of the more extreme Liberty men, it was on the whole favorably received in antislavery circles. Garrison's *Liberator,* although opposed on principle to political abolitionism, congratulated the Liberty party "on having got at last a reputable candidate." But that it had got such a candidate only at high price, many had no doubt. To Wendell Phillips it seemed that the events of 1847 had borne out his prophecy of seven years before—that when pressed, Liberty men "would be forced to gain strength by soliciting for candidates men not of their party." The Liberty party was dying, it seemed, "& merging under other names in other movements." [29]

There were other movements aplenty during the fall and winter of 1847–1848, giving to those who anticipated the forging of a grand Wilmot Proviso coalition in the spring, additional cause to regret Hale's acceptance of the Liberty nomination. In Massachusetts, Conscience Whigs, long at odds with their "Cotton" brethren, were prepared to bolt rather than support General Taylor who, in addition to his complicity in the Mexican War, owned slaves in Louisiana.[30] At the Whig State Convention at Springfield in September 1847 the Conscience group had tried without success to carry a resolution endorsing only candidates "known by their acts or declared opinions to be opposed to the existence of Slavery." Defeated, they came away from Springfield convinced that they could not long remain in the Whig party.[31] In New Hampshire, also, Whigs balked at accepting Taylor, whose candidacy seemed more and more likely as the national convention approached.[32]

Not only within the Whig party was there serious discontent during these months. Northern Democrats also had their differences, especially in New York where disagreement over slavery and local issues exploded in September 1847 into full-scale political warfare. Angered at a long train of slights and abuses by the conservative

"Hunker" faction, culminating in the rejection of resolutions endorsing the Wilmot Proviso, the Van Buren or "Barnburner" Democrats bolted the state convention and met by themselves at Herkimer in October. There, with the eyes of the North focused on their deliberations, they proclaimed their devotion to "Free Trade, Free Labor, Free Soil, Free Speech and Free Men." Antislavery men everywhere cheered the Barnburner revolt, none more than the Liberty party nominee. It was, said Hale, a "noble . . . demonstration . . . against the encroachments of slavery, & in behalf of the principles of the Wilmot proviso." [33]

The Conscience Whig and Barnburner upheavals, while encouraging, further complicated Hale's position. The national Wilmot Proviso convention that Chase had been anticipating for months, now seemed all but certain, barring unexpected nominations by the Whig and Democratic national conventions in the spring. Letters were already flying back and forth between Ohio's political abolitionists (Chase, Giddings, E. S. Hamlin), the Massachusetts Conscience Whigs, and Van Buren Democrats in New York, looking toward "a great Convention of all Antislavery men" in 1848, and speculating on possible candidates. Hale's name cropped up repeatedly in these speculations, usually to be quickly passed over with expressions of regret that he had "thrown himself away" by accepting a nomination from the Liberty party. During the winter and early spring of 1847–1848 most antislavery Whigs, in Massachusetts and New Hampshire, as well as Ohio, pinned their hopes first on Thomas Corwin and later on Judge John McLean. The Barnburners from the start inclined toward their wily old chief, Martin Van Buren.[34]

Actually, though at the time few seem to have noticed, Hale waited nearly two months before answering the letter from Sam Lewis, president of the Liberty convention, which informed him of his nomination. Not until January 1, 1848, did he formally accept the Liberty offer. Even then his acceptance was hesitant and provisional. To those who wondered if he were really a "Liberty party man," Hale answered "yes," if by that phrase they meant one who supported the Buffalo platform, but emphatically "no," if any supposed that by joining the Liberty party he thereby subjected his "public conduct to the supervision or direction of its officers or committees." In October the Liberty delegates had provided for assembling a subsequent convention if necessary. Having this in mind, and acutely aware of the events in New York, Massachusetts, and Ohio, Hale announced in his letter of acceptance that should a broader-based antislavery coalition form, joining "the good and true of every party," he would gladly step aside and "enrol myself among the humblest privates who will rally under such a banner." [35]

In view of his genuine eagerness to avoid Presidential candidacy, it would appear that Hale purposely accepted the Liberty nomination to *avoid* becoming a freesoil candidate, at the same time to smooth the way for a merging of the Liberty party in a more inclusive antislavery movement. Certainly by New Year's Day 1848 all indications pointed to the formation of a new party including Barnburner Democrats and antislavery Whigs, and Hale had had repeated warnings from Chase, Sumner, Charles Francis Adams, and others that he must not take the Liberty nomination if he wished to lead such a new coalition. He knew that acceptance of the Liberty party's offer, however qualified, would seriously impair his availability in the eyes of Wilmot Proviso Whigs and Democrats. That he took the step anyway, with great dragging of feet, suggests his reluctance to accept *any* Presidential nomination.

Yet once having accepted the Liberty party's nomination, Hale dutifully went through the motions of a candidate, albeit with the gloomy fatalism of a man bailing water in a sinking boat.[36] It was one of the perhaps unconscious satisfactions of his position as Liberty candidate that he could play the part of a man selflessly doing his duty, while to do so provided an excuse against pursuing a personally more disagreeable course. He could bravely uphold the Liberty colors, secure in the conviction that a free soil alliance would before long absorb his party and permit him honorably to resign a position he had with great reluctance assumed.

Events were moving rapidly toward just such an alliance during the spring of 1848, a development which engaged more and more of Hale's attention if not of his time. At the end of May, New York Barnburners, anticipating the nomination of Lewis Cass—an anti-Proviso Democrat from Michigan—and angry over a credentials squabble, stormed out of the Democratic National Convention at Baltimore. Returning to New York, the Barnburners called a convention of anti-Cass Democrats to meet in Utica on June 22. There, sparked by the impassioned orations of Preston King, Benjamin F. Butler, and John Van Buren, Democrats from six Northern states renounced Cass and slavery, nominated Martin Van Buren for President, and proposed a national meeting of all friends of free soil. By then antislavery Whigs, equally disturbed at the nomination of Zachary Taylor and Whig silence on slavery, were also in commotion. "Our purpose is now fixed to oppose to the last the election of Taylor," wrote Sumner to Chase. Throughout the North, Wilmot Proviso men of all parties gathered to endorse the idea of holding a national free soil assembly at Buffalo in August.[37]

These events raised ticklish problems for Hale and his party. Were Liberty men to submerge themselves in a larger free soil organization, including and perhaps dominated by former Whigs and Democrats? And if so, whom should they support as the new party's Presidential candidate? The Barnburners had already made Van Buren their choice, but most Liberty men, remembering his objections to abolition in the District of Columbia, and his pro-Southern stand on the *Amistad* case, the gag rule, and "incendiary" abolitionist mail, found the "Red Fox" a highly unattractive prospect.[38] It seemed to Joshua Leavitt, for one, that "the Liberty party *cannot* support him, without deliberately giving the lie to all our own declarations for fifteen years past. He is the 'Northern man with Southern principles,' not a hair changed." "Van Buren is too old a sinner to hope for his conversion," thought Whittier.[39] But what if the Barnburners should insist upon Van Buren, or the Buffalo convention should make him its candidate? All these questions and more troubled Liberty men during the early summer of 1848, and to them they offered a variety of answers. On one thing they were agreed: self interest demanded their attendance at Buffalo. Even Gerrit Smith's Liberty Leaguers endorsed the call and prepared to send delegates in August.

By and large most Liberty men were determined to do all that they could to secure the Free Soil nomination for their own candidate, but there was wide disagreement as to how this might best be done. Some, among them Chase and Gamaliel Bailey, editor of the Washington *National Era,* felt that Hale ought to withdraw his candidacy so that his name might be placed before the convention as an unaffiliated candidate. As Charles Francis Adams rightly observed, Conscience Whigs and Barnburners would be more inclined "to create a candidate" than "to adopt one." [40] Others agreed with Lewis Tappan that Hale should stand firm. "Should you resign previous to the Convention," the New Yorker warned Hale, "it would look like conscious weakness on our part, & strengthen the feeling on the part of the Barnburners that Mr. Van Buren will be the nominee of the Buffalo convention.[41] Still others insisted that "the time has not yet come when we can coalesce with the Barnburners" without sacrificing "our moral position, in which our strength lies." They urged a combination with the Conscience Whigs of Massachusetts and Ohio, but without the New Yorkers, and they too adamantly opposed giving up their nominee without a battle.[42]

Early in July, Hale wrote a long letter to Lewis Tappan which, after an appraisal of the current state of political affairs, suggested a conditional resignation of his candidacy, not *before* but *during* the convention. Having carefully studied Northern opinion, Hale said, he had realistically concluded "that a very large proportion of the Antislavery sentiment of the Country, and of the Liberty party portion of it too, will unite in the Buffalo Convention," and that Van Buren was the most likely choice. He noted that the Cincinnati *Herald,* Ohio's leading Liberty paper, had dropped his name from its masthead, and that Chase had recently come out for Van Buren. Was this not a "significant sign of the times?" asked Hale. "And if men of Mr. Chase's character, and stability of purpose see their duty in such a course, what can be expected of the great mass of men who are not so fixed in purpose, or so enlightened as he?"

He therefore proposed that Liberty men attend the Buffalo Convention and "exert as favorable an influence as possible." He would "write a letter declining to stand," to be put into the hands of Samuel Lewis or some other reliable person. Lewis would then use the letter or not, as he thought best. If the convention adopted a platform that Liberty men found satisfactory, the letter of declination should be used. If not, it should be withheld and the Liberty party proceed independently.[43]

Tappan at once raised a cluster of objections to this plan (which seems to have been as much the work of Gamaliel Bailey and John G. Palfrey as of Hale). In the first place, there was no good reason to believe that the Barnburners would approve a platform in agreement with Liberty principles, so why act on the assumption that they would? Even should the New Yorkers endorse a satisfactory platform, what assurance had Liberty men that Van Buren would stand by its principles? Finally, Tappan feared that a letter such as Hale suggested "might be used injudiciously—under excitement—even by your best friends." It therefore seemed wisest to make no decision about resigning until after the convention and after further consultations with Liberty leaders. Lewis concurred, and declined holding Hale's letter of resignation.[44]

To this advice, Hale seemingly submitted, though Tappan was later greatly distressed to see in the *National Era* a paragraph, allegedly with Hale's approval, saying that Hale wished to retire from the canvass. So little support and encouragement did Liberty men receive from their candidate, that by the end of July even the steadfast Lewis seemed to be wavering, wondering whether Van Buren might not be, after all, the best man on whom "to unite all of antislavery influence." Matters remained in this unresolved state until the delegates assembled in Buffalo on August 9.[45]

As was the custom of the day, railroads and steamboat lines offered transportation at half-fare to all who wished to attend the convention, be they delegates or lookers-on. Even at reduced rates they must have turned a pretty penny, for more than ten thousand Free Soilers (some estimates ran twice that high) poured into Buffalo during the second week of August. They came from every Northern state and three slave states, and represented all shades of political antislavery opinion. Among those present were Barnburners Preston King, B. F. Butler, David Dudley Field, and Samuel J. Tilden; Conscience Whigs Charles Francis Adams, Stephen C. Phillips, Richard Henry Dana, Jr., and Francis W. Bird; Liberty men Leavitt, Lewis, and Stanton. Also on hand when the convention opened were Salmon Chase, nominally still with the Liberty party but in fact already in league with the Van Burenites; Joshua Giddings; Frederick Douglass, the runaway slave turned orator; and an assortment of disappointed Clay Whigs, Liberty Leaguers, New York land reformers, workingmen, and champions of cheap postage. From New Hampshire came George G. Fogg, Moses Cartland, Joseph G. Hoyt, and W. A. Marston.[46]

Because of the unwieldy number of spectators and delegates, two meetings went on simultaneously. One was a mass convention, "consisting of all persons who had come up to Buffalo for Free Soil," which met under a huge tent in the park. The real work, however, was done by a select "Committee of Conference" which met in the Universalist Church opposite the tent. The "conferees," as the delegates to this select assembly were called (and who represented equally the Whig, Democratic, and Liberty parties) made all the important decisions, referring them afterward to the mass convention for ratification.[47]

In the opinion of Oliver Dyer, who kept the official record of the proceedings, at the start of the convention preference for Hale "was strongly predominant and seemingly irresistible."[48] Dyer underestimated the strength of Van Buren, yet he correctly gauged Hale's broad popularity. With few exceptions Liberty men warmly endorsed him; he had many friends among Whigs, particularly those from New England where the workings of the New Hampshire Alliance were well known; and many Democrats, even those committed to Van Buren, thought well of him. Yet there were also many obstacles between Hale and the Free Soil nomination, some of which he had placed there himself. One was his own widely-known disinclination to continue as a Presidential candidate. Those who from the beginning had managed his candidacy were now either absent from the convention, like Lewis Tappan, or, infected by Hale's reluctance, had become less insistent on his nomination than before. Both Leavitt and Stanton, for example, now stood ready to swap Hale's candidacy for platform concessions.[49]

In fact, at the same time most Liberty men were shouting themselves hoarse over preliminary details and making fiery speeches in Hale's favor, Stanton, Leavitt, and Chase were striking a bargain with the Barnburners which helped to assure Van Buren's nomination. Either because they believed Hale's chances were not good anyway, or because they were convinced that the powerful New Yorkers would bolt the convention if thwarted, the Liberty leaders agreed to back Van Buren's nomination and make it "harmonious & unanimous if possible" in exchange for Barnburner support of a "thorough Liberty platform." In particular, they demanded a plank calling upon the federal government "to relieve itself from all responsibility for the existence or continuance of slavery wherever the government possesses constitutional power to legislate on that subject."[50]

The bargain was soon sealed. On the morning of August 10, the second day of the convention, the platform committee reported out the fruit of its labors. Mainly the work of Chase—an old hand at such matters—and Van Buren's confidant, B. F. Butler, the platform offered something for everyone. Not only did it satisfy the Liberty men with its resolutions against slavery extension and in favor of separating the national government from slavery, but it pleased Westerners with its demand of free homesteads for actual settlers, placated Whigs by advocating internal improvements, and won Democratic approval by endorsing cheap postage, economy in government, and a tariff for revenue only. As Butler read the proposed platform to the sweltering throng in the giant tent, "Every sentence, every paragraph was cheered into its legal existence." When Adams, as president of the mass convention, put the question on their adoption, there followed wild applause, shouting, waving of hats and handkerchiefs. "In my whole life, I never witnessed such a scene," exulted the normally phlegmatic Adams.[51]

With the platform out of the way, the Committee of Conference repaired once more to the relative calm of the Universalist Church and undertook to nominate a candidate for President. The conferees first demanded to know precisely where each candidate stood— leaving "nothing to letters in gentlemen's pockets." [52] Chase, speaking for his fellow Ohioan McLean, immediately dashed Whig hopes by withdrawing the judge's name from consideration. That effectively narrowed the field to Van Buren and Hale and left the Whigs holding the balance. All listened attentively as Butler next presented with consummate skill the case for Van Buren. He began by assuring the delegates that the ex-President had agreed to enter the convention on equal terms with all candidates, and would abide by whatever decision were made. Then, with great eloquence, he expatiated upon the virtue and integrity of the Barnburner chief. Carried away by his own rhetoric, Butler had wandered into a picturesque if somewhat irrelevant description of Van Buren the farmer who took pride in his rolling fields of wheat, cabbage, and turnips, when Jacob Brinkerhoff of Ohio shrilled out: "Damn his cabbages and turnips! What does he say about the abolition of slavery in the Deestrict of Columby!" Sobered but unruffled, Butler thanked his "friend from Ohio" for raising this important issue. He spoke from personal knowledge of Van Buren's present beliefs, Butler said, when he assured the convention that if elected President, and if a bill outlawing slavery in the District should come from Congress, Van Buren would sign it into law. Having thus put to rest the most nagging doubts of the conferees about Van Buren's eligibility, Butler took his seat.[53]

Stanton spoke for Hale. He had the New Hampshire senator's authorization, he announced, "to abandon his [Liberty] nomination, and put him fairly upon the Convention, to serve the cause either as captain, officer, or private." [54] Before Stanton had finished his intended remarks, "the call for the roll became deafening," and he gave way.[55] There followed an informal polling of the conferees who, state by state, named their preference for President. When counted, the ballots showed Van Buren 244 votes, Hale 183, Giddings 23, Adams 13, and four votes scattered. Except for Chase, Leavitt, and

Stanton, Liberty men stuck loyally by Hale. Whigs, led by the Massachusetts Conscience group, gave Van Buren his majority. The New Yorker's greater prestige, which made him "the best man to knock in pieces the main prop of Slavery, the Northern Democratic party," seems to have most influenced their decision.[56]

After the informal ballot, Leavitt and Stanton, mindful of their pledge to the Barnburners, persuaded Sam Lewis, William Jackson, Owen Lovejoy, and other Liberty leaders that Van Buren's nomination should be made unanimous. Leavitt then made his way to the platform. Amid great stillness, his voice filled with emotion, he pronounced the Liberty party "not dead, but TRANSLATED," and moved Van Buren's unanimous nomination. Lewis made a brief seconding speech, and the conferees carried the motion by acclamation. To balance the ticket, the Free Soilers selected rectitudinous Charles Francis Adams for Vice President. With "VAN BUREN AND FREE-SOIL, ADAMS AND LIBERTY," they would carry their cause to the people.[57]

Taking their lead from Leavitt, Stanton, Lewis, and Chase, most Liberty men approved the Buffalo nominations, though, as Albert G. Hart, a delegate from Ohio, recalled, "We knew perfectly that he [Van Buren] and the 'Barnburners' were only anxious to 'beat Cass' and the Baltimore Convention, and that they had no hearty hatred of slavery."[58] The "glorious" platform went far toward assuaging misgivings about Old Kinderhook's softness on slavery, and it was worth a good deal to "have consolidated the forces of freedom."[59] Even so, some made no attempt to conceal their disappointment, nodding with approval when "Hosea Biglow" admitted

> I used to vote fer Martin, but, I swan, I'm clean
>   disgusted,—
> He aint the man thet I can say is fittin' to be
>   trusted;
> He aint half antislav'ry 'nough, nor I aint sure, ez
>   some be,
> He'd go in fer abolishin' the Deestrict o' Columby;

and supporting grudgingly or not at all the New Yorker's campaign.[60] A few, among them Lewis Tappan, bitterly complained that Stanton and Leavitt had acted counter to Hale's wishes in capitulating so readily to the Barnburners. The complaint appears groundless. Both Leavitt and Stanton, upon hearing of it from Tappan, wrote immediately to Hale, asking that he publicly deny their having acted without his authorization, and that he announce his acquiescence in the convention's decision and his readiness to do all in his power to promote the election of the Free Soil ticket. Had they been guilty of betrayal, they would hardly have asked their victim to make a public statement.[61]

Hale generally complied with their request in an open letter to Lewis. In it he declared his determination to withdraw his candidacy and urged "a hearty, energetic and unanimous support" of Van Buren and Adams.[62] He thereafter worked hard to insure a strong showing by the Free Soilers in November. Throughout New England Hale addressed political rallies, and in public letters sought to arouse the antislavery men of other states. His hopes for the Free Soil movement of 1848 were more realistic than some. Van Buren's chances of carrying even New York were slim. But it was still possible that the Free Soilers might "utter a voice which, if it be not potent enough to overthrow the foundations of the power of the Tyrant, may nevertheless, like the miraculous visions coming of a judgement, revealed to an eastern monarch, cause his countenance to change, his thoughts to trouble him, his joints to be loosed, and his knees to smite one against the other." [63]

It was well he did not expect too much. On election day Taylor won in a close fight over Cass. Van Buren polled barely ten percent of the popular vote, more than half of his total coming from New York and Massachusetts alone. Still, Free Soil strength was nearly five times that of Birney and the Liberty party in 1844. Perhaps the tyrant's knees *were* beginning to knock.

CHAPTER VII

"The Place of an Ishmaelite"

THE Free Soil upheaval of 1847–1848 coincided with Hale's first year in the United States Senate. As Liberty candidate he found that his Senate speeches attracted unusual attention during that eventful winter, from friends and enemies alike. Conscious of the drama as well as the responsibility of his position, Hale battled alone against the Calhouns, Douglases, Websters, and Bells, revealing in debates on the war and slavery expansion a brand of abolitionism which, though moderate by Garrisonian standards, was more radical than the Senate had ever known. This was his finest hour.

As in 1843, Hale had set out from Dover alone, planning to find suitable accommodations before Lucy joined him. His trip south took him first to New Haven where on November 30 he lectured before "the Officers of the College & the Literati of the place generally." The high intellectual caliber of his audience worried him a bit. "However the lecture went off very well, the people were exceedingly attentive, and I was told were well pleased." The next morning Yale's president Theodore Dwight Woolsey graciously acted Hale's cicerone, showing him about the campus. Continuing his trip by steamship and railroad, Hale arrived in the capital on the evening of December 4 and promptly took a room at Coleman's Hotel.[1]

The Washington of 1847 had all the appeal of a gawky and slightly corrupt adolescent. Caught midway between the "rural beauty of its youth" and "the tasteful elegance" of a maturity still years away, the federal city looked unkempt and unfinished. Pigs, chickens, and geese wandered through unpaved streets, foraging among noisome piles of garbage. The District's parks still awaited the professional attentions of A. J. Downing, the Capitol and Washington's Monument were uncompleted and would remain so until the Civil War, work had just begun on the Smithsonian Institution and the Treasury Building. "It was still the 'City of Magnificent Distances,'" one observer recalled, adding "Little else about it was magnificent." More disturbing to Hale than its rudeness, was the "decadence and licentiousness" he found in Washington's many saloons, gambling dens, and houses of prostitution. Equally distressing to Hale—indeed to all Northerners—was Washington's prominently situated slave pen and auction block where human flesh was bartered and sold in full public view.[2]

The convening of Congress in December always overshadowed for a while the seamy side of Washington life. It was a time of gaiety and excitement—senators and representatives meeting again old friends and making new ones, chatting amiably over candlelight dinners in hotels and boarding houses, preparing for the debates to come. In its composition, the Thirtieth Congress was truly impressive. From his seat on the Whig side of the Senate Chamber, to the left of Vice President George M. Dallas, Hale could see the "Godlike" Daniel Webster; Thomas Hart Benton of Missouri; John C. Calhoun, the ardent and doctrinaire defender of Southern rights; Michigan's Lewis Cass, already the leading candidate for the Democratic nomination in 1848; John J. Crittenden, the capable and conscientious Kentucky Whig; John M. Clayton; Reverdy Johnson; Willie P. Mangum; and Thomas Corwin—all Senate veterans. Among the newcomers were many who would leave their mark on the American scene: Calhoun's heir apparent, Jefferson Davis of Mississippi; scrappy and shrewd Stephen A. Douglas of Illinois, at thirty-four already experienced in national politics; Tennessee's John Bell, an early leader of the Whig party and a former speaker of the House; and Robert M. T. Hunter of Virginia.

The House was scarcely less distinguished. Doughty ex-President John Quincy Adams at eighty-two still carried on his dogged fight against slavery. On hand to assist him were Joshua Giddings; John G. Palfrey, the scholar turned politician; David Wilmot of Pennsylvania, whose proviso had made him instantly famous; Amos Tuck; Caleb Smith of Indiana; and others. Balancing this small but talented band of freesoilers was a proslavery group headed by the brilliant Alexander H. Stephens and fiery Robert Toombs, both Georgia champions of state rights. Although none guessed it at the time, the House numbered among its members two future Presidents of the United States: Andrew Johnson of Tennessee, and, the lone Whig in Illinois' delegation—Abraham Lincoln.[3]

Many of these men were "old acquaintances" of Hale. Adams, Stephens, Johnson, Giddings, Smith, and Douglas had served with him in the House during the Twenty-Eighth Congress; Benton, Mangum, Clayton, and Crittenden had then been in the Senate. By all he was "very cordially greeted, & by none more than by the ultra Southerners," he reported to his wife. "How it will be when I have broken ground on some exciting subject I do not know."[4] He need not have worried. There were plenty of exciting subjects during his years in the Senate, and on all Hale took a strong stand in accordance with his antislavery principles. Yet he never lost the friendship of his fellow senators, not even those whose views he most strenuously attacked. His "imperturbable good nature and wise forbearance" were well known. In debate he never lost his temper or indulged in personalities. He fought for and against measures, not men, and did so with a disarming blend of sincerity and wit. Some felt that "In point of ability he is overrated by the people," and many remarked his "constitutional indolence," but slaveholder and abolitionist alike agreed that Jack Hale was "a prince of good fellows," "a free-and-easy, fat-and-social man, who can relish a dish of oysters, or a good joke, as well as any member of the Senate." But there was more than mere bonhomie. There was also a boldness and an independence with which Hale defended his deeply felt beliefs which won the respect of all who heard him—even his political enemies.[5]

It was well that Hale possessed such popularity, for his role in the Senate was a difficult one. For two years he stood virtually alone in that body as spokesman for the antislavery movement. Although there had been men before him who had expounded political aboli-

tionism in the Senate Chamber—notably Thomas Morris of Ohio—
Hale was the first senator elected by an antislavery coalition, the
first who had openly embraced antislavery principles *before* his
election. That he came to the Senate the Liberty candidate for
President, beyond the pale of the regular parties, made his position
all the more difficult. It meant, among other things, that in the
organization of the Senate he was excluded from power[6] and that he
had no voice in the distribution of patronage. It meant also that
other senators, feeling the bonds of party, would only with great
reluctance support him on unpopular issues.

Set against these liabilities of Hale's status as a *tertium quid* were
certain real advantages. In the first place, his election by a disparate
group of Democrats, Whigs, and Liberty men—whose single common denominator was a hostility to slavery and the Mexican War—
left him free to speak his mind on all questions without concern for
party policy. It also gave him license to devote most of his energy
solely to the antislavery cause. There was no point preparing elaborate speeches on tariffs or internal improvements if by delivering them
he could only lose support. Finally, his position as the lone antislavery senator was helpful in two ways: it meant that his words
attracted the special attention of all political groups (including those
who considered Hale a dangerous incendiary) and it gave him the
moral support of antislavery men from all parts of the United States
—not just New Hampshire. Some, in fact, offered practical assistance as well. Henry B. Stanton helped Hale prepare some of his early
speeches in the Senate, and Palfrey, Theodore Parker, Chase, and
countless others plied him with information and advice. Even Senator Benton, a peerless storehouse of facts, provided Hale ammunition
for his assaults on slavery. As a legislator, Hale's position was hopelessly weak; as a propagandist of his cause it was strong.[7]

An administration bill to raise an additional ten regiments of
army regulars for service in Mexico gave Hale his first opportunity
to display his antislavery views in the Senate. Since September 1847
General Winfield Scott had been firmly ensconced in Mexico City,
and except for guerrilla action fighting had ceased. But the peace

negotiations of Nicholas P. Trist had as yet proved fruitless, and Polk, unwilling to withdraw from Mexico without a treaty providing "indemnity for the past and security for the future" (by which he meant a sizable, though undefined, cession of Mexican territory to the United States), had asked for extra troops.[8] Lewis Cass, as chairman of the Military Affairs Committee, sponsored the Ten Regiment Bill in the Senate. On December 30 he moved its consideration, urging swift action in the interest of an early and honorable end to the war. After remarks by Calhoun, Clayton, and others, Hale rose and briefly but eloquently expressed his objections to the bill. He opposed the increase in military strength, he said, because it meant continuing a criminal war for indefinite ends. It was, he maintained, a war "commenced in falsehood, and prosecuted in injustice," with the avowed object of perpetuating slavery. He would fight the expenditure of a single dollar on the army "until the President informs us how much he supposes will be required to bring the army home by the shortest and cheapest route."[9]

His extemporaneous maiden speech, which lasted no more than fifteen or twenty minutes, was well received by all but Polk Democrats. Willie P. Mangum and several other Southern Whigs congratulated him, saying "that if it had not been for that 'magot' of Anti slavery which I had got into my head and into the speech, it would have been an excellent one and calculated to do good over the whole country." Back in New England, Sumner seized his pen and exulted to Whittier: "Thank God! at last we have a voice in the Senate. Hale has opened well."[10]

In his opposition to the Ten Regiment Bill, Hale found support from an unexpected quarter. John C. Calhoun, believing that the complete conquest of Mexico would be "subversive of our free and popular institutions," not only opposed the proposal to strengthen the army, but advocated its withdrawal to a defensive line along the thirty-second parallel.[11] On January 4, before packed galleries, the gaunt, intense South Carolinian cogently stated his case for disengagement in Mexico, outlining the dire economic and political consequences of a conquered peace.[12] Two days later Hale, in a long and carefully prepared speech, argued for the same result—evacuation of American troops—but for markedly different reasons.

His opening remarks he aimed at the Whigs. Congress as well as the President had a responsibility for events in Mexico, he reminded them, pointedly scoring the moral inconsistency of those who thought the war a radical wrong yet voted supplies for its continuation. If one believed as he did that the war was wrong, "the first, the plainest, and the simplest duty" was to withhold supplies, and force Polk to do what was right. Developing his thesis that the propriety of granting men and supplies devolved upon the justice of America's cause, Hale next launched upon a lengthy discussion of the origins and merits of the Mexican War. Once again he pronounced his conviction that the war was rooted "in the avowed policy of the American Government . . . to make the extension of human slavery one of its primary motives of action," supporting this contention with evidence from the diplomatic and political correspondence of Upshur and Calhoun.

Warming to his subject, Hale turned his guns on President Polk, the man he had helped to elect three years before. Polk's oft-repeated assertions that "war exists by the act of Mexico" (he had said as much fourteen times in his last annual message to Congress), Hale took as the overly vigorous claim of a guilty man who "doth protest too much." Reminding the Senate that the joint resolutions for annexing Texas had called for the adjustment of "all questions of boundary," he asked: "Well, is it necessary for me to stand here to-day to tell the American people that if there is a question of boundary existing, and one party goes and occupies the territory to the extreme verge of the claim, that is an act of war?" With obvious relish he needled the President for so readily surrendering what in his inaugural address he had called America's "clear and unquestionable" title to Oregon, while at the same time carrying war to Mexico on the flimsiest of pretexts. Polk had "exhibited meekness to a surprising degree," Hale noted sarcastically. "But he did not inherit the blessing of the meek. He did not get the land."

Such were Hale's views. It was unpleasant "to occupy the place of an Ishmaelite," but it was a critical period in American history, a time when "the great question of the capability of man for self-government" hung in the balance, and he acted only out of conscience and a sense of duty when he reminded his listeners that no good could come from a war for slavery.[13] Northern antislavery advocates reacted enthusiastically to Hale's indictment. In Boston, Joshua Leavitt read it aloud to a group of Liberty men at the *Emancipator* office, and Sumner again announced his "great satisfaction" at having a man of Hale's stamp in Congress.[14] Wilmot Proviso Whigs also found much in Hale's speech that was praiseworthy—especially his shots at Polk, but also his outspoken condemnation of the war. William Plumer, Jr. credited Hale with bringing timid New Hampshire Whigs to open denunciation of the Mexican conflict.[15] The senator from New Hampshire had made people sit up and take notice. "Hale is no cipher," telegraphed the Washington correspondent of the New York *Herald*. "He leaves his mark where he walks— and where he speaks, he has, at least, the merit of a boldness which stops neither for friend or foe."[16]

In the Senate, Hale's speech poured fuel on the fire which kept debate on the Ten Regiment Bill boiling for weeks. He added to his notoriety in February when alone of all senators he voted against joint resolutions, already passed by the House (where only Giddings dissented), thanking Generals Scott and Taylor, their officers and men, for valor in Mexico. Using a precedent suggested by Sumner to Palfrey, Hale likened his action to that of John Wilkes and Charles James Fox who had opposed in Parliament a motion to thank Sir Henry Clinton and Earl Cornwallis for their services against America during the Revolution. "The resolution speaks of glory. That glory I look upon as our shame!" he trumpeted.[17]

Debate on Mexico took a new and more constructive turn on February 23 when Polk laid before the Senate the Treaty of Guadalupe Hidalgo. Three weeks earlier Nicholas Trist, ignoring his instructions to break off negotiations and return to Washington, had signed a treaty which disappointed the demands of the most ardent American expansionists but still gave much to the United States.

Mexico agreed to recognize the Rio Grande as her boundary with Texas, and ceded to the United States all of New Mexico and Upper California. In return the United States was to pay Mexico fifteen million dollars in addition to assuming claims of American citizens against Mexico amounting to $3,250,000. Polk, angered at Trist's insubordination, thought briefly of tearing up the treaty, but since it contained most of what Trist had been instructed to obtain, and since the clamor against continuation of the war was rising, Polk at last decided to send it to the Senate.

For two weeks the Senate worked overtime in closed session considering its merits and demerits. More than once the debates carried well into the evening, and Hale complained that he repeatedly missed dining at the regular hour with his wife, who had recently joined him in Washington. He did what he could to make the treaty as unobjectionable as possible. He voted in favor of Whig-sponsored resolutions to reduce the territory ceded by Mexico, and supported Roger S. Baldwin's proviso which would have excluded slavery from the lands about to be acquired.[18] But when on March 10 the treaty came to a vote without these amendments, Hale approved it just the same. He did so, he later explained, "because I thought, in the words . . . of Benjamin Franklin, that there never could be a good war or a bad peace . . . I tried to make the peace better, but when I found that we had got the best that we could get, I took it." [19] Thirty-eight voted for ratification, fourteen against. In May the Mexican Congress formally added its endorsement, and the war of two years was officially at an end.

The Treaty of Guadalupe Hidalgo added 850,000 square miles to the United States. Out of these wild and vast new lands Congress would soon be called upon to create territorial governments. Most difficult of all, it would have to decide the volatile question of slavery in the territories. Heated debates over the Wilmot Proviso had already indicated how explosive that question could be. Slaveholders angrily resisted all attempts to exclude their "property" from the new lands, and Northerners argued with equal vehemence in favor of preserving free soil. In April, a month after the Senate had approved the peace treaty with Mexico, there occurred an incident in the District of Columbia which showed frighteningly just how inflamed congressional tempers were over slavery and which served as a warning that compromise would be difficult wherever that subject was concerned.

On the evening of April 13, 1848, as Washington joyously celebrated with speeches, bonfires, and a torch-light procession the French revolution that deposed King Louis-Philippe, a small schooner, the *Pearl,* sailed slowly up the Potomac. She had come from Philadelphia with a shipment of wood. Two nights later, having in the meantime traded her wood for a more valuable cargo, the *Pearl* quietly made sail and headed downstream toward the open sea. In her hold were seventy-seven fugitive slaves.

Directing this bold rescue was tall, taciturn Daniel Drayton, already experienced in such maneuvers. With the backing "of persons of wealth and intelligence" he had approached Edward Sayres, captain of the *Pearl,* who for $100 agreed to transport the black cargo to Frenchtown, New Jersey. From there the underground railway would shuttle the runaways to freedom. At first all went well. Toward dawn on Sunday the 16th a strong breeze came up from the North, and bending on sail the *Pearl* spanked along briskly. By the time she reached Point Lookout at the mouth of the river, however, the wind had stiffened so much that Captain Sayres refused to enter the choppy waters of Chesapeake Bay until the wind abated or backed around to the West. Drayton reluctantly agreed to wait until morning, and, dropping anchor in Cornfield Harbor, all hands went below decks to get some rest.[20]

Meanwhile, distraught slaveholders in Washington, Georgetown, and Alexandria—among them Dolly Madison—had reported the disappearance of their chattels, a Negro informer had revealed the *Pearl's* flight, and by Sunday afternoon an armed posse aboard the steamship *Salem* was in hot pursuit. About 2 a.m. the following morning a lookout aboard the *Salem* spotted the *Pearl* peacefully riding at anchor. Taken entirely by surprise, the hapless fugitives surrendered without a fight. Their captors transferred Drayton,

Sayres, and Chester English (a white cook and able seaman) to the *Salem,* took the *Pearl* in tow, and began the long voyage back to Washington.[21]

Arriving at the capital early on Tuesday, April 18, the captives were bound together by twos and marched off to jail. Along the way an angry mob gathered, shouting "Lynch them! lynch them!" Rumors that the runaways had been seized only after a bloody struggle had agitated already excited feelings. That night and the next a crowd milled about the jail, promising violence to Drayton and Sayres, while another mob, reminiscent of the murderers of abolitionist editor Elijah P. Lovejoy, gathered at the offices of the antislavery *National Era,* threw bricks and stones through its windows, and threatened to heave the press in the canal unless its editor, Gamaliel Bailey, ceased publication in the city.[22]

Antislavery members of Congress were deeply disturbed at this ugly display of mob action, as well as heartsick for the unfortunate Negroes who had so narrowly missed freedom and would now be sold into harsher bondage in the deep South. In the House, Giddings, who had braved the fury of the mob to visit Drayton and Sayres, demanded to know by what authority the District jail was used to hold fugitive slaves, and Palfrey moved the appointment of a special committee to investigate the necessity of further legislation to cope with mob violence. On April 19 Hale announced his intention of introducing "a bill relating to riots and unlawful assemblies in the District of Columbia."[23]

Hale felt "very much grieved" at the capture of the *Pearl* and the disturbances that followed. He poured out his feelings in long letters to his daughter Lizzie. The plight of the captured slaves moved him profoundly. "Oh, it is sad to think of it," he wrote, "to think of husbands and wives, parents and children, brothers and sisters torn from each other in violence and consigned to such a cruel fate as awaits these poor creatures." Drayton and Sayres were to be tried for the crime of helping slaves to escape, but at this even Hale's legalistic mind boggled. "It may be considered a crime by the slaveholders & their aiders and abettors," he declared, "but it can hardly be so received by that God who sent his son on Earth to announce a system of Religion, whose first principle is deliverance to the captive, & the opening of prison doors to them that are bound." [24] These were strong words, words that suggested his belief in a "higher law" than the law of Man. Although he refrained from any public expression of such a belief, it nonetheless burned within him and colored his outlook and actions.

It was typical of Hale's approach as a senator that while acutely aware of slavery's moral aspect, he often attacked it on a more superficial, legalistic plane. Thus although distressed at the fate of the *Pearl's* victims, his first public response was not to denounce the trade in human souls (though he soon took steps to abolish it in the District) but instead to curb proslavery mobs in the name of civil liberty and property rights. He hoped, perhaps naïvely, that by stressing the constitutional rights of freemen he might not only win Northerners to abolitionism but convert moderate Southerners as well. Not that he forsook ethical comment altogether, or that he decried agitation. On the contrary; agitation kept antislavery alive and moral argument was one of the agitator's best weapons. Yet Hale's persistent efforts to reach the Southern mind (he did not quit until the Civil War began), as well as his own constitutional conservatism, frequently produced the kind of oblique assault on slavery that he now launched after the capture of the *Pearl*.

This attack Hale embodied in the bill which he brought before the Senate on April 20. Much like a law already in force in Maryland and other states, it would simply have made any community "within the District liable for all injuries done to property by rioters or tumultuous assemblages." [25] Hale made a pretense of divorcing it from any connection with slavery, but Southern senators discerned its intent clearly enough. Calhoun minced no words in urging immediate rejection of the bill. Long since, he had predicted that only one question could destroy "this Union and our institutions, and that is this very slave question," he said, cutting straight to the real issue. Its continued agitation was rapidly forcing matters to a crisis, the approach of which was near when "such a bill upon such an occurrence" could be introduced "to repress the just indignation of our people from wreaking their vengeance upon the atrocious perpetrators of these crimes . . . without a denunciation of the cause that excited that indignation." In threatening tones Calhoun warned the North: "if you continue to disregard the provisions of the Constitution in our favor, we shall, on giving you due notice, retaliate by disregarding those in your favor."

James D. Westcott of Florida and Jefferson Davis followed in much the same manner. Then Davis' excitable colleague from Mississippi, Henry S. Foote, gained the floor. Foote began calmly enough, but soon worked himself into a fury. He insinuated that Hale was a party to the "kidnapping" of the slaves, and declared that the bill he now proposed was "obviously intended to cover and protect negro-stealing!" It was, moreover, a "covert and insidious" attempt to abolish slavery in the District, since if enacted it would discourage slaveholders from bringing their chattels to Washington. Hale he vilified as little better than a highway robber, one who was "evidently filled with the spirit of insurrection and incendiarism." If the New Hampshire senator really wished glory in the perfidious cause of emancipation, Foote fumed, "let him visit the good State of Mississippi . . . I invite him there, and will tell him beforehand, in all honesty, that he could not go ten miles into the interior, before he would grace one of the tallest trees of the forest, with a rope around his neck, with the approbation of every virtuous and patriotic citizen; and that, if necessary, I should myself assist in the operation."

Hale responded to Foote's undignified outburst with customary aplomb. He denied "in general and particular" any foreknowledge of the *Pearl* plot, and challenged Foote to furnish proof to the contrary. The Mississippian lamely admitted that he had no proof, but if not Hale himself, certainly some of his brethren abolitionists "had much to do with it." The emptiness of Foote's rebuttal gave Hale the upper hand, and with a calm which contrasted effectively with the other's angry diatribe, he reminded the Senate of the wild words Foote already "would have really given worlds to recall." [26]

He invites me to the State of Mississippi [said Hale], and kindly informs me that he would be one of those who would act the assassin, and put an end to my career. He would aid in bringing me to a public execution—no, death by a mob. Well, in return for his hospitable invitation, I can only express the desire that he would penetrate into some of the dark corners of New Hampshire, and if he do, I am much mistaken if he would not find that the people in that benighted region would be very happy to listen to his arguments, and engage in an intellectual conflict with him, in which the truth might be elicited.

Turning to Calhoun, Hale spoke with increasing passion. He protested once more that his bill was but a copy of a long-existent Maryland statute, that it made no allusion to slavery. "Yet I am accused of throwing it in as a firebrand, and in order to make war upon the institutions of the South!" he cried. "In God's name, is it come to this, that in the American Senate . . . the rights of property cannot be named, but the advocates of slavery are in arms, and exclaim that war is made upon their institutions . . . ? It has long been held by you that your peculiar institution is incompatible with the right of speech; but if it is also incompatible with the safeguards of the Constitution being thrown around property of American citizens, let the country know it!" Hereafter tempers rose steadily. Calhoun became so excited that at one point he interrupted Hale to shout: "I would just as soon argue with a maniac from bedlam, as with the Senator from New Hampshire"; Foote's language became so abusive that the chair declared him out of order; even the usually imperturbable *Globe* reporter noted that the debate was "most personal and exciting."

The rancor in the Senate attracted nationwide attention. Hale's fame—or notoriety—grew overnight. Southerners, whose sensitivity to "Negro stealing" Hale had underestimated, deplored his "firebrand resolution," and urged him to forbear his "maddened, parricidal hand."[27] But the unseemly conduct of Foote and Calhoun was an embarrassment to them. Stephen A. Douglas was right when he said that Foote's fanaticism would only win votes for Hale. Everywhere Northerners spoke of the "deep impression" the Riot Bill debate had made. "It has done more to *bring out* the abolition feeling of the Country than any occurrence for a year past," thought E. S. Hamlin.[28] Chase, Giddings, Sumner, Adams, and many others warmly praised the cool skill with which Hale had returned the Southerners' fire.[29] The Rochester, New Hampshire Athenaeum invited Senator Foote (now known throughout the North as "Hangman" Foote) to lecture to its members, assuring him a "cordial welcome." [30] Rev. Parkman jokingly asked Hale if he had read Charles Lamb's essay "On the Inconveniences Resulting from Being Hanged." [31]

Not only did the *Pearl* incident exacerbate sectional feelings and enhance the prominence of the senator from New Hampshire, but it at last brought Hale openly to advocate abolishing slavery in the District of Columbia. The appalling fate of the captured runaways continued to trouble his thoughts. "No one can tell how much of misery this system of human slavery is causing even here in this District," he wrote to Lizzie a week after the uproar over the Riot Bill. "No tongue can describe, nor heart conceive of the mass of bitter agony which we are thus causing." From time to time he helped individual bondsmen to purchase their freedom, but such piecemeal efforts, while morally satisfying, seemed painfully ineffectual. By June 1848 his moral indignation at the evil of slavery had all but subdued his constitutional scruples, and he was fast bending before the pressure of Sumner and Chase to bring "forward some aggressive measure on slavery." [32]

It was the opinion of Chase and others that slavery was illegal in the District of Columbia and ought to be abolished. Slavery was illegal, Chase argued, because it depended for its establishment and maintenance upon the Act of 1801 which extended the existing laws of Maryland and Virginia to the District. And since that Act was unconstitutional because it deprived Negroes of their liberty "without due process of law," slaveholding in the District was "an usurpation and a crime." [33] Hale agreed in principle that slavery should be eradicated in the District, and felt that its existence there was "a great and constant reproach to the whole Country." Yet there was one point of law, "tolerably well established by authority," which gave him pause, namely that when one nation acquired another nation or part of a nation, by whatever means, the laws of the ceded nation remained in force "until the new Sovereign imposes new laws." Since slavery existed in Maryland and Virginia before they ceded the District of Columbia to the United States, "did not those laws sanctioning slavery remain in force after the cession?" In other words, did not slavery lawfully exist in the District independently of the Act of 1801?[34]

Chase admitted that he too had been "somewhat troubled" by this line of argument, but had found a way out. "The general rule that laws of ceded or conquered territories remain in force after coercion or conquest must be qualified with the limitation that such laws be not . . . such as the legislature of the acquiring state is itself incompetent to enact," he advised his New Hampshire friend.[35] Seemingly reassured, on June 23, less than a week after receiving Chase's opinion, Hale offered a resolution that the Committee for the District of Columbia be instructed to bring in a bill to abolish slavery in the District. The Senate voted it down without debate, 36–7.[36] Hale was not at all discouraged. "I consider [it] a very good beginning," he confided to Lucy, and he was no doubt pleased at the favorable attention his effort received from antislavery men.[37] He could not know that a bloody civil war would begin before his proposal would at last be enacted.

On the same day that Hale introduced his resolution against slavery in the District, the Senate began serious consideration of a bill providing a territorial government for Oregon. So sensitive a subject had slavery become, that even the organization of this mountainous and forested region excited acrimonious debate over its status. Preliminary skirmishing had, in fact, already defined four distinct schools of thought on the question of slavery in the territories. Hale and Jefferson Davis spoke for the two most extreme groups when they greeted the Oregon Bill with provisos that, respectively, extended the Ordinance of 1787 to the inhabitants of the territory, and forbade the exclusion of slavery from Oregon while it remained a territory. More moderate were those who advocated the extension of the Missouri Compromise line to the Pacific and those who preferred "popular sovereignty"—by which they meant letting the settlers decide for themselves the question of slavery.[38]

During the broiling hot summer of 1848 all of these doctrines received full expression. As one of the few spokesmen for prior exclusion of slavery from the territories, Hale was on hand for most of the Oregon debates, making no set speeches, preferring instead to thrust and parry extemporaneously. Occasionally he escaped the capital's heat, making short trips to visit acquaintances who owned country estates nearby. Early in July he spent a weekend as the guest of a Mr. Sasgar, whose eighty slaves worked a thousand-acre plantation in Prince George's County, Maryland. Unlike some abolitionists— Garrison and Salmon Chase, for example—Hale easily distinguished between slaveholding and slaveholders. Although hating the institution, he found many friends among those who exploited and defended it.[39] Over tea at Sasgar's, therefore, Hale amicably debated slavery with his host and three other wealthy planters, and reported later to his wife: "We had a pleasant time." [40]

Discussions in the Senate were less friendly and no more productive. After three weeks of fruitless debate the Senate referred the vexing territorial question to an eight-man committee headed by John M. Clayton of Delaware, in hopes that a smaller group could hammer out an acceptable compromise. Hale, who voted against the proposal to create the Clayton committee, was pessimistic. Far from providing light, he felt sure, "it would only make the mist thicker." [41]

On July 18 the Clayton committee reported "A bill to establish the Territorial Governments of Oregon, California, and New Mexico." This lengthy compromise measure, supported by six of the eight as the best possible "under all the embarrassing circumstances of their position," would have organized Oregon without restriction on slavery. California and New Mexico were to receive temporary governments—again without restriction, though provision was made for appeal to federal courts if slaves introduced into those territories should claim their freedom.[42]

The Clayton bill seemed to Hale to confirm all his apprehensions. Least of all he liked the provision referring the slavery question to the courts. Even in the Supreme Court, as then constituted, he had no confidence, and was unwilling that it should decide the question. To say, as Clayton had, that the bill "left the question to the laws of God and the Constitution" was to admit that it settled nothing, for, Hale pointed out, "the Constitution was interpreted as variously as the Bible." Doggedly he proposed amendments which would have given the suffrage to *all* male adults, and which would have extended the provisions of the Northwest Ordinance to the western territories.[43] Southern senators at the time, and historians since, accused "extremists" like Hale, Corwin, Hamlin, and John A. Dix, of gratuitously insulting the South by insisting on the Wilmot Proviso even though "Everybody knew that climate, soil, and the views of the early settlers made all idea of slavery in Oregon preposterous." [44] But, as Hale himself put it: "Pray, sir, who, then, is fighting for an abstraction?" [45] Surely those who, admitting that slavery would never take root in Oregon, nonetheless fought bitterly against giving legal sanction to the law of nature were at least as "extreme" ideologues. There were men North *and* South in whose eyes a principle was at stake, and a principle that had nothing to do with geography.

In the end Hale's side won the Oregon battle. The Senate, after "a most exhausting session of twenty one hours," passed the Clayton bill on the morning of July 27, 33–22. Northern senators cast nineteen of the twenty-two dissenting votes.[46] But the House tabled it without debate, insisting on its own bill which extended the Ordinance of 1787 to Oregon and endorsed all enactments of the existing territorial legislature, including one excluding slavery. On August 13 a weary Senate approved the House measure, 29–25, and adjourned the next day.[47]

It was a victory for the champions of free soil, but tougher struggles lay ahead. California and New Mexico still lacked territorial governments, and their needs could not be long ignored. Especially California, rapidly filling up with gold-mad prospectors, demanded the early attention of Congress. The deliberations of the second

session of the Thirtieth Congress left these touchy matters unresolved, but showed more clearly than ever "the widening rift"
between North and South and the intention of extremists on each
side to stand implacably for what they believed right. Alarmed at
proposals to abolish the slave trade in the District of Columbia, and
fearful of Northern "aggression and encroachment," several Southern congressmen, led by Calhoun, published in January 1849 a
"Southern Address." In it the grim South Carolinian and his forty-
seven cosigners denied the right of the federal government either
"to extend or restrict slavery," and insisted that they "not be prohibited from migrating with our property, into the Territories of
the United States, because we are slaveholders." [48] Simultaneously,
as a leading advocate of free soil, Hale demanded that the issue "be
settled, and settled upon principle." Compromise, he shouted, would
not do. First and last he called for the unqualified exclusion of
slavery from "the territories of which we have robbed the Mexican
Republic." [49] The lines of battle were drawing tight.

CHAPTER VIII

Crisis and Compromise

D URING the summer of 1849 Hale pondered deeply the "momentous crisis" of his times. There was, he believed, a "great and imminent danger" that slavery would force its way into all the newly won territories, including California. Attempts at self deception were ill-advised. The peril was real and apparent:

It is even now upon us [he warned] and while the interested & venal are lulling us with the syren [*sic*] song that there is "no danger" slaves are being carried into those territories, the clanking of whose chains, and the cries of whose agony shall fill the ear of the Most High, calling for vengeance upon us, if through timidity, party spirit or any other cause, we hold our peace, and do not do what we may to prevent so great a wrong.

More, too, than just slavery expansion was at stake. Unless checked, the Slave Power threatened to pervert the whole democratic system by making the Northern majority subservient to the Southern minority. To Hale the whole drift of American history seemed in this direction. For sixty years the South had "made war and peace[,] passed and repealed tariffs, moulded our legislation, controlled our diplomacy, and made the operation of the whole machinery of Government subsidiary to her interests." With the sole exception of the Oregon Act, the South had invariably imposed its will on Congress, and that one setback served "only to enrage the slave-power and excite it to greater efforts." Equal exertions were demanded "of the friends of Freedom," Hale observed. "The crisis is near, the day and the hour are near at hand. May God grant that . . . [we] may not be wanting."[1]

It delighted Hale greatly that he would not face the impending crisis alone. In February 1849 his confidant and adviser—Salmon P. Chase—had been elected to the Senate by a coalition of Ohio Free Soilers and Democrats.[2] "I confess," Hale rejoiced at the time, "that I do not remember when I have heard of an election which has afforded me more pleasure than that of Mr. Chase."[3] Shortly thereafter the Ohioan paid a brief visit to Washington where for the first time the two men met face-to-face. They hit it off well from the start. To Chase, Hale seemed "one of the most pleasing men I ever met with," and Hale took great delight in introducing "his brother Freesoiler from Ohio" to Foote, Andrew P. Butler, Solon Borland, and other defenders of the peculiar institution.[4]

In a number of ways the two were strikingly similar: each had moved into Free Soil politics through the Liberty party, each was deeply religious, each was a strong advocate of temperance reform, each with a lawyer's training insisted that the war on slavery be waged within constitutional bounds.[5] At the same time, there were interesting differences. Chase now thought of himself as a regular Democrat with antislavery principles. "I am a Democrat, and I feel earnestly solicitous for the success of the Democratic organization and the triumph of its principles," he had written in July 1849. Not so Hale, whose bitter fight with the party machine soured his affections irreparably. "Hale has no love for the Democracy," Chase lamented during his first term in the Senate. "I alone sympathize with the Democrats on general questions."[6] Of the two, the Ohioan was the more methodical, industrious, deeply learned in the law. In debate Chase was apt to be ponderous, preferring laboriously prepared speeches to extemporaneous exchanges, and was at all times deadly serious. It seemed to George Julian, after hearing both speak in the Senate, that Hale, whose wit "was effective and unfailing," was a superior debater, and Chase himself said of Hale: "I wish I had his read[i]ness & good humor." Yet whatever their differences of temper, the two Free Soil senators were as one in opposing the extension of slavery and agreed that on that issue there could be no compromise. Hale warmly welcomed such a capable ally.[7]

Two inches of wet snow covered the ground as Hale made his way from the National Hotel to the Senate on December 3, 1849, in time for the opening of the Thirty-First Congress. The Capitol glistened "splendidly" under a new coat of paint, as if reflecting the luster of those who then assembled within its walls. Back once more at his Senate seat was Henry Clay, beginning to show his seventy-three years, but still a man of great ability and influence. Webster, Calhoun, and Benton—fellow veterans of earlier political wars—were on hand to greet him, as were a host of only slightly less illustrious figures: Sam Houston, Lewis Cass, Stephen A. Douglas, Jefferson Davis, and others. Among the newcomers was William H. Seward, former Governor of New York, a known foe of slavery extension whose word had enormous influence with President Taylor.[8]

The intensity of sectional feeling on the slavery issue showed itself first in the House where for weeks extremists, both North and South, prevented the election of a speaker. Howell Cobb, a moderate Georgia Democrat, was finally chosen on December 22 after sixty-three ballots, but by then recriminations had poisoned the air. While the House indulged itself in acrimony, the Senate whiled away its days on inconsequential executive business, repeatedly adjourning early. Hale even found time to make a speech to a local society for poor relief. Finally, on December 24, 1849, with the House at last organized, President Taylor sent to Congress his annual message and the way for constructive legislation was at last clear.[9]

Taylor's message, strongly nationalistic in tone, upset Southern hotspurs on several counts. The work of many hands (among them John M. Clayton, Alexander C. Bullitt, and Thomas Ewing), the President's address recommended the admission of California as a state with its antislavery constitution. New Mexico, too, would soon be seeking statehood—likely also as a free state—and Taylor hinted broadly that it should be admitted when the time came. Referring to the executive's veto power as "an extreme measure, to be resorted to only in extraordinary cases," Taylor gave Southern radicals further cause for alarm by suggesting that he would not veto the Wilmot Proviso should it be written into any territorial bill.[10]

On January 3, 1850, Henry S. Foote offered a "compromise" resolution which proposed the establishment of *territorial* governments for California, New Mexico, and Deseret (Utah). Hale at once moved to amend the Mississippian's proposal by adding a clause "Securing to the inhabitants of those Territories all privileges and liberties secured to the inhabitants of the Northwest Territory by the ordinance of July 13, 1787." Far from extending new liberties and privileges, Foote stormed, Hale's misguided proviso would be "oppressive, tyrannical, and eminently subversive of popular freedom." He hoped the New Hampshire senator would not "persist in imposing the yoke of the Wilmot proviso upon the necks of freemen . . ." Hale replied that he was happy "to find the Senator from Mississippi and myself looking to the accomplishment of the same purpose; that is, to keep the yoke off the necks of the people. That is the object of my amendment . . ." Words, it seems, had already lost much of their meaning.[11]

Although Foote's scheme scarcely deserved to be called a compromise, its author was responding to insistent national promptings in seeking what he believed to be a reasonable, moderate resolution of the territorial problem. The great body of citizens from all sections feared for the safety of the Union and looked to some form of give-and-take to settle the slavery question in all its forms. Instinctively they turned for leadership to the Great Compromiser himself—Henry Clay. They were not disappointed. On January 29 the aged Kentuckian rose to offer a compromise plan much broader in scope than that proposed by Foote.

Clay proposed first of all that California be admitted as a free state and Utah and New Mexico organized as territories without mention of slavery. Congress, moreover, should induce Texas to surrender its extreme western boundary claims by offering to assume the Texas debt. Finally, slave trading (though not slavery itself) was to be suppressed in the District of Columbia, but Southerners would be mollified by a stiffer Fugitive Slave Act and assurances that Congress contemplated no interference with the interstate slave trade.[12] This potpourri, for the most part a carefully blended mixture of old and unsuccessful proposals, was generally well received.[13] Even some

Wilmot Proviso men, alarmed at the "distant thunder of disunion," thought well of it. But there was also loud and immediate opposition. Southern fire-eaters objected strenuously to the admission of California as a free state and to the suppression of the District slave trade, while to most Free Soilers it seemed that Clay's resolutions were "like the handle of a jug, all on one side." Not only extremists found fault with Clay's compromise, either. President Taylor stuck firmly to the plan he had sketched in his annual message, and moderate Whigs like Robert C. Winthrop, as well as Seward, refused to desert him for Clay.[14]

Debate on Clay's resolutions, which began February 5, soon revealed a curious alignment of factions in the Senate. Radical Democrats, such as Benton and Hamlin, joined Northern Whigs (Webster and James Cooper excepted) in supporting Taylor's proposal for piecemeal settlement, while Democratic senators Douglas, Cass, Foote, and William R. King worked behind the scenes in behalf of Clay's compromise package. Opposing any form of compromise were the lone Free Soilers—Hale and Chase—and extreme advocates of Southern rights, among them Calhoun and Jefferson Davis.[15]

Hale listened carefully as one by one his illustrious colleagues set forth with great passion their views of Clay's plan. Mrs. Hale, who had come to Washington in January, spent much of her time in the visitors' gallery, sometimes arriving hours before the Senate was called to order so as to get a good seat for the exciting debates.[16] Clay—a messmate of the Hales at the National Hotel—led off the discussion of his resolutions with a two-day speech on February 5 and 6 in which he dwelled on the dangers of disunion and insisted that the concessions his plan demanded of Northerners and Southerners were minor ones. The Wilmot Proviso, said Clay, was superfluous; nature had decreed that slavery would not go to the territories.[17] A week later, Jefferson Davis expatiated on the "dangerous doctrines" contained in Clay's proposals. Arguing that neither the federal nor territorial governments had the sovereign power to prohibit slavery in the territories, Davis complained that as between the Wilmot Proviso and popular sovereignty, he preferred the former, "because the advocate of the Wilmot Proviso attempts to rob me of my rights, whilst acknowledging them . . . The other denies their existence."[18]

On March 4 a crowded and attentive Senate listened as James M. Mason of Virginia read the dying John C. Calhoun's speech "upon the great question which has agitated the country." One by one, said the Great Nullifier, the bonds of the Union were snapping, and the blame rested solely on the abolitionist agitators of the North. If the Union were to be saved, the aggressive North would have to make concessions; the South could make none. Rather than accept such a scheme as Clay proposed, Calhoun hinted, the slave states might better withdraw from the Union. It was an extreme speech, one undisguisedly disunionist in tone, and one which, far from rallying the South to a defense of its rights, alienated all but a handful of Southern fire-eaters.[19]

More in accord with the national mood was Daniel Webster's famous address of March 7, 1850. "I wish to speak to-day, not as a Massachusetts man, not as a northern man, but as an American . . . ," Webster began, standing "grave and sombre as a sphinx" before a Senate chamber packed nearly to suffocation. Like Clay, whose compromise he by implication endorsed, Webster asserted that to extend the Wilmot Proviso to the territories won from Mexico would be a gratuitous insult to the South, since "the law of nature—of physical geography" already excluded slavery from those lands. "I would not take pains to reaffirm an ordinance of nature," he thundered, "nor to reenact the will of God." Although he found the South as well as North to blame for sectional discord, and although he exposed in vigorous language the impossibility of peaceful secession and the horrors of civil war, Webster went out of his way to tongue-lash "irresponsible" abolitionist agitators and indicated his support for a stronger fugitive slave law.[20]

In appealing to men on both sides of the Mason-Dixon line to forbear in their mutual recriminations and by compromise to settle the issues that threatened the Union, Webster no doubt struck a responsive chord in a large part of the nation. But in his native

Massachusetts—indeed in all New England—his placatory words excited widespread indignation. "His speech falls upon N. E. like a cold northeast wind from the icebergs," one New Hampshire Whig informed Hale. "Had a southern man expressed such sentiments as D. Webster did on some points, he would have been sent down to Pluto's regions . . . by those very men who are now so vainly attempting to sustain him," wrote another. The free soil heresy had spread widely in New England, and Theodore Parker spoke for many more than himself when he told Hale: "Webster has disgraced himself, beyond hope of recovery. I hope from *you* something worthy of N. E. & of Mankind." [21]

Hale was, in fact, already preparing an elaborate refutation of both Webster and Calhoun. Parker, Lewis Tappan, and Wendell Phillips, as well as his coterie of Free Soil congressmen and Washington abolitionists, plied him with data which he ordered and shaped for delivery in the Senate at an early date.[22] Seward's speech on March 11, which declared "all legislative compromises radically wrong and essentially vicious" and which affirmed the existence of "a higher law than the Constitution," stole some of Hale's thunder, but he proceeded with his preparations nonetheless.[23] Finally, on March 19, he gained the floor and held it for the better part of two days while he labored "to set history right," to correct the inaccuracies and misleading statements recently uttered by Calhoun and Webster.

First he addressed himself to Calhoun. Singly he examined the series of "aggressive" acts which the Carolinian claimed had destroyed that precious equilibrium so vital to the South. The first such act, Calhoun had said, was the Ordinance of 1787. But, Hale pointed out, this precursor of the Wilmot Proviso had at the time received the unanimous vote of every Southern state—only New York voted against it—and was reenacted by the First United States Congress expressly that it might conform to the new Constitution. In 1803 that outspoken champion of Southern rights, John Randolph, had himself upheld the Ordinance and counselled against setting it aside. The second in Calhoun's catalogue of Northern aggressions was the Missouri Compromise. "Well, sir," Hale asked, mindful of the fate of recent attempts to insert its principle into the Oregon bill, "if . . . the Missouri compromise was such an odious measure, and has had such an injurious effect upon the South, is it not singular that we find nearly every southern man voting for it, whenever it is offered?" Was it not, then, the South that was aggressive and upsetting the equilibrium? As for the Oregon Bill, it was preposterous to think that in the brief time since its passage, it could produce any genuine effect on the South. At length Hale dealt with Calhoun's contention that most Northerners, while disavowing the abolitionists, had "co-operated with them in almost all their measures." By wrenching Calhoun's words out of their context, he allowed himself to pass without notice the measures to which the Carolinian referred—personal liberty laws, legislative resolutions affirming the Wilmot Proviso and criticizing slavery—and instead to read into the record a long list of anti-abolitionist outrages committed in the North, most of them before 1836. Much more summarily, Hale rejected Calhoun's claim that Northern business interests had driven the slave states into economic vassalage. As for Calhoun's indictment of the North for centralizing governmental power at the expense of states' rights, Hale replied that if such a shift had occurred, it had been with at least the tacit consent of Southerners who had monopolized the Presidency and always constituted a majority on the Supreme Court.

Leaving off his verbal assault on Calhoun, Hale switched his fire to Webster. The Black Knight had declared that nature had excluded slavery from the territories, that he would not reenact the laws of God. Well, said Hale, he would. What were the laws against murder, stealing, and perjury if not reenactments of the laws of God? "And when he tells me that the law of God is against slavery, it is a most potent argument to my mind why we should incorporate it in any territorial bill." The stringent Fugitive Slave Bill which Webster now endorsed seemed to Hale an anathema. If preservation of the Union could be bought only at the price of trampled civil liberties, he for one would say "come disunion, and come to-day."

In closing, Hale appealed to gentlemen of the South "to cease from representing the North as oppressive." "I ask them," he said, "to cease from representing that there is a design, or a purpose, or a wish to do wrong or injustice to any portion of this Confederacy." Those whom he represented desired the abolition of slavery, that was true. But their action would come "not out of the Constitution, or against the Constitution, but in and under it."

We do not expect that public or political measures are to effect it [abolition of slavery]; but by appealing to the hearts and consciences of men; by bringing home the principles of Christianity, and the appeals of humanity to those who have the power to influence men around them, and who have hearts to feel, we trust they will be induced to remedy or remove the evils under which the Country, in this connexion, labors . . . We ask not the aid of this Government to bring it about; for we know that under the Constitution you have no power to move in the work, and therefore any such appeal of ours would be ill-timed. What we do have a right to ask, and do ask, in the name of justice, of humanity, of liberty, is that you place not this Government in the way—that you do not, by any action of yours, interpose to extend the boundaries of slavery, or retard the progress of human freedom or improvement.[24]

In his crusade against slavery Hale thus applied the same premise that had shaped his views on temperance: reform depended not on legislative proscription but on pricking the conscience of the wrong-doer.

Although a big hit with Northern Free Soilers, Hale's speech (the longest of his Senate career) was remarkably ineffective. It was plainly the work of a skilled debater who by concentrating his fire on weak points and by distorting statements seeks to discredit his opponent's argument. And in this case his main opponent was a dying man who represented a tiny minority in the Senate. Hale was much more forceful in short, impromptu exchanges in which he eschewed political and economic for moral arguments. For at bottom slavery was a moral issue.

In April, the Senate referred Clay's compromise plan, along with alternate proposals, to a committee of thirteen.[25] Hale strenuously opposed this action, chiefly because he objected to all steps leading to a compromise solution, but also because he distrusted private caucuses to which, as an independent, he was never invited and whose actions he learned of only at second hand—"from Philadelphia and New York, and sometimes from the West," he complained.[26] On May 8, Clay, as chairman of the committee of thirteen, reported three bills which tied together his earlier resolutions. The first of these linked free statehood for California, territorial organization of Utah and New Mexico without restriction on slavery, and resolution of the Texas boundary problem. The second was a fugitive slave bill (a modification of one drafted by Virginia's James M. Mason), and the third restrained the slave trade in the District of Columbia.[27]

Clay evidently hoped that by joining California statehood to the New Mexico and Utah bills, he would make the pill sweet enough for Taylorites to swallow. But in this he was disappointed. The President and his followers gave this "Omnibus" bill a decidedly chilly reception, as did radicals both North and South. "This bill turns the whole of the territories into a slave pasture," cried Hale, while Jefferson Davis proposed an amendment which would forbid territorial legislatures from interfering with the property rights of slaveholders.[28] Still, the forces favoring the compromise were strong and talented—Clay, Cass, Douglas, Foote, and Webster—and no one could predict its fate. "We are all in the dark here, as to what our prospects are, even in the Senate, in regard to Mr. Clay's great compromise," Hale told Theodore Parker on May 15. "If we can judge from the indications of a few days since, we shall have the ultra pro-slavery Senators of the South to fight our battles for us against the bill of Mr. Clay. But we may be deceived, & they may come in & support it." [29]

Much to the distress of Chase, Hale preferred to oppose the compromise measures independently. Rarely and reluctantly did he sit down with other friends of free soil to map strategy. Having made his reputation as a maverick, a political independent who scorned party ties, Hale balked at letting any faction tie his hands or obscure his identity. Ever since his disillusioning experience with the Concord Clique he had insisted on perfect freedom of action. He willingly aligned himself with political groups committed to the fight against slavery, but always his allegiance was loose and provisional.

Besides, for a lazy man whose forte and passion were for impromptu debate, it was easier to launch piecemeal counterattacks than to plan and execute systematic assaults on the Slave Power.

Despite attempts to regiment him, therefore, Hale remained a guerrillist. "He confers with no one," Chase lamented, "—cannot even bear to sit down and talk over a subject in its various bearings. He wants no campaign upon a systematic plan, but bold dashes here and there and fun & frolic in the intervals. He is a clean, good-natured, prompt, quick-witted debater and fills a most important place, but he is not a patient thinker, a wise deviser, or persevering executer of measures." It would have shocked the singleminded Ohioan had he known that at the height of the battle over Clay's compromise Hale had taken time to compose a seventeen-page story for his daughter Lucy about her pet canary and the cleaning of its cage.[30]

Yet in his guerrillist way, Hale kept up an unrelenting attack on the Omnibus Bill and its defenders. He was particularly sharp with Webster whose "law of nature" argument he found especially infuriating. Northerners viewed Webster's course "with loathing and contempt," Hale informed his wife. Personally, though he thought Daniel "both cowardly and corrupt," he felt pity that the once-great warrior "should have so degraded himself in his old age and sacrificed his honorable fame so basely."[31] These opinions, however, Hale expressed only privately; in the Senate he scrupulously avoided personalities. Not all his colleagues could say as much. On June 8, William C. Dawson of Georgia, attempting to embarrass Hale, brought to the Senate's attention the Rev. George Storrs' 1835 letter to the *Herald of Freedom* describing Hale's part in the disruption of his abolitionist lectures in Dover. It seemed to Dawson ample proof that the New Hampshire senator's motives were less than pure and that ambition rather than principle had directed his subsequent actions. Vice-President Millard Fillmore cautioned Dawson against making personal allusions, but Webster roared with laughter and Clay cheered the Georgian on. Before Hale had a chance to defend himself, Webster and Clay, together with Cass, George E. Badger, and others, ostentatiously left the Senate Chamber in what the *National Era* called a preconcerted attempt "to mortify and abash Mr. Hale." [32]

Admitting that his beliefs had undergone a decided change since 1835, Hale asked "is that a sin? Is it a sin when light shines to walk in the light?" As for Dawson's charge of having pursued an ambitious course, he need say no more than that he planned "to retire not only from public life, but from this Senate, and to leave these scenes and these troubles to those whose tastes are better suited to the strife and turmoil of political life." Although he would have had Dawson believe otherwise, Hale had given no previous inkling of his intention to resign his seat, and it seems to have been precipitated by Dawson's attack. Not until June 11, the day after his reply to Dawson, did he tell his wife that he contemplated any such move. "You will not understand by this that I have made and perfected any arrangement for leaving the Senate at present," he told her. "But I feel constantly more and more dissatisfied with the situation of a member of Congress here." He had decided to investigate likely places to practice law and if he found something attractive he would resign at the end of the next session.[33]

The senators might view his professions as the pouting of a wounded man, but word that Hale was contemplating an early retirement from the Senate shocked his antislavery friends. Soon scores of letters began arriving in Washington, urging that he reconsider. "Your services to the cause are of incalculable importance," wrote Sumner, "& with your increasing experience & influence, must continue to increase in importance." Even political enemies admitted "the ability, tact, & readiness" with which Hale had defended antislavery principles in the Senate, and Sumner urged him to stick.[34] Notwithstanding such praiseful entreaties as this, Hale continued to talk of retiring and of setting up law practice, probably in New York City. Mrs. Hale readily fell in with her husband's plan. Indeed there is no doubt that family separation, the inevitable result of Hale's career, in large part explains his desire to leave the Senate. He may also have been discouraged at the seeming futility of his senatorial labors and disappointed that they were so little appreciated. And he may have decided that he could earn more money as a lawyer and lecturer than he could as a senator. But for the time being he put off any final decision and continued to war against the compromise.[35]

In July the opponents of Clay's Omnibus settlement suffered a grievous loss. After a five-day illness, President Zachary Taylor died on the evening of July 9, 1850, leaving executive power in the hands of Millard Fillmore. Paradoxically, no one lamented the slaveholder President's passing more than the Free Soil extremists who had so fiercely denounced him before he took office. "Every day, his position & policy were becoming more & more Northern," commented Gamaliel Bailey, "and constituted the most formidable obstacle to the passage of the Compromise." Taylor's death, mourned Hale, was "a very great and serious public calamity." It was especially calamitous, he thought, because of the Texas crisis "in which . . . the course of the President would have been salutary and his influence good . . ." Texas had laid claim to all of New Mexico east of the Rio Grande and was "threatening to maintain that title by arms." Old Zack's known determination to protect New Mexico (which had recently adopted an antislavery constitution) "was considered a great point gained to the cause of free soil & free principles," Hale reported, "as President Taylor was a slave holder & from a slave State. Thus situated he could exert more influence on the question than a man from a free State however well he may [be] disposed." There was also a personal element in Hale's reaction to the President's death. He had come to know Taylor well, and had visited him often. "I really feel deeply grieved at his death," he privately confessed.[36]

The accession of Fillmore brought a shift in administration policy favorable to Clay's compromise. Webster, elevated to Secretary of State once more, replaced Seward as the power behind the throne. Yet even so, it proved impossible to enact the Omnibus Bill in one chunk. Congress seemed bogged down. "Life here is quite monotonous," wrote Hale. "The compromise bill still drags its way slowly along . . . I begin to think however that the bill in some shape will pass, as the most strenuous efforts are made to bring over individuals who have heretofore been supposed to be opposed to the bill, & I fear these efforts are having their influence with some of our Northern members." [37]

It was, however, less such "strenuous efforts" than a change of tactics that got the compromise through. On the last day of July the foes of compromise won what seemed a victory when they succeeded in stripping the Omnibus of all its provisions save those relating to the organization of Utah. Davis grinned, Chase shook hands with Pierre Soulé, Seward danced "about like a little top," Benton's face bore a look of triumph. Hale, reported the New York *Express,* was beside himself with delight.[38] But their joy was short-lived. On August 1 the Senate passed the Utah bill. Then, after Clay had left to recuperate his failing energy at Newport, Rhode Island, Stephen A. Douglas took charge and one by one steered the compromise bills safely through the Senate and House. First came the admission of California to the Union as a free state, then the act organizing New Mexico with popular sovereignty (the boundary dispute with Texas had been settled first, the Texans getting ten million dollars for relinquishing their extreme claims), then the Fugitive Slave Act, and finally a statute suppressing the slave trade in the District of Columbia. By September 20, 1850, President Fillmore had signed them all into law.[39]

After voting for the admission of California, Hale had left Washington for three weeks in New Hampshire, returning in time to help pass the bill curbing the slave trade in the District. The reason for his long absence from the capital at this critical juncture was that Mrs. Hale was pregnant and apparently very apprehensive about giving birth at her comparatively advanced age. After duty forced his return to Washington, he tried, not always with success, to convince her of his solicitude. "I never loved you more fondly or more devotedly than at this moment," he assured Lucy. "I can imagine no calamity that could befall me, so dreadful as to lose you." He had, he told her, been "praying especially that God would be with you to comfort[,] sustain and aid you in the hour of peril attending your approaching confinement." Unhappily, although her own life was saved, she lost the child.[40]

Amid all the uncertainty and gloom that Hale faced in 1850, there was one bright light. On September 28 Congress at last abolished flogging in the navy. Ever since 1843 Hale had worked to achieve this humanitarian reform. As a freshman representative in the Twenty-Eighth Congress he had the "great satisfaction" of getting the House to approve his proviso abolishing corporal punishment in the navy; but the Senate had disappointingly rejected it.[41] Thereafter during his every session in Congress, Hale reintroduced his amendment. Always the Senate refused to change the existing law —one which had been in effect since 1800. Finally, in July 1848, he won approval for his resolution requesting the Secretary of the Navy to furnish the Senate with information about punishment inflicted on ships, frigates, and sloops of war.[42] Armed with this report, petitions from Northern humanitarians, the support of the *National Era,* and the assistance and encouragement of some naval officers and enlisted men, Hale pressed his campaign against flogging with renewed vigor.[43]

Secretary of the Navy John Y. Mason's report proved a gold mine for Hale's purposes. Men had been severely whipped, he was able to show, for such minor offenses as bad cooking and not being properly dressed at quarters. Worst of all were floggings in punishment of drunkenness—drunkenness induced by a legalized spirit ration.[44]

I find that on board the United States ship Marion, from the 1st of December, 1847, to the 8th of January, 1848, only thirty-eight days, four hundred and thirty-nine lashes were given by the cat; and of the number thus punished by twelve lashes each, twenty-three sailors were flogged for drunkenness and desertion . . . Thus you degrade and brutalize the sailor by law, and then by law flog him for being just what you have made him.[45]

Arbitrary justice, meted out before the mast, had on more than one occasion taken the life of an American seaman. Why was it, Hale asked, that this vestige of barbarism, abolished in the army and from which even the meanest felons were exempt, remained to torture "the sons of the battle and the breeze?" At a time when "humanity is lifting up her voice . . . for every other class of unfortunate and oppressed," the sailor was as much degraded as a dog, he protested. It may have been with this injustice in mind that he named his daughters' beloved mongrel "Sailor." [46]

Senator George E. Badger of North Carolina, speaking, it must be said, for most naval officers, best stated the arguments against banishing the cat-o'-nine-tails. "Flogging remained the best means of maintaining naval discipline," he alleged. The only alternatives were death for minor offenses, or confinement—a form of chastizement welcomed by shirkers. Hale's proposal was "the result of a mistaken philanthropy," Badger concluded, one which all officers and good seamen would disapprove.[47]

At the first session of the Thirtieth Congress only a handful of senators supported Hale's motion to abolish flogging and the spirit ration in the navy; at the second, sixteen (all but three of them from the North) voted with Hale to outlaw "whipping in the naval service." [48] By 1850 Hale's public and private arguments were wearing the opposition's majority thin. The showdown occurred on September 28, 1850, when James M. Mason presented an amendment which would have deleted from the naval appropriations bill the House's provision that flogging in the navy be abolished. Hale answered the Virginian in a short but forceful speech. Without repeating earlier arguments, he addressed himself first to the contention that it was the unique disciplinary problems of ships at sea which made flogging a necessary punishment, and second to the oft-repeated statement that only the few "cowardly, skulking rascals" felt the lash's sting. The captain of the U.S.S. Pennsylvania, a receiving ship moored snugly in port, he pointed out, had ordered whippings in inordinate number—239 times during 1848—and the list of offenders showed few repeaters. Time and again, "by an overwhelming and increasing majority," Hale reminded his fellow senators, the House of Representatives had voted to put an end to flogging, "and year after year has this Senate stood here as the bulwark of the cat-o'-nine-tails." Having spent so much of the present session discussing the interests of "those that are subject to a discipline of a different kind," having "done so much to heal the 'bleeding wounds' of a violated Constitution," he hoped the Senate would "not consent that the bleeding wounds of the lacerated backs of white citizens of this republic shall be longer submitted to this brutalizing punishment." A brief debate followed in which Seward and Hamlin backed reform, and Dawson, Yulee, Jefferson Davis, and Andrew P. Butler opposed it. Cries of "Question!" "Question!" "Question!" cut discussion short, the yeas and nays were ordered, and to Hale's great delight Mason's amendment failed to carry, twenty-three voting for, twenty-five against. Flogging—that "relic of feudalism and barbarity" Hale called it—had at last been outlawed.[49]

This humane reform had not been the work of one man. Many hands, both in and out of Congress, had helped to carry it forward. But no one had been more persevering or influential than Hale, and his leading role in its ultimate success was well understood and appreciated by the men of the fleet whose welfare he had at heart. The crew of the frigate *Brandywine* sent him a testimonial of their "sincere thanks and grateful feelings," and sailors aboard the *U.S.S. Germantown* gave him a medal valued at one hundred dollars for his campaign against the lash.[50] Even some commanding officers applauded the reform. Captain J. C. Long of the U. S. Frigate *Mississippi* thanked Hale for helping to abolish a form of punishment "which has always to me been as painful to inflict, as for the poor Jack to receive," and Commodore Nicholas of the *Germantown,* who admitted that "No man could have been more opposed to the bill than I was," came back from a cruise to Africa "delighted with its operation. It raises the character of the men astonishingly," he confessed. "I could not have believed it." In 1853 Hale accepted the Commodore's invitation to visit the *Germantown,* and as he departed, "the crew manned the rigging and gave him three cheers." It was reward enough, and more.[51]

"There is, I believe, peace now prevailing throughout all our borders," Henry Clay proclaimed in September 1850. "I believe it is permanent." President Fillmore, in both his first and second annual messages to Congress, announced his belief that the Compromise of 1850 was "a final settlement of the dangerous and exciting subjects

which they embraced." Indeed, it is true that the compromise temporarily cooled tempers in Congress and out; that bête noire slavery
in the territories was for the time being put to rest. But with
large and influential groups in North and South, the one committed
to a crusade against the sin of slavery and the other to a defense of
human bondage as a "positive good," any compromise involving the
issue of slavery was bound to be fragile and short-lived. Hale saw
this as clearly as anyone. "Gentlemen flatter themselves that they
have done a great deal for the peace of the country," he said in reply
to Clay. "Everybody is pleased but a few 'wild fanatics' . . . Sir, let
not gentlemen deceive themselves. The pen of inspiration teaches us
that there was a time when a set of men cried 'Peace! peace! but
there was no peace.' Let me tell you there is no peace to those who
think they have successfully dug the grave in which the hopes, the
rights, and the interests of freedom have been buried. No, sir, that
peace will be short, and that rejoicing will most assuredly be turned
into mourning." Events soon proved him correct.[52]

Debates in the second session of the Thirty-First Congress quickly
showed that the slavery issue was still very much alive. Ironically it
was Southern friends of the compromise who reopened old wounds:
Foote with an entirely gratuitous resolution declaring the Compromise of 1850 a "definitive settlement of the questions growing out
of domestic slavery," and Clay with a request for a reexamination of
means to suppress the African slave trade.[53] To Hale, as to most
Northerners, the most obnoxious part of the compromise was the
new Fugitive Slave Act. That statute—which denied alleged fugitives the protection of habeas corpus, jury trial, and the right to give
evidence—appeared to him a dangerous perversion of fundamental
civil liberties, and he joined Chase and Sumner (who entered the
Thirty-Second Congress) in attacks on it in the Senate. But his most
conspicuous efforts to thwart its working took place outside the
Capitol.

One of the first runaways seized under the Act of 1850 was
Frederick Wilkins, alias Shadrach, who had fled from Virginia to
Boston where he had found employment at the Cornhill Coffee

House. On February 15, 1851, United States Deputy Marshal Patrick Riley, acting under the new act, arrested Shadrach and held him in the Suffolk County Court House, pending a hearing before a special federal commissioner and probable return to his master. Before the law could move further, however, a group of twenty Boston Negroes, led by Lewis Hayden, broke into the Court House, grabbed Shadrach, and spirited him away by carriage to the north and freedom. "I think it the noblest deed done in Boston since the destruction of the tea in 1773," said Hale's friend, Theodore Parker.[54]

Not all agreed with the radical Unitarian. In the Senate, Henry Clay, not satisfied with the arrest of Hayden and three others accused of directing Shadrach's rescue, called for an inquiry into the affair. The question was, he cried, "whether the majesty of the Government shall be maintained or not; whether we shall have a Government of white men or black men in the cities of this country." The action of the Boston mob, moaned Jefferson Davis, seemed to indicate an incapacity of the people for democratic government. Hale mildly and briefly answered these complaints. He would not oppose Clay's request for an inquiry, he announced; but he cautioned against the mistake of using military force to oppose "the moral sentiment of the people," (learn from the lesson of George III, he advised), and, perhaps with a glance at the senators from South Carolina, recalled that Hayden and his accomplices had not been the first to nullify a federal law. Soon he was more directly involved in the rescue cases.[55]

The Boston Vigilance Committee engaged two lawyers to defend Shadrach's rescuers: Richard Henry Dana, Jr. and John P. Hale. The trials began on May 27, each of the accused being tried individually. Dana, who had sought Shadrach's release by legal means before his rescue, was glad to have Hale's assistance.

What I have seen of Hale has pleased me [he noted in his diary after the first week of trial]. He has strong sense, quickness, fairness & a habit of thinking over cases & points, with a good memory, although not a book man nor fond of mere learning. He is an excellent companion, unobtrusive & sociable. There is a queer mixture of the natural gentleman & the rough country trader or farmer about him. He is a man of good birth and education, but wasted his youth, and [was] saved by an excellent wife.[56]

Hale presented most of the oral arguments, doing so, in Dana's words: "nobly, with great skill in feeling the jury, and with passages of true eloquence." [57] One example of that eloquence won a small renown in antislavery circles:

John Debree claims that he owns Shadrach. Owns what? Owns a man! Suppose John Debree should say that he owns the moon, and has an exclusive right in its beams! Would a Massachusetts jury find it so? And yet, moons shall wax and wane no more; the earth itself shall crumble and decay, while the soul of the poor, hunted, persecuted Shadrach shall live on with the life of God himself! [58]

Whether it was owing to Hale's persuasive eloquence, Dana's legal erudition, or the repeated votes of "not guilty" by a juror who had assisted Shadrach's rescuers,[59] all four defendants were eventually exonerated. Hale had been present at only the first two trials, but they set the pattern for the remaining two, whose progress he watched attentively. The Vigilance Committee paid him $500 for his labors. No less gratefully received was an eight-volume set of Hallam's *History of England* which the colored citizens of Boston presented to Hale in appreciation of his "invaluable services" during the rescue trials.[60]

Hale was glad for a chance to keep his hand in the practice of law. Although sometime during the winter or spring of 1851 he had decided against leaving the Senate before his term expired, he knew that when that time came he would have to fall back on his profession, for he cherished no hopes of reelection.[61] Ever since 1847 the Democrats of New Hampshire had controlled the state nearly as tightly as before the "Hale Storm." By expediently assuming a slightly radical position on slavery, they had wooed back many who had followed Hale out of the party. They also profited from rifts in the enemy's camp.[62] Impediments had been admitted to the unnatural marriage of Whigs and Independent Democrats, so that by 1852 the Alliance of 1845–1846 was defunct. In fact, it had been all but dead since 1848, its only successes coming at the biennial congressional elections in the first and third districts where Amos Tuck and a free soil Whig were twice reelected.

In this weakened condition, Hale's friends approached the March election in 1852. Their ranks were somewhat swelled by followers of John Atwood, who in 1851 had been deposed as Democratic gubernatorial candidate because of his public statements of dissatisfaction with the Compromise of 1850.[63] But Atwood's army proved much smaller than expected, Whigs were apathetic, and the Maine Liquor Law—which the Free Soilers backed strongly—was still a liability in New Hampshire. Democrats, exhorted to "remember that the paramount question in the choice of Representatives, is *the re-election or defeat of John P. Hale*," turned out in large numbers.[64] Not even Hale's vigorous electioneering could turn the tide. In December 1852 the predominantly Democratic legislature selected Charles Atherton to replace Hale in the Senate, and Dover's leading citizen prepared to resume private life.[65]

CHAPTER IX

Law, Lyceums, and Free Soil

EIGHTEEN-FIFTY-TWO was also a Presidential election year —one of more than usual interest to New Hampshire. For not only did Concord's Frank Pierce win the Democratic nomination, but his "neighbor," John P. Hale, opposed him as the Free Soil candidate.

The years 1849–1850 had witnessed a collapse of the Free Soil party. For many reasons—most of all the feeling that getting anti-slavery men into public office had precedence over the building of a third party—Free Soilers drifted back into the old parties. The Whig and Democratic disposition to meet the recusants halfway made this coalescence easy, and by the end of 1851 the Free Soil star had reached its nadir. Even Salmon P. Chase returned to the Democratic fold.[1]

Hale, almost alone among politicians of national reputation, struggled to preserve and revitalize an independent, antislavery party, and not only in New Hampshire. In 1850 he was calling on Sumner to "Stir up the fourth [Massachusetts] District," (where John G. Palfrey was running for Congress) and urging that meetings be held in each town to insure effective Free Soil organization.[2] Both major parties were corrupt beyond regeneration, Hale believed; both were the tools of the Slave Power. Only within a third party might anti-slavery advocates act in good conscience and with hope of ultimate success.[3] More important than Hale's exhortations and entreaties in checking the drift away from the Free Soil party, were the actions of Whigs and Democrats at their national conventions in June 1852. First the Democrats, who nominated Pierce, and then the Whigs, who made Mexican War hero Winfield Scott their candidate, affirmed that the Compromise of 1850 had laid the slavery question to rest. The effrontery of these "pro-slavery" resolutions shook many Free Soilers out of their complaisancy. Former Whigs like Charles F. Adams and Joshua Giddings, and quondam Democrats like Chase at last admitted what Hale had preached all along—that nothing could be expected from the old parties and that Free Soilers must act independently in the election to come.[4]

By the time Sam Lewis issued a call for Free Democrats (as the Free Soilers now dubbed themselves) to assemble at Pittsburgh in August, speculations abounded about possible candidates.[5] The name most often mentioned was that of John P. Hale. His fame had grown as a result of his senatorial labors, many old Liberty party hands wished to make amends for having dropped him in 1848, and now that the New York Barnburners were once again merged in the Democracy (Van Buren himself backed Pierce), Hale seemed the best and most logical candidate. In February 1852 the Ohio Free Soil Convention declared itself in favor of a Hale-Lewis ticket, and in May Maine's antislavery forces followed suit.[6] Elsewhere preferences were much the same, though many supported Cassius M. Clay of Kentucky for Vice-President, and a few favored Salmon P. Chase over Hale.

As in 1847–1848, Hale wanted the nomination not at all. Success appeared even less likely in 1852 than in 1848, and the prospect of months of grueling campaigning—months away from home—was not a pleasant one to a man of Hale's easy-going, even indolent, ways. At first he tried to head off his own nomination by proposing Chase, enlisting the help of Sumner and several Ohio congressmen, but his efforts proved unavailing. Chase wanted no part of the nomination "for many reasons," and most Free Soilers, suspicious of the Ohioan's flirtations with the Democracy, received his name coolly.[7]

Failure made Hale bolder. A week before the Pittsburgh convention he flatly refused to serve as Free Democratic candidate. Yet never had there been "a more pressing necessity for efficient action by the friends of Freedom and Independent Democracy, than at the present," he admitted. Whigs and Democrats were both the lackeys of slavery, and by affirming the finality of the Compromise of 1850 they had condoned the abandonment "of every safeguard of liberty" in the territories. The Free Soil cause must be kept alive, he told George G. Fogg, and he would gladly endorse the Pittsburgh nominee. But he had concluded—for reasons he declined to divulge—not to run. If necessary, Fogg was to state explicitly to any or all delegates that it was his "deliberate and final determination" not to accept a nomination.[8] The sacrificial lamb would be hard to catch.

News of Hale's decision leaked out before the convention, and pitched Free Soilers into a quandary. Learning of it from Fogg while enroute to Pittsburgh, Charles Francis Adams glumly confessed: "I think I should not have started upon this mission had I been apprised of this early enough. Its effect will be to throw us into complete confusion." Who else was left? Chase appeared out of the running, owing to bitter feeling against him in his own state; and, it seemed to Adams, Giddings, another possible choice, might better expend all his energies in the House. The best course, then, seemed to be to persuade Hale to change his mind. Austin Willey, a Free Soil editor from Maine, was thus deputized to telegraph Hale from Buffalo asking that he reconsider.[9] Independently, from Washington, Chase also brought pressure to bear. When Robert Carter, editor of the Boston *Daily Commonwealth,* sent word of Hale's letter of declination, Chase at once wired Carter to withhold its publication and dashed off a note to Hale, asking him to withdraw his letter. Nearly all Free Democrats desired Hale's nomination, Chase maintained. He could disregard their wishes only by inflicting "the most serious injury" on himself and the antislavery cause. "This must not be," declared the Ohioan, "at least it should not be."[10] But Hale remained mum, strengthened in his resolve by Amos Tuck who wrote on August 5: "I still continue of the opinion that you are of too much value to be used up, by being run at this time."[11]

Hearing nothing from the New Hampshire senator, Free Democratic delegates nonetheless decided to press for his nomination. There was really very little else they could do. Despite his disclaimer,

Hale remained the strongest candidate. Adams and Chase had only minor support, and neither wanted the nomination any more than did Hale.[12] On August 11, after some 2,000 sweltering delegates and lookers-on had poured into Pittsburgh's Masonic Hall, Sam Lewis, as chairman of the national committee, called the convention to order. Ohio's delegation caught the prevailing spirit perfectly with a huge banner proclaiming: "No Compromise with Slaveholders or Doughfaces." Delegates elected Henry Wilson of Massachusetts convention president and selected a platform committee that included among others Fogg, Adams, Willey, Giddings, and Gerrit Smith.

Midway in the second day Giddings reported the platform. Although it included new planks denouncing the Compromise of 1850 (especially the hated Fugitive Slave Act), calling for recognition of Haiti, and recommending arbitration of international disputes, it was essentially a copy of the Free Soil credo of 1848. In committee, Smith and Dr. Francis J. Lemoyne had fought unsuccessfully for recognition of the principle that slavery and the laws protecting it were illegal, but in the face of strong opposition from Adams had to settle for resolutions which implied the *ethical* illegality of human bondage. The convention with proper enthusiasm adopted the platform, diplomatically tabled Smith's alternate proposals, and turned to nominations. An attempt to push through Hale's nomination by acclamation failed, but it made little difference, for on the first ballot he received 192 of 208 votes cast. His nomination was at once made unanimous, and the hall rocked to "nine cheers for John P. Hale!" In a much closer fight, George W. Julian of Indiana defeated the popular Lewis for second place on the Free Democratic ticket, thanks in large part to the efforts of Henry Wilson.[13]

Spirits had been high at Pittsburgh, and men like Adams came away from the convention with greater confidence in the vigor and practicality of the political antislavery movement. Others were less enthusiastic. Sumner remained aloof, and Chase, while prepared to back the Free Democratic candidates and platform, feared sinking his "individuality in this organization, which it seems to me, must be temporary." Those who came to Pittsburgh hoping to nominate a ticket that would appeal more to Democrats than Whigs—and so facilitate the election of Scott whom most antislavery men viewed as a lesser evil than Pierce—found the nomination of Julian, a Whig turned Free Soiler, dispiriting.[14]

The profound silence from Dover also dampened Free Soil enthusiasm. Throughout August, Hale refused to accept or reject the Pittsburgh nomination. Henry Wilson, while predicting that Hale would not decline, nevertheless feared the effect of Whig entreaties. Some nationally prominent Whigs—among them Thurlow Weed of New York—fearful at first that Hale's candidacy would cost Scott Ohio and Indiana, apparently sought to get him to decline the Free Democratic nomination. But if some pressured Hale to decline, a great many more (including young Walt Whitman of Brooklyn, New York) implored him to accept. On September 6, Hale at last wrote to Wilson, reluctantly accepting the Pittsburgh decision.[15]

Once having made up his mind, Hale acted in good faith to fulfill his duties as Free Democratic candidate. Within a week of his acceptance, he was swinging west through New York, carrying the campaign to the people. In Peterborough he passed a pleasant day and a half with Gerrit Smith, whom he found "a very religious and devout man," but one who had "many eccentric and peculiar notions." At the time, the colorful philanthropist was endorsing Hale and Julian, but soon after Hale left Peterborough Smith switched his allegiance to a more radical Liberty party ticket of his own creation: William Goodell and S. M. Bell.[16]

Realizing that most of their strength lay in the Old Northwest, Free Democratic strategists directed their heaviest attack at that sector. Hale left the East to the care of Adams, Palfrey, Lewis Tappan, Frederick Douglass, and others, and in mid-September joined Chase, Giddings, and Julian, then actively stumping the Middle West. Everywhere the Free Democrats campaigned with an eye to 1856. Yet they had an immediate goal as well: they hoped to woo enough votes from antislavery Democrats to throw the election to Scott. Such hopes appeared brightest in Ohio, and Hale made a special effort there.[17] Nowhere was he better received than in the

Western Reserve—for two decades a hotbed of abolitionism. In Oberlin ("probably the most thoroughly anti-slavery place in the U States," Hale noted) 3,000 persons filled President Charles Grandison Finney's church to overflowing in order to hear Hale excoriate the slaveholders and doughfaces.[18] In October he moved west into Michigan, Wisconsin, and Illinois. Sundays excepted, he spoke every day, usually two or three times. Often he gave his speeches out of doors, or standing near an open window, so that all who wished could hear. Always proud of his skill on the hustings and genuinely fond of people, Hale enjoyed the campaign once he had been forced into it. The crowds and cheers were therapeutic—washing away fatigue—as well as satisfying to his ego, and in long letters he shared each new success with his wife.[19]

Despite the noise and fuss stirred up by Hale and his followers, the campaign was one of unparalleled dullness. "In our recent travels in New York and New England," observed the *National Era,* "we should not have known, from any indications of popular feeling, that a Presidential election was pending." "Genl *Apathy* is the strongest candidate out here," wrote one Whig from Cincinnati. Only the Free Democrats, it seemed, showed any enthusiasm or any anxiety about the outcome. Both Whigs and Democrats studiously avoided the slavery question and did their best to ignore their antislavery tormentor.[20]

The result in November was much as expected. Pierce, the Northern friend of the South, easily defeated General Scott, capturing all but four states. Hale received only 156,149 popular votes—little more than half Van Buren's total in 1848—and nowhere did the Free Democrats tip the scales in favor of either major candidate. Many antislavery men were disheartened at this weak showing. To Garrisonians it appeared to vindicate opposition to political methods. But the more optimistic Free Soilers found reasons for hope. Hale's small vote was no matter of serious discouragement, they contended. To be sure, it was much less than Van Buren polled four years earlier, but that canvass had been deceptive. Many, especially in New York, had then supported the Free Soil ticket for reasons unconnected with antislavery. "They were not Free Soil men, but Van Buren men, who had hated Gen. Cass," George Julian recalled. "The vote for Hale represented the *bona fide* strength of our cause after this element had been eliminated, and its quality went far to atone for its quantity." Better to compare Birney's vote in 1844 with Hale's in 1852—a 150 percent increase. It was this trend which heartened men like Julian. But they still had a long way to go.[21]

After his political defeats in the fall of 1852, Hale still had one more session in the Senate before stepping back into private life. Since Congress had little important business that winter, and since he was a lame duck, Hale entered Washington's busy social life more fully than ever before. Mrs. Hale and Lucy were with him much of the time (Lizzie stayed at her Connecticut boarding school) and the three made the rounds of private receptions, embassy parties, and dined with President and Mrs. Fillmore at the White House. The affable and gregarious senator no doubt enjoyed making social visits accompanied by his shyly attractive daughter, now approaching young womanhood, and his charming, popular wife ("a quiet, most pleasant and rather pretty woman," Chase described her). Both he and his wife had always taken the "courtesies and attentions of society" seriously, making all the requisite calls and feeling slighted whenever they were not promptly returned. In March, after staying long enough to witness Pierce's inauguration, the Hales packed their belongings and returned to Dover.[22]

For nearly two months Hale puttered about the Pleasant Street home, enjoying the company of friends and family, free from the cares of office. But he did not long remain at leisure—nor, indeed, in Dover. He had already made plans to enter into partnership with Peter Starr, Jr., a Wall Street lawyer with strong antislavery beliefs. For political as well as economic reasons (the spark of political ambition still glowed enough to make him wish to keep his New Hampshire residency) Hale decided to leave his wife and daughters at home. He would put up at a Manhattan hotel and exchange visits with them as often as possible. Accordingly, during the second week of May 1853 he kissed his womenfolk goodbye and entrained for New York City, stopping enroute to attend the grand dinner given in his honor at Boston.[23]

By May 12 Hale had moved into his office at 35 Wall Street. Starr had just had new carpets laid down and the rooms repainted. "The signs will be printed this week & I shall be fairly launched on the great tide of life as it flows in this Great City," Hale announced in his first letter home. "I have nothing definite in the way of expectations or hopes as to business or patronage, but still I feel in good spirits and courage and hope for the best." This brave façade was not long in crumbling, for in truth he was often very lonely and tortured himself with doubts about the wisdom of his decision to practice in New York. "I . . . have many hours in which I have no familiar faces to see or friends to talk with . . . ," he complained to Lizzie, and repeatedly implored his family to write more often.[24]

After a week or two, Hale was more cheerful again. He glowed when New York papers noticed "in handsome terms" his setting up practice in the city, and he began to get his first fees, mainly from Boston bankers and merchants. Equally important in raising his spirits were the many prominent people who befriended him. Horace Greeley, crusading editor of the *Tribune,* called on Hale at his hotel and chatted at length about politics and reform. At a dinner party Hale met the mighty Henry Ward Beecher, and twice went to Plymouth Church in Brooklyn to hear him preach. He became very friendly with legal reformer David Dudley Field, Captain Uriah P. Levy, owner of Monticello and a former supporter of Hale's naval reforms, John Jay, a prominent antislavery attorney, and James John Roosevelt, associate justice of the New York Supreme Court. But best of all, he could always count on a warm welcome at the home of John Parkman, for many years his minister in Dover, who had recently moved to Staten Island. Save for his occasional trips home, or his wife's visits to New York, Hale was happiest during the weekends he often spent with the Parkmans.[25]

Yet on balance it was a lonesome life, not only for himself but for Mrs. Hale who spent most of her days in Dover with Lucy, and for

Lizzie at her school in Hartford. He put up with it only because it seemed the only way he could earn a sizable income without burning his political bridges in New Hampshire. Actually, his partnership with Starr seems to have been only moderately profitable. Most of his practice (which was busy enough to keep him at his desk from nine to five on most weekdays) Hale conducted in New York City, though he occasionally went to Washington, Boston, and New Hampshire for trials. Whatever money he did receive for his legal labors, he managed—or tried to manage—with Yankee frugality. No sum was small enough to throw away. Although generous in providing for the wants of his family, Hale expected that they be economical. Lizzie he required to keep a cash book of receipts and expenditures, which he audited from time to time.[26]

Hale argued both criminal and civil cases, and may also have peddled his influence with members of Congress, although the evidence on this last point is muddled.[27] His best known legal services were those rendered in behalf of Theodore Parker, Thomas Wentworth Higginson, Wendell Phillips, and other Massachusetts abolitionists accused of obstructing the execution of the Fugitive Slave Act at the time of the rendition of the escaped slave Anthony Burns in 1854.[28] The defendants in that celebrated case were pleased to secure such impressive counsel. "John P. Hale takes off his outside coat more sturdily than any man living can do it, I presume, and looks so hearty and solid that I should think a jury would come down like Davy Crockett's coon, without waiting for a shot," Higginson reflected at the time of the trial.[29] Parker, with whom Hale stayed during the legal preliminaries and the trial itself, was unwilling to rely solely on his attorney's imposing figure or courtroom eloquence. Believing that phosphorous was good for the brain, he forced Hale (who hated all seafood) to eat fish at every breakfast and dinner while the legal battles lasted. Even so, Hale enjoyed himself.[30] Once begun, the trial was quickly over; the indictments were quashed on a technicality. It had, in fact, ended too soon to please Parker who had longed for a chance to deliver a carefully prepared speech in his own defense. Nothing daunted, he published his remarks privately, dedicating them to Hale and Charles Mayo Ellis, the second counsel for the defense—"such generous advocates of humanity as equal the glories of Holt and Erskine, of Mackintosh and Romilly." Hale's $350 fee, paid by the Boston Vigilance Committee, was as handsome as any he received during these years.[31]

Never did Hale display the same generosity as Richard Henry Dana, Jr., who regularly reduced his fees when arguing antislavery cases. Either Hale lacked Dana's deep commitment to the antislavery movement or, more probably, he was harder pressed financially. Despite his economy drives and lectures on frugality, Hale never fully overcame the free-spending ways of his father. Nor were his womenfolk—budgets and accountbooks notwithstanding—much better. As a result, Hale always took his dollars where he could find them, and that he sometimes depleted the antislavery war-chest troubled his conscience not at all. His none-too-scrupulous quest for income (although never approaching corruption) would in time stain his reputation and cost him his public career.

As important a source of income as his law practice was Hale's lyceum lectures. Since 1850 Hale had been capitalizing upon his eloquence,[32] and by 1853 he was one of the most sought-after speakers on the Northern lyceum circuit. His orotund talks on "The Last Gladiatorial Spectacle at Rome," "A Day in the U.S. Senate," "Trial by Jury," "The Agrarian Laws of Rome," and "The Compromises of 1850" drew crowds of a thousand and more. At a time when Theodore Parker, Horace Greeley, Josiah Quincy, Henry Thoreau, and others were receiving top fees of $25 for their lectures, Hale commanded as much as $100 an address, averaging about $35.[33] His rates were "about double what we have paid to any one," complained one lyceum director;[34] but he was greatly in demand and usually got what he asked. By conservative estimate, Hale's lectures augmented his income by $4,000 during 1853–1855. He wrote all the talks himself, and, once he had learned them, orated from memory. Occasionally premature reliance on memory produced amusing results, as when at

Manchester, New Hampshire, his extemporaneous speech began with "the gladiatorial & concluded with the jury trial." But even then "It was well received." [35]

As the months passed, the financial rewards of Hale's new life seemed less and less to compensate for the disagreeable separation from his family. "One thing I am determined upon," he assured his wife at Thanksgiving, 1854, "and that is that this is the last year that we will live as we are now living, we must be together and with the children." [36] Already, however, political tremors in New Hampshire—the result of a renewed national upheaval over slavery—indicated that his reelection to the Senate might still longer postpone any such permanent reunion.

The event which raised Hale's political stock and whetted his desire once more to return to the Senate, was the passage in May 1854 of the Kansas-Nebraska Act. That controversial measure, which explicitly repealed the Missouri Compromise and in theory at least opened the Kansas and Nebraska territories to slavery, aroused immediate and widespread indignation throughout the North. During the months it was being debated in Congress, angry mass meetings in city after city decried its passage, clergymen denounced it from the pulpit, workers and professional men signed and circulated petitions of protest, and the Northern press attacked it "with an energy for which the history of American journalism had no parallel." As its author, Stephen A. Douglas, had predicted, the Kansas-Nebraska Bill had raised "the hell of a storm." [37]

Hale did his part in whipping the storm into hurricane force. At giant anti-Nebraska rallies in New York and Concord he lambasted Douglas' bill as a diabolical scheme designed solely to extend "that accursed wrong," slavery. Only the people, he proclaimed, the common people, acting directly and vigorously could forestall this impending calamity. It was of great importance, he wrote to his Free Soil followers, that the "premeditated outrage" of repealing the Missouri Compromise be emphatically rebuked at the polls. Ministers might be especially helpful in channeling public opinion, he thought, and he urged them to publicize the infamy of the Kansas-Nebraska Bill in their churches.[38]

In New Hampshire, as in other Northern states, Douglas' bill shivered the Democratic party and crystallized antislavery elements of all parties into a formidable new political coalition. In Congress, Representatives George W. Morrison and George W. Kittredge advertised the Democratic split by breaking with their colleague Harry Hibbard and Senators Moses Norris, Jr. and Jared Williams to vote against the Kansas-Nebraska Bill. At the March elections in New Hampshire "a solid phalanx" of Conscience Whigs and Free Soilers, capitalizing on Democratic dissension and demoralization, nearly won control of the state House of Representatives. What had been a Hunker majority of eighty-nine in 1853 was only three in 1854. And the Kansas-Nebraska storm had far from blown itself out.[39]

With the political scales once again in near balance, Hale's friends raised with him the question of his candidacy for reelection to the United States Senate. The 1854 legislature would have at its disposal two Senate vacancies, one for four years (created by the death of Atherton in 1853 and temporarily being filled by Jared Williams) and one for the full six. Hale longed to return to Washington. He relished the thought of beating the Clique, and after his year in New York the Senate seemed more like the gladiatorial arena he described in his lectures than the bear pit he had complained of before. But there were dangers in committing himself too soon. After careful consideration and consultation with political associates, therefore, Hale decided against running in 1854. Instead, he advised his lieutenants to do all possible to prevent the election of any senator until the following year. By then, he felt sure, "with prudent management" and "proper effort," victory would be assured.[40]

But it would be no easy trick to block the election of Democratic senators in 1854. With a slim majority in the House and complete control in the state Senate, the Hunkers' prospects looked bright. Franklin Pierce could be counted on to use the powers of his office to keep Democratic lines firm. "If we should succeed in staving off this question till next year," one of Hale's backers reported, "it will be but little short of a miracle, as the whole power of the Administration is in the field ag[ain]st us—agents here from Washington with money, & the New York, Boston & Portsmouth Custom Houses are literally *emptied* upon us." [41] Against this potent combination, Hale relied on a mounting disaffection in New Hampshire for the Pierce administration ("It is looked upon by a great many 'democrats' as a corrupt & 'small potatoe' concern," noted one observer) and on the remarkable talents of Mason Weare Tappan. [42]

It was Tappan, most loyal and hardworking of the Hale men, who managed the cumbersome anti-Nebraska alliance in the legislature. As representative from Bradford, Tappan skilfully turned every Democratic weakness to Hale's advantage. Playing upon the rivalry of the three Hunker candidates—John S. Wells, Hibbard, and Morrison—he succeeded at first in postponing election of United States senators from Tuesday, June 13, to Friday, June 16, a move the *Patriot* correctly divined as one "to gain time to trade and create division among Democrats by getting up discussion and excitement upon the Nebraska question." [43] He then forced the House to consider proposed anti-Nebraska resolutions *before* balloting for senator so as to force all candidates to reveal their views on the Kansas-Nebraska Act. [44] When balloting did begin on the 16th, Morrison, the anti-Nebraska Democrat, swung enough votes away from Wells to prevent his election. The next three weeks saw nine more ballots, but each time Wells fell short, though on the sixth he came within five votes of victory. Tappan had taken care to concentrate the Free Soil vote upon himself, rather than on the more prominent Amos Tuck or Jared Perkins, for, as he later explained, Hale's friends feared that "if we once put them on the track, and next year there should be a chance to elect, that they might consider us in some sort bound to go for them . . ." instead of Hale. Tappan therefore became the Free Soil candidate on the understanding that he would "*clear the track*" whenever it became necessary or there was any chance of electing Hale. Few men have had a more devoted or able man Friday than Mason Tappan. [45]

The late summer and fall of 1854 found anti-Nebraska men of all parties groping for some new political organization. At mass meetings across the state, Free Soilers, Whigs, and anti-Nebraska Democrats resolved "That without reference to party ties or our peculiar party opinions, we will stand shoulder to shoulder in our opposition to any increase of the slave power, or extension of slave territory." [46] By 1856 these disparate political elements had united in a new, broadly based Republican party, born of the Kansas-Nebraska explosion. But their first union came within the semi-secret Native American or "Know-Nothing" party, whose rise Hale watched with interest and concern.

Northern Know-Nothingism of the middle-1850's was a product of nativism, anti-Catholicism, and antislavery. At different times and at different places one or the other of these elements would receive greater attention than the others, but all three were always present and to a certain extent interrelated: antiforeign feeling centered on the Irish, most of whom were Catholics and steadfast enemies of the antislavery movement. Although its roots reached far back into American history, what Horace Greeley dubbed the Know-Nothing party was organized in 1849 by Charles B. Allen of New York as the Order of the Star Spangled Banner. During the 1850's—as a result of amorphous party alignments, the surge of antislavery feeling following the Kansas-Nebraska Act, and "the growth of a sincere nativist sentiment"—there occurred a series of spectacular Know-Nothing successes. In 1854 Know-Nothings made a clean sweep of Massachusetts, electing a governor, all state officers, all state senators, and all but two of 378 state representatives. [47]

New Hampshire possessed all the necessary ingredients of Know-Nothingism, and by the autumn of 1854 the order in that state was surging forward. Some who took one of the party's three degrees did so chiefly out of antipathy for the German and Irish immigrants who were filling up manufacturing cities along the Merrimack and on the coast, immigrants whose competition in the labor market was not always welcome and whose allegiance to Rome offended Protestant sensibilities. (Anti-Catholic feeling was never more rampant than in the 1850's and was at least partially responsible for New Hampshire's refusal to abolish its religious test act in 1852.) Others, however, men like Tappan, James Bell, Ralph Metcalf, and Anthony Colby, joined the Know-Nothing party as Henry Wilson had done in Massachusetts—"determined to use it to further the antislavery cause." And, it might be added, to destroy the Democratic party.[48]

For Hale the "great accession of strength" of the Know-Nothings posed certain problems. Reelection to the Senate, he had decided, "would be highly gratifying," and if New Hampshire went the way of Massachusetts in 1855 the Know-Nothings would have it within their power to give him that prize. He himself had no very strong feelings about the Native American movement. From what he knew, he wrote Tappan, "much which it proposes I heartily approve, though I cannot see the wisdom of the course adopted to effect it." Many of his friends, Tappan among them, belonged to the order. But he was troubled by intimations that to insure his election he would have to become a member himself. This he adamantly refused to do, for, as he explained to Tappan in November 1854, "if I were at this time to seek an introduction to the society, charity itself could hardly fail to attribute it to a desire to further the ends of personal ambition." Unless he could count on "a tolerably good chance of success" without becoming a Know-Nothing, he would prefer not to be again a candidate for the Senate. Tappan replied that Hale's chances of reelection looked bright anyway, and enlisted his aid in the impending campaign.[49]

The various anti-Nebraska factions held separate conventions during the fall and winter of 1854–55, but except for governor and railroad commissioner, their nominations were nearly identical. Whigs, Independent Democrats, and Know-Nothings all chose Tappan, Aaron H. Cragin, and James Pike as their candidates for Congress, and there was considerable overlapping at the state representative level.[50] It was well that there was close cooperation among antislavery men, for the Pierce Democrats were out early and in force. Lewis Cass, California congressman Milton S. Latham, "& a whole menagerie of other animals" were "coming on from Washington to help the Hunker[s]," Tappan excitedly reported in January 1855.[51]

Democratic strategy was to distract attention from Kansas-Nebraska by dwelling exclusively on the dangers of Know-Nothingism. Their opponents, however, publicly soft-peddling nativism and popery, strained to keep the "invidious" repeal of the Missouri Compromise constantly before the people.[52]

Hale responded to Tappan's pleas for assistance in a number of ways. He solicited funds from out-of-state politicians and himself gave $75, which Tappan promised to put "to good use" in support of anti-Nebraska candidates.[53] In February and early March he returned to New Hampshire where he stumped energetically against the Democrats. There were encouraging signs that at long last the people had aroused from their moral slumber and were swinging to the antislavery cause. At Haverhill, John Davis of Orford, long a Democrat, opened the meeting by saying that for years he had thought it would be a merciful intervention of Providence should Hale fall dead in the street. But now, he told the enthusiastic throng, he was convinced that Hale had been right all along.[54]

This was the kind of vindication and support Hale had always craved. An essentially extroverted man, he thrived on popular acclaim. He had been perfectly sincere in telling the Senate that he found it "unpleasant to occupy the place of an Ishmaelite." Hale was enough his own man to be willing to sacrifice popularity before principle, but he hated to do it. Now that his principles were at last becoming popular, Hale's world looked rosier than it had in a decade. He longed to return to public life.

In addition to his financial and oratorical contributions, Hale saw to it that the *Independent Democrat* adopted a friendly stance toward the Know-Nothings. "The people will hardly deem it hazardous to unite with any organization which receives the hostility of the panders to Rum, Catholicism and Slavery," Fogg editorialized. So long as the Order remained "the handmaid of Freedom and Reform," the *Independent Democrat* wished it "God-speed." To those of its readers who balked at the basically undemocratic tenets of Know-Nothingism, the paper urged wise restraint. "Now is not the time to strike. We cannot strike without striking the sincerest friends of freedom in the State. We cannot strike it without helping the Administration in their conspiracy against Liberty and the Constitution." [55]

Vigorous campaigning and small sacrifices to expediency paid off at the polls. On election day, March 13, the anti-Nebraska forces swept the field. Ralph Metcalf, Know-Nothing gubernatorial candidate, won easily, and Tappan, Cragin, and Pike were elected to Congress. Best news for Hale was that nearly all state senators and three-fourths of the representatives would be Whigs, Know-Nothings, or Free Soilers. His election to the United States Senate seemed assured. [56]

Although sanguine, Hale's champions were unwilling to leave anything to chance. There were "many new men elected as *K-N's* who must be looked after," Tappan concluded, and he at once set to work securing pledges of support from anti-Hunker representatives to the 1855 legislature. [57] In early May, an unforeseen obstacle raised itself in the form of the "third degree" which New Hampshire Native Americans voted to add to their liturgy. The third degree, or "Union degree," was established by the national Know-Nothing convention in November 1854 as a sop to slaveholders. Those who took it bound themselves energetically to "uphold, maintain, and defend the Union," to guard all secrets of the degree, and to "vote for and support for all political offices third or union degree members of this Order in preference to all others." At the New Hampshire convention in May, Tappan countered with a set of antislavery resolutions that passed with near unanimity, "so that the antidote goes with the bane," but the threat to Hale's election contained in the final clause of the third degree was clear. "Some of our patriotic, Union Saving candidates for the Senate may attempt to tie up the hands of members of the Legislature on the Senator question," Tappan feared. [58] The threat became even greater in June when friends of James Bell, a leading Whig aspirant for one of the vacant Senate seats, let it be known that Bell would take the third degree before the legislature met. [59]

By June rumors were rife that Bell had the full-term vacancy all sewed up and that others would have to scramble for the short one. Hale, who had returned to New Hampshire to discuss his candidacy with Tappan and Fogg, found this prospect disturbing. He cared little whether he got the long term or the short, but he wished to act with dignity and not, like "a bear wounded in the top of a tree, catch every branch as he falls to the ground." If Bell did have the long term in his pocket, Hale would rather his own name be withdrawn, unless some dignified arrangement could be made whereby he could be elected *first* for the short term. Or, an honest battle with Bell for the full term would be honorable. "If there is any occasion for a fight go in," he instructed Tappan. "Do not hesitate to sacrifice me if necessary. Next to an election for the long term, I should enjoy a good old-fashioned fight with an open field on the slavery issue." [60]

Although pretending for a time that the outcome of the senatorial elections would "not disturb me a tittle," [61] as the day of reckoning drew near and a three-way struggle shaped up between Bell, Daniel Clark, and himself, Hale grew increasingly anxious. His worry expressed itself in mildly querulous letters to the hardworking Tappan, hinting that his chances were not being as carefully managed as they might. Tappan, whose efforts on Hale's behalf were so diligent that he went for several days with practically no sleep, answered reassuringly. It was true, he wrote his chief, that "we have strong & bitter enemies." Still, even Bell's election by no means meant defeat for Hale. Faithful to his instructions, he would press for Hale's nomination in caucus for the short term, conceding the long one to the opposition "if they will let us elect you first." [62]

The Native American caucus met in the evening of June 12, 1855. Earlier that day Tappan had informed Hale: "the thing is a good deal mix'd up . . . All hunkerdom is on hand & the fossil remains of defunct Whiggery meet you at the corner of every street." [63] Yet in caucus, matters went smoothly. Tappan pushed through a resolution to nominate for the short term first, beat down Joel Eastman's amendment to reverse that order, and watched with satisfaction as 154 of the 222 present voted to back Hale. Thanks to Tappan, no serious difficulty arose over the third degree. (After the doors of the caucus room had closed, a delegate from the national Know-Nothing convention at Philadelphia arrived with a directive "to cut off" Hale; but he came too late—Hale had already been chosen.) As expected, Bell was quickly nominated for the long term.[64]

The House concurred automatically. On the 14th the Senate endorsed the House's action and Bell and Hale became United States senators-elect. A joyful Tappan informed Hale of his election. "'Now is the winter of our discontent made glorious summer,'" he cheered.[65]

CHAPTER X

The Coming of the Civil War

A S Hale prepared to return to Washington in November 1855 violence broke out in Kansas. The murder of a free-state man over a disputed land claim was the immediate cause of the flare-up, but the real causes struck much deeper and kept the slogan "Bloody Kansas" alive for years to come.

Even before the passage of the Kansas-Nebraska Act, Northerners and Southerners had begun maneuvering for control of Kansas. Free-state pioneers—wasting no love on the Negro, but determined to exclude slavery—began to arrive in the newly organized territory during the summer of 1854. There they encountered hostile and aggressive proslavery settlers, mainly from neighboring Missouri, willing to fight if necessary to keep Kansas open to slavery. With the overt aid of "border ruffians" from Missouri, the proslavery forces rigged elections, preempted much of the most desirable land, recruited slaveholding immigrants, and sought to frighten off anti-slavery settlers. By force and fraud the slavery men won complete control of the territorial legislature, enacted outrageous laws protecting slavery, and forced the removal of Governor Andrew H. Reeder who objected to the illegality of their methods. In protest the free staters held their own, admittedly extralegal, constitutional convention at Topeka in October-November 1855, abolished slavery, and applied for recognition from Congress. Under the capable leadership of James H. Lane and Charles Robinson, they organized a strong Free-State party and armed themselves with Sharps rifles. The Wakarusa War, which followed from the murder of young Charles M. Dow on November 21, 1855, was nearly bloodless, but Kansas remained in a state of armed unrest. None knew what explosion the next spark might ignite.[1]

Kansas, then, was uppermost in the minds of the politicians who arrived at Washington for the opening of the Thirty-Fourth Congress. Hale found the Senate much the same body he had left in 1853. Back again were his antislavery allies William Seward, Charles Sumner, Hannibal Hamlin, Ben Wade—all now listed as Republicans. Only his friend Salmon P. Chase was missing, having returned to Ohio as governor. Many of Hale's old senatorial foes were also still at their posts: Mason and Hunter of Virginia, Butler of South Carolina, Cass, Douglas, and Bright. Jefferson Davis was serving Pierce as Secretary of War, but Georgia's boisterous Robert Toombs, Louisiana's Judah P. Benjamin, and newcomer John Slidell ably expressed his sentiments in the Senate Chamber.[2]

The Senate's composition was much the same as when Hale had left, but already his position in it had changed significantly. No longer was he the cynosure of abolitionist eyes. Having dropped from public view during two critical years, he returned to find himself but one of a growing band of antislavery senators, all now tagged Republicans. In coming days, as radicals like Zachariah Chandler joined Wade and Sumner in slashing attacks on the Slave Power, Hale, whose hatred of slavery was as strong but whose tone was more temperate, lost some of the notoriety (as well as fame) which had been his before. Neither gifted nor industrious enough to dominate his burgeoning party, Hale resigned himself to an independent and honorable position in the second rank.

As in 1849, Congress was slow in getting down to business because of a protracted fight over the speakership. With Know-Nothings holding the balance between Democrats and the more numerous Republicans, representatives cast inconclusive ballot after ballot. Hale fussed over the delay which he attributed to unprincipled Northerners voting against the wishes of their constituents. "Such men are so utterly despicable that it is revolting and disgusting to think or speak of them," he fumed. Happily, New England's skirts were most nearly clean: "Not one who was elected by the people as an Anti-Nebraska man has yet faltered . . . I believe the NE States were never so nearly united before on the great Anti-slavery issue." In the end a Massachusetts Republican and ex-Know-Nothing, Nathaniel P. Banks, won out, but not until February 1856.[3]

President Pierce, whose conduct regarding Kansas had been weak and vacillating, scarcely mentioned that troubled region in his annual message of December 31, 1855. Instead, he dwelled at length on Latin American affairs, political theory, and the danger of disunion brought on by the irresponsible actions of "sectional agitators." [4] Hale, who had always loathed Northern "doughfaces" like Pierce ("friends of the Constitution," Pierce called them) more than Southern fire-eaters, replied three days later in a speech more rancorous and personal than any he had delivered before.

In breaking precedent to deliver his message before formal organization of the House, Hale implied, Pierce had been motivated by a desire to make known his proslavery position before the meeting of Southern state Democratic conventions in January. But if he cherished hopes of renomination, the President was sadly deluded, Hale correctly observed, for there was "no more chance of his being renominated, than there is of one of our pages receiving that honor." The message itself seemed to Hale no better than the shabby motives behind its premature delivery. All its talk of Central America was a red herring, an attempt to divert attention from "a subject which will really agitate the people." What little Pierce had said about Kansas simply showed how utterly subservient to the interests of the South he had become. Most galling of all to Hale was Pierce's labelling as "enemies of the Constitution" all those who opposed the admission of Kansas as a slave state.

He has no right to designate any men who are here under the same oath to support the Constitution which he has taken, as enemies of the Constitution [Hale indignantly declared]; and when he does it he comes down from the high place which God, in his wrath for the punishment of our national sins, and for the humiliation of our national pride, has permitted him to occupy. I say he comes down from that high place into the arena of a vulgar demagogue, and strips himself of everything which should clothe with dignity the office of President of the United States. I deny the issue; I hurl it back in his face; I tell him, when he undertakes to designate these men as enemies of the Constitution, he abuses and defames men whose shoe-latchets he is not worthy to untie.[5]

After this savage and quite uncharacteristic personal attack, Pierce understandably turned his back on Hale at a White House reception, a rebuff which set Washington tongues wagging.[6] The Washington *Union* rushed to the President's defense with an editorial on January 5 that denounced Hale's "wild and angry assertions," his "violence and vituperation," and put him down as "essentially a low man, and a low demagogue . . ." But on Capitol Hill, Hale's volley drew no return fire, for the truth was, as Slidell had written Buchanan in December, that "the feeling of contempt for Pierce in the Senate is general."[7]

Hale may have felt secretly ashamed of his *ad hominem* outburst, for thereafter he reserved his most violent denunciations of Pierce for letters to Mrs. Hale. ("I do not know but I am prejudiced, perhaps I am," he wrote in mock humility, "but, upon the coolest reflection which I can bestow upon the subject, it appears to me that no man in modern times has inflicted such serious and lasting injury upon his country as Franklin Pierce."[8] Yet he had no intention of softening his criticisms of the President's Kansas policy, which he viewed as wilfully and flagrantly wrong. All that Hale read in the press confirmed his belief in Administration appeasement of the border ruffians who were making a mockery of popular sovereignty. The army, though instructed to put down "insurrections," had been given no word about repelling "invasions," with the result that armed Missouri interlopers roamed at will through Kansas, rigging elections and running off free settlers. Letters he received from Kansas confirmed his own guesses and the reports of the Northern press. One Free-Stater asked Hale for a copy of Scott's *Tactics* ("to be able to receive *our friends* from Missouri with all due military honor"). "Our prospects are bad," the settler confided in February 1856. "Congress or the Free States must help us. We are constantly threatened with the destruction of life & property."[9]

Early in January, Hale began preparing a major address on "The Wrongs of Kansas." That long and discursive speech, delivered before crowded Senate galleries on February 28, fell into two parts: an indictment of Pierce's policy and a defense of the Republican response to events in Kansas.

His chief purpose, Hale announced, was to expose the absurdity of Pierce's contention that conditions in Kansas did not warrant executive intervention. One had only to read the papers to learn the magnitude of the outrages the President was willing to overlook. Quoting from published letters of Senator David R. Atchison, he demonstrated that that border ruffian leader had urged Missourians to cast proslavery ballots in Kansas; and he recalled the words of Governor Reeder: "It was, indeed, too true that Kansas had been invaded, conquered, subjugated by armed forces from beyond her borders . . ." United States citizens had been forcibly prevented from exercising the constitutional right of self-determination, Hale proclaimed, his voice rising in indignation. "Their Territory was overrun and conquered; and yet it is said there was nothing calling on the President to interfere." Pierce had shown no such reluctance to use his executive power in returning a single fugitive slave, Hale noted sarcastically, alluding to "Young Hickory's" energetic use of his office and the public purse to secure the rendition of Anthony Burns.

As for his defense of the Republican position, Hale repeated old arguments upholding the right of Congress to legislate for the territories, denied that the North wished any "crusade against Southern rights," and defended the much-maligned New England Emigrant Aid Company as but one of a long line of such enterprises by which America had been settled. Had not nearly every original state been planted by just such companies? And had not the North been invited to go to Kansas and compete fairly with the forces of slavery? Why, then, the furor over Northern emigrant aid societies? Repeatedly he denied aggressive designs on the part of the North, but warned Southerners "that on the subject of human slavery, we have convictions which we cannot sacrifice . . ." He felt that dissolution of the Union was as unlikely as it would be unfortunate, but concluded presciently:

I believe that if, listening to evil counsels, pushed on by the purposes of ambition or any other, a party, large or small, shall be so far forsaken of God and of good counsels as to venture on that rash experiment, the conservatism, the patriotism, the intelligence, and the humanity of this great people will teach such men a lesson which [neither] they, nor their children, nor their children's children to the latest posterity will forget.[10]

In many ways the "Wrongs of Kansas" was one of Hale's best speeches. Moderate yet forceful, it was warmly received throughout the North, although Garrison took umbrage at Hale's "supplicatory tone and on-bended-knee position" toward the slaveholders. Even Southerners found it a fine oratorical effort, and fire-eater Judah Benjamin congratulated Hale on it afterwards.[11]

In sharp contrast to Hale's temperate address was Charles Sumner's angry, insulting philippic "The Crime Against Kansas," delivered after the most elaborate preparation on May 19 and 20. More shocking than the vindictive and vituperative personal references which studded Sumner's oration, however, was the violence it provoked. On May 22, Congressman Preston S. Brooks of South Carolina, a cousin of the aged Senator Butler whom Sumner had viciously maligned, accosted the Massachusetts senator as he sat at his desk writing letters. "Mr. Sumner," he announced with cool formality, "I have read your speech twice over carefully. It is a libel on South Carolina, and on Mr. Butler, who is a relative of mine——" With that he began raining blows on Sumner's head with a sturdy gold-headed cane, continuing his brutal "chastisement" until Sumner fell to the Senate floor, bloody and unconscious.[12]

Like most Northerners, Hale recoiled in shock from the "cowardly and brutal" caning of his fellow Republican.[13] "The assault on Sumner excites feelings that can hardly be expressed," he informed Theodore Parker. Nearly as great a disgrace as the attack itself was the composition of the Senate committee picked to investigate the affair—"Not a single political friend of Mr. Sumner being placed on the Committee . . ." Yet greatly though he decried Brooks' ruthless attack and the sanction Southerners gave to it, Hale saw that its galvanic effect might produce much good in the North. Already, free-state congressmen were drawing closer together. "Next to the indignation at the outrage on Sumner," he wrote, "I think the feeling that has been aroused here among Northern men is a deep and settled purpose to maintain our position at all hazards." Equally important, the assault promised to alarm the complaisant and fortify the timid. "My first thought when I heard of the blows on Sumner," he told Parker, "was that every voter in the Free States wanted just such blows on his own head, especially those conservative and cautious ones who are asking 'what has the North to do with slavery?' and counselling quiet and the putting down of agitation. It seems as if it required something of that kind to arouse the North." [14]

All spring and summer violence ran just below the surface. In Kansas it erupted into clashes between proslavery men and free staters; charred homesteads scarred the plains, and blood stained the earth at Pottawatomie Creek. News of the arson, murder, and pillage in Kansas exacerbated already strained tempers in Washington and prevented calm discussion. Equally important in keeping congressional fevers high, were the repercussions of the Sumner affair. While Republicans worked to martyrize Sumner, and condemned his assailant as a brutal proslavery ruffian, Southerners in and out of Congress leapt to Brooks' defense. The "chivalrous" South Carolinian had done no more than mete out a deserved punishment to a "nasty scamp," a "blackguard," they insisted. Brooks himself, in no way repentant, challenged Henry Wilson and Anson Burlingame to duels after their stinging speeches against him. Hale's contribution to the Sumner-Brooks post mortem was a remarkably moderate speech on June 26 which treated the incident solely as a threat to the hallowed right of free speech.[15] "I have no idea that it will satisfy Sumner's ultra friends, or the ultra anti-slavery people of the Free States," Hale admitted to his wife. "But it satisfies my own judgment, & I hope it does yours & the children's, if so I am content." [16]

Hale's response to the Sumner-Brooks affair was characteristic.

As at the time of the *Pearl* incident, his public protest—calm, reasoned, legalistic—reflected little of the moral indignation which underlay it. He rejoiced that Brooks' attack had shocked the apathetic North, and he privately applauded the oratorical counterblows of his friend Burlingame.[17] Yet still hopeful of influencing moderate Southerners, and perhaps dimly aware of the dangers of agitation, Hale preferred to couch his own criticisms in constitutional terms.

All the while Sumner's vacant seat reminded the Senate—indeed, the nation—of his beating and the angry debate which occasioned it. As weeks passed and the Massachusetts senator failed to appear, Republicans (mindful of the approaching election) exploited "Bloody Sumner" as fully as "Bloody Kansas." Most Southerners, however, and many Northerners, maintained that Sumner was shamming, that his injuries "were nothing but flesh wounds," and that he was "playing the political possum." [18] Hale, while welcoming the political benefits of Sumner's wounds, also had some doubts about their severity. Early in July 1856 he paid a visit to Sumner at the Silver Spring estate of Francis P. Blair where the ailing senator was then convalescing, both to convey his condolences and to see for himself. He found Sumner feeble and haggard. The head wounds had healed, but there was no doubt that he was genuinely suffering and Hale came away feeling "for him more keenly . . . than I did the first day he was struck." Over dinner with Seward, Wilson, and Lyman Trumbull a few days later, Hale subtly suggested that Sumner's recovery was retarded by the delights of his quasi-fantasy world—a world overflowing with sympathy, condolence, and praise—which made the harsh realities of the Senate all the more hard to face.[19]

To some extent Hale's diagnosis was influenced by his own dissatisfaction with the life of a senator. His spirits were never lower than during the summer of 1856. The weather was so oppressively hot that he found it difficult to sleep and was usually up by 5 A.M. When the heat abated he still got little rest "owing to the flies." Sessions of Congress often ran long into the night, but to little effect, since the Democratic Senate and Republican House found it impossible to agree on Kansas. After one fruitless twenty-hour meeting Hale frankly gave himself up to his "complaining mood." In a long letter to his wife he poured out his frustrations and self-pity. "Here I am alone with nobody that I care for, or that cares for me," he wailed, "spending my days amid savages with whom one feels that life itself is not safe, with serious and great duties to be performed in the midst of those who misunderstand and misrepresent the most honest and conscientious endeavors to perform the plainest and most imperious duty, and no letter for days from those whom I love, & for whom I could do anything which I can do. I am sick and tired, and long for home."[20] But Congress did not finally adjourn until late August, and not long after that Hale had again left his family, this time to electioneer in the East and Middle West for the Republican candidate, John C. Frémont.

Actually, campaign preliminaries had begun while Congress was still at work. Continued civil war in Kansas made the troubles of that territory the prime issue for the ensuing canvass, and Democrats and Republicans in both houses began early to assign blame for "Bleeding Kansas." Stephen A. Douglas, incensed by opposition to his bill for a constitutional convention in Kansas, accused Senate Republicans of inciting "murder and bloodshed in Kansas for political effect." They had sent their minions, he shrilled, "to get up rebellion, to commit crime, to burn houses . . . Their capital for the presidential election is blood . . . An angel from heaven could not write a bill to restore peace in Kansas that would be acceptable to the Abolition Republican party previous to the presidential election." Hale and his fellows indignantly denied this charge. Violence in Kansas, Hale replied, plainly originated in the repeal of the Missouri Compromise, and those responsible for the abrogation of "that ancient landmark of liberty" must shoulder the blame.[21]

As a pioneer political abolitionist and recent Free Democratic candidate, Hale inevitably received consideration for the Republican nomination in 1856. But only the radical wing of the Republican party showed much enthusiasm for Hale, and even it rarely made him first choice. Not only did he represent a small state in a region already committed to Republicanism, but he had been out of office and out of the public eye during the critical months when the party was born. Moreover, as he had foreseen, by leading the doomed Free Democrats in 1852 he sacrificed all hope of ever occupying the White House. Hale might privately curse the fates that ran him when defeat was sure and dropped him when victory seemed at hand, but the new party understandably preferred a new candidate satisfactory to all factions and free of the stigma of defeat.

Resigned to a supporting role, Hale attended the Republican national convention at Philadelphia in June. In a short speech he reminded the delegates that the question before them was not whether the Union should be preserved, but whether it should be "a blessing to the people, or a scorn and a hissing the world over." He rapidly acquiesced in the nomination of the romantic pathfinder Frémont whom the delegates preferred to Hale's more radical friends Chase and Seward, and, happy over the solid if moderate antislavery platform, agreed to work in the fall campaign.[22]

Republican strategists correctly discerned that the election hinged on Pennsylvania, New Jersey, Indiana, and Illinois. Those states, therefore, received their most effective campaigners: William Seward, David Wilmot, Joshua Giddings, Henry Wilson, Anson Burlingame, and John P. Hale. The New Hampshire senator had barely a month in Dover with his wife and daughters before taking the stump for Frémont and the Republican party. During September and October, he campaigned at a leisurely pace, combining lyceum talks for profit with political addresses—"Bloody Kansas" in the afternoon and "The Agrarian Laws of Rome" in the evening. Much of September he spent in New Jersey and Pennsylvania, electioneering with Wilmot and Burlingame. Everywhere large and enthusiastic crowds greeted them; in Hatboro' 10,000-15,000 persons turned out to hear Hale and his associates roast the Democrats and their "doughfaced" candidate, James Buchanan. As always, the excitement of campaigning—the crowds, the cheers, the handshakes, the greetings—boosted Hale's spirits and he enjoyed himself immensely.[23]

Toward the end of October he honored an earlier promise to help Republicans in Illinois. His successes in the West matched those in the East, and Hale became hopeful about Frémont's chances. "There never was a time when there was more need of courage, and more ground for it," he informed the despondent Elihu Washburne. "We shall carry Pennsylvania beyond a doubt & Illinois *may* decide the battle." [24] In the event, Hale's optimism proved unwarranted. Not only Illinois, but Pennsylvania as well, went to Buchanan, and with them the election. The new, and still ill-organized, Republican party had showed strength enough to frighten the South (Frémont carried eleven Northern states with 114 electoral votes, while Buchanan took nineteen states and 174 electoral votes), but its day in the sun was not yet.

Returning to Washington for the short session of 1856–1857, Hale settled his family in a suite at the National Hotel, one of the capital's largest and finest. It proved an unfortunate choice, for in mid-January, the Hales, along with nearly all others at the hotel (including President-elect Buchanan) came down with the "National Hotel sickness." The disease—apparently paratyphoid fever—struck Hale hard. As soon as he was able he fled Washington for Dover, but even in New Hampshire's bracing climate recovery was slow. Not until May could Hale pronounce himself "well," and even then he admitted: "I am not quite so strong, nor so heavy as I have been." Never again, in fact, was his health as good as it had been before.[25]

During his absence, Washington witnessed two events which greatly alarmed all antislavery men and which provided the subject for Hale's first major speech after his return: the Dred Scott decision and the so-called Lecompton Constitution for Kansas. In the Dred Scott case, Chief Justice Roger B. Taney and five other justices invalidated the Missouri Compromise—or any other law which excluded slavery from the territories. Taney and two other Southerners also maintained that Scott, as a former slave, was not entitled to United States citizenship. Only the Northern judges John McLean and Benjamin R. Curtis upheld Scott's citizenship and the constitutionality of the Missouri Compromise.[26]

While the Dred Scott decision theoretically undercut popular sovereignty—the right of territorial settlers to prohibit slavery if they wished—the proslavery Lecompton constitutional convention threatened to make a mockery of it in practice. That body, after drafting a document which forbade the legislature to emancipate slaves without their owner's consent, excluded free Negroes from Kansas and demanded strict enforcement of the Fugitive Slave Act, provided for a referendum not on the constitution itself, but only on the "constitution with slavery," or the "constitution without slavery." In other words, the people of Kansas might decide only whether they would prevent the *further* introduction of slaves, since even if they chose the constitution without slavery its proslavery clauses would protect slavery as it already existed in Kansas. A howl of protest heard throughout the North greeted news of the Lecompton Constitution. Even Stephen A. Douglas, father of the Kansas-Nebraska Act, cried out in indignation at the sham the restricted referendum made of his pet doctrine of popular sovereignty. But President Buchanan—anxious to bring Kansas into the Union as a Democratic state and taking his advice from Southerners Howell Cobb, Jacob Thompson, and John Slidell—stubbornly pressed Congress to accept the Lecompton Constitution. Not even unmistakable evidence that a clear majority of Kansans opposed it, swayed his resolve.

Against these twin "outrages"—Dred Scott and Lecompton—Hale, like other Republicans, raised his voice. On January 18 and again on January 20, 1858, he lectured to the Senate on "Kansas and the Supreme Court." At the outset he made it plain that however much he welcomed Douglas' support in the fight with Buchanan, he disagreed as much as ever with the Little Giant's fundamental approach to slavery in the territories. He joined Douglas in opposing the Lecompton Constitution, not, however, because it was contrary to the "principles and policy" of the Kansas-Nebraska Act, "but because it is in exact conformity with them," in spirit if not in letter. The Act of 1854, Hale charged, had been "designed to break down the barrier which separated free territory from slave territory; to let slavery into Kansas and make another slave State . . ." The Lecompton Constitution, he argued, was but the latest of a long series of perversions of popular sovereignty in Kansas, not, as Douglas seemed to feel, the first.

After these gentle swipes at Douglas and sharper jabs at the Administration, Hale struck out full force against the Supreme Court. By their decisions in the Dred Scott case, Hale charged, those worthies had "come down from their place, and thrown themselves into the political arena," attempting "to throw the sanction of their names in support of doctrines that can neither be sustained by authority nor history." His distrust of the Supreme Court was not new. Its predominantly Southern composition made it at once suspect, and Hale had repeatedly declared his lack of confidence in its slavery decisions. In attacking the Dred Scott decision he kept step with the New Hampshire legislature which had denounced it as contradictory to the facts of history, "repugnant to the Constitution and subversive of the rights and liberties of the people."

Hale confined his criticism to two points: the court's finding that property in slaves was of the same right as all other property (and hence could not be excluded from a territory without violating constitutional guarantees of "due process"), and its contention that the right to hold and trade slaves was universally recognized in England and the United States at the time of the adoption of the Constitution (and hence the Founding Fathers had not meant to extend the rights of citizenship to Negroes). The first was the more important point, and with great thoroughness he paraded authorities arguing that slavery, as a form of property, depended upon the municipal or local law of the states in which it was established and ceased to exist when removed from the jurisdiction which imposed slavery. Likewise he quoted eminent British and American jurists and political thinkers to confute the court's argument that the guarantees of the Declaration of Independence and the Constitution did not extend to black men. Taney and his associate judges would make "the immortal authors of the Declaration of Independence liars before God and hypocrites before the world . . ." Hale boomed. He would have none of it. Friends of the Administration, Hale remarked in closing, now proposed to implement the Dred Scott

decree by forcing upon the people of Kansas an unwanted constitution. Such folly, he warned, would "kindle the fires of civil war in
that country" and awaken a great crusade "to redeem this fair land,
which God has given to be the abode of freemen, from the desecra-
tion of a despotism sought to be imposed upon them in the name of
'perfect freedom' and 'popular sovereignty.' " [27]

The speech was well received in Republican quarters. Governor
Chase wrote from Ohio to say that it gave him "more pleasure than
any I have read this year," and William Herndon requested printed
copies: "one for myself—one for Lincoln." "Mr. Hale's speech takes
like 'hot cakes' here with everybody but the 'old fogy Whigs,'"
George G. Fogg notified Mason Tappan. "They think they 'smell
a rat'—that it was made to advance his chances for the Senatorship
again! " [28]

In spite of the strenuous efforts of Republicans and Douglas Democrats, the Senate voted on March 23, 1858 (33 to 25) to admit Kansas
to the Union under the Lecompton Constitution. A week later, however, the House substituted for the Senate bill one to resubmit the
Lecompton Constitution to a popular vote in Kansas. In April a
committee of conference reported a compromise—the English Bill—
which scheduled a referendum as the House had asked, but which
offered Kansas immediate admission to the Union and a customary
grant of public land if it adopted the Lecompton Constitution. Hale,
like all Republicans, blasted the English Bill as "one of the most
profligate propositions" ever submitted to the Senate, and joined the
minority who voted against it. He greatly feared that Kansans
would find its inducements (which he exaggerated) too sweet to
resist, and was happily surprised when in August they voted six to
one to reject the constitution, "bribe" or no bribe. Kansas' admission
to the Union was indefinitely postponed, but for the first time in
years that troubled land knew peace.[29]

But peace in Kansas did not appreciably reduce sectional discord.
The South, aggressive and touchy wherever slavery was concerned,
glared defiantly at a burgeoning North, where day by day the forces
of antislavery grew stronger and less prone to compromise. New

crises were inevitable. Whether Hale would be in the United States Senate when these new crises broke was something New Hampshire had to decide in 1858.

The Republican party, into which the anti-Nebraska factions drifted after their brief flirtation with Know-Nothingism, had controlled New Hampshire's government since 1856. Hale's chief agent in the Granite State (after Tappan went to Congress), George G. Fogg, had been elected state printer in 1857.[30] The *Independent Democrat,* long Hale's mouthpiece, was as influential as any Republican journal in New Hampshire. Hale himself had done what he could to keep his political fences in good repair: personally answering all correspondence, doing small favors whenever possible, distributing among his constituents documents, newspapers, books—even flower seeds. His Senate speeches refreshed his prominence and received wide acclaim throughout the state. Yet certain obstacles to his reelection remained.

Most important of these obstacles was the cry of "rotation in office." Hale would already have served ten years in the Senate, many pointed out; to elect him again would give him greater tenure as senator than any of his New Hampshire predecessors. And more than one man's career was at stake. Hale's reelection, the *New Hampshire Statesman* predicted, would establish "a dangerous precedent" for the Republican party, one which might justify men like Tappan and Cragin in asking for third terms in Congress.[31] Furthermore, it was charged, Hale's political managers had in 1855 pledged that he would not be a candidate for reelection.[32] A less serious but nonetheless irritating impediment was the Democratic party. Though discredited, it still had force; the strength of the Jacksonian tradition and the lure of federal patronage kept many within its ranks, and newly naturalized citizens—particularly Irish immigrants—regularly gave their votes to the Democracy.

To the demands for rotation, Hale's backers pleaded the critical state of national affairs. Experience and ability never counted for more in federal councils, they argued, adding: "if the present incumbent should be *returned he will at least be able to fill the place he vacates.*"[33] "People forget," said one Strafford County Republican, "that the aristocrats of the South, keep old hands constantly in the field, & to successfully meet them, we of the North ought to have well tempered & well tried weapons."[34] Those who looked ahead to a Republican victory in the 1860 Presidential campaign pointed out that the "new & additional duties & responsibilities then imposed upon the Party will require the best talents, with the largest experience, for the discharge of those duties & to meet the opposition which has been threatened."[35] The allegation that there had been a "bargain or understanding" in 1855 that Hale would stand aside in 1858, Mason Tappan and others angrily branded "a d——d lie."[36]

Hale waited until May 9 before making known his own wishes regarding the senatorship. No pussyfooting this time, no mock professions of unconcern. The hour of Republican ascendancy was too near at hand to risk being set aside. Having so long fought an uphill fight against the "slavocracy," Hale was determined to be in at the kill. Reelection now, he wrote Fogg, "would be peculiarly grateful." He was aware of support for others, and had no wish to put his friends "in an unpleasant or embarrassed position." But he left no doubt of his desire for reelection.[37] Fogg had already concluded that no other reliable antislavery man was sure of election as senator and willingly undertook to promote his old friend's candidacy. "I have made up my mind that Hale *must* be chosen," he had confided to Tappan. "I shall, in every prudent way, act accordingly."[38]

As the June session of the legislature approached, most of Hale's Republican competition melted away. Amos Tuck, who prior to the March election had actively pressed his claims to a Senate seat, quieted down when he learned of Hale's eagerness to be reelected.[39] By June, Hale's only strong rival for Republican support was sixty-three-year-old Thomas M. Edwards of Keene, and knowledgeable politicians were predicting that Hale would get from two-thirds to three-fourths of the votes in party caucus. Fogg, playing Hale's strong hand astutely, kept the *Independent Democrat* silent about "the senator question" so as to antagonize none of the rival candidates.[40]

The results of the Republican caucus, held in Concord's Frémont Hall on the evening of June 8, vindicated the confidence of Hale's backers. Not even the last hour backsliding of Tuck nor the intransigence of George W. Nesmith significantly affected the outcome, thanks largely to Fogg's management. One-hundred-twenty-seven Republican legislators nominated Hale; Edwards, his nearest rival, received only thirty votes. The next day the House gave Hale a 185-111 edge over his Democratic opponent, John S. Wells, and on June 10 the Senate balloted 8-3 for Hale, one vote going to Anthony Colby.[41] To celebrate his triumph, Hale authorized Fogg to "spend any sum you think proper by way of entertainment of friends not exceeding *one hundred* dollars, and I will hand you the money when I see you"—an uncharacteristic splurge which attests to Hale's joy at reelection. Clearly, approval of his antislavery position and the prospect of leadership in an increasingly powerful Republican party outweighed the difficulties of congressional life. A week later there was a second celebration when Hale, together with Tappan, returned to Concord at the close of Congress; but at the senator's insistence it was a private affair. There was no point in wounding the feelings of the defeated, he reasoned.[42]

Hale's reelection was the first gust of a Republican cyclone which ripped through the North in the fall of 1858, leaving broken Democratic hopes in its wake and sending shivers of apprehension through the South. In state after state, Republicans won control of state governments and sent representatives to Congress. Those Democrats who were successful in the North were usually Douglas men—opposed to Lecompton and the English Bill. Republicans would control the House in the Thirty-Sixth Congress and their strength in the Senate had increased. The Administration stood plainly rebuked. The omen for 1860 seemed clear to all.

By the time the second session of the Thirty-Fifth Congress gathered in the now nearly-complete Capitol in December 1858, intersectional bitterness was so pronounced that it precluded rational discussion of the national crisis at hand. Republicans, confident that they were riding the wave of the future and secure in the knowledge that they controlled the House, vowed to budge not an inch where principle was concerned. Southern Democrats—angered at the loss of Kansas, furious over Douglas' Freeport Doctrine, and acutely aware "that the balance in area, population, wealth, and power was tipping ever more heavily against the South"—embraced a radicalism born of desperation. Secessionists like Edmund Ruffin, Robert B. Rhett, and William L. Yancey sowed their seeds of disunion in increasingly fertile soil. In Congress, Southern extremism expressed itself in demands for effective federal protection of slavery in the territories and for the acquisition of Cuba.

President Buchanan saw in the annexation of Cuba a chance to add a little luster to his otherwise tarnished reputation and at the same time gratify vociferous Southern annexationists. It may also be that he hoped that Cuba would provide a unifying issue for the 1860 campaign. In his annual address to Congress, therefore, he asked for money to be used in negotiations with Spain for the purchase of that island. This request John Slidell embodied in a bill appropriating $30 million "to facilitate the acquisition of the Island of Cuba" which he introduced to the Senate in January 1859.[43]

Hale's response initially was a critical but reasoned address which stressed the importance of friendly relations with Spain and which ridiculed a "manifest destiny" that "always travelled South." George G. Fogg, for one, was not satisfied with this line of attack. Early in February he admonished Hale and other Republican congressmen for "wasting the best opportunities men ever had" to strike a blow at slavery when they refrained from exposing the "dangerous and infamous character" of the scheme for buying the Pearl of the Antilles. Together with Mason Tappan he built fires under the slow-moving senator who at last responded on February 15, with a full-scale address on Cuba.[44]

It differed less, perhaps, from his earlier sallies than Fogg had hoped. For the greater part of his long and frequently humorous speech, Hale rehearsed more or less conventional arguments against the Cuban purchase: the impulse behind it was basely political, it would involve "a wasteful and extravagant appropriation of money" at a time when the federal coffers were low, Cuba's strategic value was grossly overrated, a proud Spain would in all events refuse to sell her prize possession, and so forth. Only at the close of his address did he reveal basic reasons for his opposition to this "gigantic scheme of national rapine": (1) it would mean the spread of slavery, and (2) to embrace "a whole people" whose religious faith was firmly Catholic, would "exert a deleterious influence." A republican system of government, he asserted, "can only be maintained . . . on the principle of Protestant liberty." He was willing that the Cubans should have any faith they pleased, but when it was proposed that they be annexed to the United States, he had the right to consider this fundamental "fact." [45]

As an exposé of an infamous plot to give slavery new pastures, Hale's speech was disappointing. But doubting that anything would ever come of the attempt to buy Cuba, and reluctant to give needless offense to the South, Hale took the path of least resistance—a good-natured, off-the-cuff address which he hoped would satisfy his constituents without enraging the annexationists. Indolent by nature, Hale hated to box with shadows. When convinced that the cause of abolition was in real danger, he fought and fought hard. Yet when the threat was unreal or distant, as he thought to be the case with Cuban annexation, he preferred to let others sound the alarm.

Ultimately, the Cuban Purchase Bill ran head-on into a Republican bill for free homesteads. "The question will be," snapped Ohio's outspoken Ben Wade, "shall we give lands to the landless, or niggers to the niggerless?" [46] With sectional antagonism so sharp and unbending, neither bill had a chance. So it was with other issues which split North from South—especially the tariff and the Pacific railroad. Indeed the whole Thirty-Fifth Congress had been a bootless affair, barren of constructive legislation except for the admission of Minnesota and Oregon. And, unhappily, there was no reason to believe the Thirty-Sixth Congress would do better. In fact, the events of 1859 seriously worsened already dangerous sectional discord and carried the nation one long step nearer to civil war.

As long as the South had known slavery it had feared above all else the sound of a "firebell in the night"—signal of a servile insurrection. Its repressive slave codes, its restrictions on freedom of expression, its attitude toward free Negroes, were all conditioned by this fear. No wonder, then, that when in October 1859 John Brown led his little band into Harper's Ferry to seize the federal arsenal and trigger a full-dress slave rebellion, Southerners reacted furiously. The angry recriminations which followed Brown's abortive raid drowned out the voice of moderation both North and South and made calm discussion of sectional differences all but impossible.[47]

Hale, campaigning in the Old Northwest at the time, soon became implicated in the Harper's Ferry conspiracy. Little more than a week after United States Marines under the command of Colonel Robert E. Lee had captured Brown and quashed his uprising, the New York *Herald* published sensational reports charging "that the whole plot was fully known for the last year and a half to Seward, Sumner, Hale, Chase, [Ryland] Fletcher, Giddings, [Franklin B.] Sanborn, [Samuel Gridley] Howe, and the leading abolitionists on both sides of the Atlantic."[48] To a limited extent, the *Herald* was correct in what it said. Sanborn and Howe were two of the Secret Six who had long connived with Brown; and in May 1858, Hugh Forbes, an English adventurer privy to Brown's plans, had warned Henry Wilson, Seward, Gamaliel Bailey and perhaps others that the reckless patriarch was in possession of arms and intended "to use them for unlawful purposes." What the *Herald* did not know—or at least did not say—was that Forbes' confidants found his news thoroughly alarming and that at the request of Seward and Bailey, Wilson wrote at once to Howe, urging the immediate recovery of the weapons from Brown's hands. The Secret Six then prevailed on Brown to postpone his operation at least until the spring of 1859 and insisted that he keep its final details secret even from themselves.[49]

As for its charge that Hale was one of those who had foreknowledge of the Harper's Ferry scheme, the *Herald* was simply in error.

Hale publicly protested in a letter to the editors of the Chicago *Press and Tribune* on October 29, 1959. "I never had any knowledge or intimation from any one that an insurrection or outbreak or anything of the sort was contemplated by John Brown or any one else, in Virginia or elsewhere, nor had I the remotest suspicion of the fact," he insisted. Forbes himself cleared Hale of advance knowledge of the raid. "As to Senator Hale," he wrote to editor James G. Bennett, "he knew nothing of Brown's projects from me—nothing." [50]

But Hale's denial, if it did convince anyone in the South (which is indeed doubtful), in no way attenuated the angry excitement in that region. The very fact that *some* abolitionists had consorted with the wild-eyed Brown to touch off a slave rebellion was proof enough to Southern fire-eaters that all Northerners were bent on the bloody destruction of the South. In the Black Belt men were flogged or tarred and feathered, for no greater crime than Northern birth. All the while newspapers, North and South, focused attention on Brown's trial for treason against the state of Virginia. Yankee extremists like Thoreau and Parker eulogized Brown as a martyr and a saint; Southern hotspurs denounced him as a murderous insurrectionist. On December 2 he was led to the gallows and hanged. [51]

The ghost of John Brown continued to haunt the American scene long after his body lay "a-mouldering" in the grave. Bitter exchanges over responsibility for his raid marked the opening of the Thirty-Sixth Congress and for months thereafter the memory of Harper's Ferry poisoned North-South relations. In the Senate, Hale, like other Republicans, tried to dissociate himself and his party from Brown's madness. Although he believed that Brown had "displayed some high traits of character for which I have high sympathy," Hale plainly disapproved of the attack on Harper's Ferry and the projected insurrection.

So far as I know, [he declared] so far as my knowledge of the public men, with whom it is my pride to associate, is concerned, they have never made, and never will make, an appeal to slaves. They do not address them. It is not one of the instrumentalities by which they propose to work. Their appeal, so far as I know, is to the enlightened conscience and the patriotism, not of the slaves, but of their masters. [52]

Such Republican protestations of innocence were directed more at the North than the South (which after Harper's Ferry persisted willy-nilly in identifying all Republicans with radical abolitionism). Eighteen-Sixty was a Presidential election year, and to be successful the Republicans would have to win wide support in Northern states. Their best course, Hale felt sure, was to emphasize the conservatism and constitutionality with which they would act if given control of the national government. "What we want now," he wrote in March 1860, "is calm but firm annunciation of the great principles which underlie the organization of our party. We should speak as a strong[,] mighty political party about to take into our hands the reins of this Government, and our tone[,] while it should be vigorous and decided, should be conciliatory and gentle, rather than harsh and denunciatory." It was with serious misgivings, therefore, that he listened on June 4 to Sumner's bitterly reproachful address on "The Barbarism of Slavery."[53] He himself took pains to establish solid *constitutional* arguments for outlawing slavery in the territories, and although attacking the Fugitive Slave Act of 1850 as "unnecessarily harsh and severe," admitted "that the provision of the Constitution for the rendition of fugitives from service or labor should be fairly and honestly carried out."[54]

Hale responded most passionately to Southern threats of disunion. Indignantly he dismissed the charge that Republicans had weakened sectional bonds. The only real threat to the Union, he maintained, "came from the persistent attempts of the slave oligarchy and their Northern allies to pervert the government from its original purposes, to the work of extending and universalizing human slavery." He became particularly incensed at the suggestion that the election of a Republican President would force the South to secede. If preservation of the Union depended upon one section of the nation voting as the other demanded, Hale stormed, "we have been living under a delusion—an utter delusion; we are not a union of States; the free States are subject provinces, and our people do not choose a President, they but perform an idle ceremony." Cavalier talk of secession was dangerous, he believed, and sprang mainly from misconceptions about the nature of the Union itself. "What is this Union?" he asked rhetorically, "a thing of to-day? Did it spring up in the night like Jonah's gourd, and is it to perish with the morning's sun?" That was not the way he saw it. "I look upon this Government and this Union and this Constitution as the consummation of the education of the race by a beneficent Providence through all the ages that are past . . . I look upon it, sir, as a consummation which a good God, by six thousand years of discipline, has brought humanity to." Northerners, he solemnly warned, loved and cherished this Union. If necessary, "they would pour out their life's blood" rather than see it in ruins.[55]

By the time Congress adjourned, at the end of June 1860, all parties had held their national conventions and selected candidates for the supremely important Presidential canvass in the fall. The Democrats, unable to resolve differences of opinion concerning slavery, split at last into two groups, one nominating Stephen A. Douglas for President, the other selecting Kentucky's John Breckinridge. The Constitutional Unionists—chiefly former Whigs and Know-Nothings—presented a separate ticket. Republicans chose Abraham Lincoln.

Hale had not been a delegate to the Chicago Republican convention but he followed its doings with interest. As in 1856, his own name had from time to time received mention as a possible candidate, but he quickly disavowed such talk and was never seriously considered.[56] During the preconvention maneuvering he promoted his friend Salmon P. Chase and tried to undercut front-running William Seward.[57] When the delegates at Chicago chose Lincoln on grounds of his greater "availability," Hale swallowed his disappointment. In August he began stumping through northern New England, September found him campaigning across New York, and by mid-October he had reached Chicago. Election day brought a good return on the investment. Abraham Lincoln, a Republican of moderate but firm antislavery beliefs, was elected President of the United States.[58]

Southern hotspurs found Lincoln's election unbearable. It was not that it immediately menaced real Southern interests: the threat was vague and distant.[59] What mattered was that Northern voters had insulted the South by putting in the White House the candidate of a sectional party dedicated to the gradual extermination of slavery. Within weeks of Lincoln's election, therefore, South Carolina, Mississippi, Alabama, Georgia and Florida had taken initial steps toward secession and other Southern states seemed likely to follow. In this atmosphere of crisis and disintegration the lame-duck session of the Thirty-Sixth Congress gathered in Washington on December 3.

Hale arrived in the capital at dawn on the third, having traveled overnight from New York.[60] Later that day he participated in a Republican caucus which plotted party strategy for the critical weeks ahead. At that meeting it was decided that rather than reveal internal rifts on the secession crisis Republicans would adopt a policy of "masterly inactivity." Like their chief in Springfield, "they would sit quietly by while their opponents held the floor." Egged on by such Southern firebrands as Clingman of North Carolina, Iverson of Georgia, and Wigfall of Texas (who boasted that if war came "the next treaty which was signed would be in Faneuil Hall, in the town of Boston, in the state of Massachusetts"), Republican "irreconcilables" were soon on their feet, replying in kind.[61]

In the van was Hale. Although often moderate in method, he had consistently refused to compromise with slavery. Now, truculent talk of disunion stripped away even his moderation. Berating Buchanan for his indecision in the face of secessionist activity, he warned that such a policy looked "to a surrender of that popular sentiment which has been uttered through the constituted forms of the ballot-box; or"—the words had an ominous ring—"it looks to open war." If there were gentlemen who believed the current crisis could be resolved "by further concessions from the North," he averred, "I think they miscalculate and mistake."[62] Many, though by no means all, Republicans followed Hale's lead. Ben Wade, Lyman Trumbull, Preston King, and Hale's New Hampshire colleague Daniel Clark all made similar pronouncements.[63]

Northern opinion confirmed Hale in his uncompromising course. His mail bulged with letters praising his resolute stand and urging "the Republicans in Congress . . . *not to yield to the demands* of Slavery *one iota.*" They were *"entirely in the right"* and the Southerners "clearly & utterly wrong." Compromise now would violate principle and destroy the Republican party. "Anything is better than compromise," wrote one New Englander, "even civil war." [64]

Given this broad agreement between his own opinions and those of his correspondents, it is not surprising that Hale received the Crittenden compromise coolly. The Kentuckian's resolutions, presented to the Senate on December 18, proposed constitutional amendments extending the Missouri Compromise line to the Pacific, giving guarantees to slavery in the slave states and the District of Columbia, protecting the interstate slave trade, and compensating slave-owners for runaways. Hale willingly conceded the purity of Crittenden's motive, as well as his integrity, disinterestedness, "and the fervor of his patriotism," and admitted that there were some things in the resolutions to which he would agree. But he would not recommend them to his constituents. "I do not believe that the remedy is to be sought in new constitutional provisions," he proclaimed; "but in an honest, faithful execution of the things that are already written in the compact and in the bond." Nothing that Congress might do or say would effect a settlement of the controversy, one way or the other, he was convinced. [65]

It infuriated Hale that the one man who might act effectively to check secession—Buchanan—did next to nothing, seemingly still the tool of Southern Democrats.

The chief evil of the day, [he was sure] arises from the imbecility, & cowardice, not to say treachery[,] of Buchanan. He seems to be perfectly paralyzed . . . so that we present to the world the humiliating spectacle of a . . . first officer whose sworn duty is to support the Constitution & see that the laws are faith[fu]lly executed, if not in actual complicity with those who are striving for its overthrow, certainly offering no obstacle to their threatened attacks against the Government. [66]

To make sure that the incoming President would not repeat

Buchanan's timorous fumbling, Hale used all his influence to secure a cabinet nomination for his radical ally, Salmon P. Chase. After Lincoln indicated that Seward (whose course in the secession crisis had been conciliatory) would be his Secretary of State, it became all the more important, in Hale's eyes, to place in the new Administration one who might be relied on to oppose dishonorable concessions to the South. Furthermore, Chase's unquestioned probity marked him as an ideal candidate for the Treasury. His being in the cabinet would ease fears that the only result of the election would be "to turn one set of public robbers out of the Treasury to let another in," Hale told the Ohioan on January 11. Chase replied, perhaps disingenuously, that "as to going into the Cabinet my own feeling is quite against it," but admitted that if pressed he would accept the secretaryship of the Treasury. It was all the encouragement Hale needed. On January 19 he wrote his first letter to Lincoln, earnestly urging Chase's appointment. His exclusion, Hale advised the President-elect, "will cause a degree of mortification, disappointment and regret second only to what would have been felt, if we had been defeated at the Presidential election." Besides, he noted, "there is entire propriety in an honest President having an honest Secretary of the Treasury." Hale's flattering entreaty no doubt counted much less with the man in Springfield than did hard political considerations, but it may have helped Lincoln override conservative Republicans who objected to the radical Ohioan.[67]

Although he counted himself among the Republican "irreconcilables" who would risk war rather than compromise, Hale loved the Union too deeply to view its fragmentation with equanimity. He felt no rancor for the South, and the thought of civil war he found profoundly repugnant. As one by one the states of the deep South broke away, it seemed that the only way to avoid conflict was to keep the border states (especially Virginia) from following suit. If secession could only be confined to the Lower South, many believed, the Union might quickly and peaceably be restored. Hale shared this opinion. Not only did he endorse the Washington Peace Convention,[68] called by Virginia as a final attempt to adjust sectional differences, but he appealed movingly to the Upper South to remain in the Union. Hale's speech of January 31 exuded a reawakened reasonableness. "We meet together here, and it is agreed upon all hands that something is out of joint," he began. But what was needed to set things right? A constitutional guarantee that the federal government would never interfere with slavery in the states? "Sir, it is not in human language to give it stronger than you have it now," he asserted; the reserved powers clause was guarantee enough. Did Southerners want a restoration of the Missouri Compromise? The idea seemed absurd. "It saved the Union in 1820 by being passed; it saved it in 1854 by being repealed; and now it has to save it again by being passed again . . . How long do you suppose the Union will last patched up in this manner," asked Hale, "if the Missouri Compromise . . . is the only medicine that it is ever to have?"

He was willing to make any concession consistent with his sense of moral duty. But, he insisted, the nation needed no concessions. "We want time," he said, "that is all. We want a little of the healing influence of time, and"—he borrowed a pet phrase of Van Buren— "we want to appeal to that sober second thought of the people of this whole Union . . ." To give time for tempers to cool and reason to assert itself, he pleaded with "the great State of Virginia" to remain faithful to its heritage and to the Union. No state had served the cause of freedom better in the past, he conceded. But, he warned, "all the fame that your glorious ancestors have won for your glorious State . . . will go out in that eternal darkness which shall shroud the liberties of this Republic, if Virginia leads or follows in this raid of secession." [69]

Predictably, the Washington Conference produced no plan of adjustment acceptable to either North or South.[70] Within two months of its adjournment, Confederate forces bombarded Fort Sumter and Virginia cut loose from the Union, taking most of the Upper South with her. Watching the slave states depart, like intractable children leaving the parental roof, Hale had reminded them that the Union would endure nonetheless. "And when you that have gone off," he had said in the magnanimous words of Luke, "like the prodigal son, in the far country, filling your belly with the husks which the swine do eat, turn at last to the Union, then, sir, and not until then, will we kill the fatted calf, and rejoice that the lost is found and the dead alive again." [71] The reunion came with time. But after Shiloh and Vicksburg, Antietam and Cold Harbor, there was less rejoicing than Hale had wished.

CHAPTER XI

Radical Republican

H ALE had lingered in Washington nearly a month after President Lincoln's inauguration and the adjournment of the Thirty-Sixth Congress, so that he returned to his red-brick home in Dover just in time to learn of the Confederate assault on Fort Sumter. Much as he must have expected an explosion, this first stroke of civil war rudely jolted Hale. The time was suddenly past for talk of good will and reconciliation; the errant child must be punished and made contrite.

It was in this grim spirit that Hale addressed a huge mass meeting in Dover on April 15. With obvious feeling he appealed to men of all parties to help put down the Southern rebellion. The very existence of the Union—indeed the whole democratic experiment—was at stake, and those who sought by force to nullify that experiment had to be met by force. The present crisis, Hale lectured his townsmen, was but a continuation of America's century-old struggle for freedom. How it was met would "decide whether the Revolution itself was not a failure." If the secessionists were not crushed, he cried, "then indeed have our Fathers lived and died to little purpose." Were his services needed in the field, Hale pompously proclaimed, he would be happy to risk his life: "I have no desire to outlive my country." [1]

Fortunately for all save the South, Hale never pressed his services on the Union army.[2] Yet even as he spoke, President Lincoln was calling for 75,000 three-month militiamen to suppress the rebellion. New Hampshire's militia lay in such disrepair that Governor Ichabod Goodwin had to ask for volunteers to meet the state's quota of one regiment. Before the month was out he had enough for two. Nowhere was recruiting more brisk than in Dover where, perhaps owing in part to Senator Hale's exhortations, 230 Strafford County men signed up.[3]

The task of raising, organizing, training, and equipping these green troops was a demanding one, but one enthusiastically undertaken by nearly all New Hampshiremen. At citizens' meetings across the state, Republicans and Democrats alike swore their loyalty to the Union and their determination to stamp out the rebellion. "The traitors have taken the sword, and they must perish by the sword," warned the *Independent Democrat,* while opposition journals announced the willingness of Democrats "to throw all party issues aside and unite with all true patriots to crush out the rebellion which has reared its hydra head against our government, and threatens to overthrow it."[4] "The enthusiasm of the people is unprecedented," Hale informed Gideon Welles ten days after the fall of Sumter. "Say to the President and to all the Cabinet that they cannot outrun it whatever they may do provided it be prompt, energetic and efficient, in vindicating the National honor and the National flag."[5] Hale was glad for once to ride, instead of breast, a great wave of popular enthusiasm. Far different it was from 1846–1847, when in May a company of Dover volunteers serenaded him at his home on Pleasant Street and afterwards accepted his offer of "as good a glass of cider as you ever tasted."[6]

While New Hampshire and her sister states mobilized for war, Abraham Lincoln, extending his executive power to the limit, moved swiftly to meet the national emergency. Following his call for militiamen, the President issued proclamations blockading Southern ports, directed Secretary of the Treasury Chase to disburse two million dollars in public funds "for the defense and support of the government," asked for three-year volunteers, took steps to beef up the regular army and navy, suspended writs of habeas corpus between Philadelphia and Washington and in other ways acted to ready the nation for war. Although many of these steps were constitutionally the right and duty of Congress, Lincoln, working furiously against time and confident of public support, put off convening the national legislature until July 4. Ratification of his extralegal emergency measures could wait until then.[7]

To lay the groundwork for the special Congressional session, cabinet members wrote in June to the chairmen of key Senate committees, inviting them to come early to Washington for consultations. Hale, as chairman-elect of the Senate Naval Affairs Committee, received such an invitation from Secretary of the Navy Gideon Welles on June 17. He promptly replied that he had an engagement in Dover which would detain him for a few days, but that he expected to leave for the capital within a week. This he did, and after brief stops at Boston and New York he reached Washington on June 29.[8]

Hale found the capital an armed camp. For two months, troops had been pouring into the District, so that by the time Hale arrived a hundred thousand soldiers bivouacked nearby. Enroute from the railroad depot to his boarding house on Capitol Hill, he could see orderly rows of army tents and disorderly drifts of haversacks, bedding, overcoats, kitchen utensils and other military supplies. The strains of army bands floated on summer breezes and husky voices could be heard singing "Yankee Doodle," "Listen to the Mocking Bird," and "The Girl I Left Behind Me." And everywhere the swarm of soldiers: galloping through dusty streets; marching and countermarching over green fields and parks, rifles aglisten in the sun; gathering in colorful knots to swap the latest rumors or share a plug of tobacco. The Capitol itself (now at long last nearing completion) had until recently served as a barracks, and army bakers still sweated and swore over ovens in its basement.[9]

Among the regiments camped in and around Washington were the 1st and 2nd New Hampshire volunteers. The 2nd New Hampshire, under the command of Congressman Gilman Marston, had arrived just a week before Hale and had pitched "Camp Sullivan" on sun-baked Kalorama Heights, about a mile and a half from Capitol Hill. On July 1, Hale drove out to survey their encampment. Satisfied that the eager, young Granite Staters were amply provided for, he chatted and joked and did what he could to keep spirits high.[10] This visit was but the first of many which Hale paid to

New Hampshire soldiers during the war. Soon his portly figure became a common sight around the camp-fires of New Hampshire regiments stationed near Washington. He found it refreshing to put political worries temporarily behind him, to borrow a horse and ride into Maryland or Virginia where he could see with his own eyes and hear with his own ears how his uniformed constituents were faring. On one such excursion a rebel battery lobbed two shells within half a mile of Hale and his party, a distant brush with danger which thrilled the senator but which shocked his family when they learned about it.[11]

An active member of the New Hampshire Soldiers' Aid Society in Washington, Hale also regularly made the rounds of the District's hospitals. His distrust of army doctors, who he believed all too often used their military authority to force wounded men to submit to "surgical" butchery, made him a valued protector against medical quackery.[12] Even more than army doctors, Hale abhorred the vinegary, arbitrary Dorothea Dix, appointed Superintendent of Women Nurses in June 1861. She had "become elated and inflated by the reputation she acquired from her efforts in behalf of the insane," he decided, "and presuming on that she fancies herself equal to anything, & has become a perfect nuisance to the hospitals, making herself as odious as possible both to the nurses, and especially to the patients, who hate her most cordially." He complained of this "greatest female humbug of the day" to the Surgeon General, but without effect.[13]

Not all of Hale's energy went so directly into the war effort. Of necessity he spent much of his time outside the Senate as a kind of middleman in the patronage market—a new and not altogether happy experience for one so long "outside of any healthy political organization." Ever since the Republican victory in 1860 he had been bombarded with requests from friends and strangers alike that he use his influence to get them government jobs of one kind or another: clerkships, positions in customshouses, paymasterships, diplomatic posts, postmasterships. Sometimes he recommended a claimant for a particular office; more often his endorsements were general: to Lincoln he recommended Belle Garcia, "a *very good girl,* whom I have known for a long time, and is deserving of patronage."[14] The claims of old associates in the antislavery movement he pressed doggedly, as for example the request of John Jay for a European mission.[15] He followed with some attention the careers of those he had placed, was chagrined when they turned out badly and proud when they turned out well. After Sumter, the demands of men seeking military promotions and commissions still further cut into his time.

As a jobber in the fruits of patronage, Hale was neither an outstanding success nor a bankrupt failure. Although early in the war he lost all favor with the Post Office and the Navy Department, and although his relations with Secretary of State Seward were cool, he was *persona grata* with the other departments and used his personal charm to advantage. Yet while reasonably successful in placing those whose claims he endorsed, he understood little of the political uses of patronage. There was never anything like a "Hale machine" in New Hampshire, for while he dutifully attended to the requests of friends for offices and favors, he never systematically used his powers to build a personal following at home. Because of inertia, if for no other reason, he continued to think of party chiefly in terms of principle and deplored crude politicking in a time of national crisis. Thus, for example, he advocated on principle a wholesale reconstitution of the pro-Southern Supreme Court; but when it was proposed that the Court of Claims be reorganized in order to replace Democratic incumbents with job-hungry Republicans, he objected, saying that he had "no heart" for such pettiness while "the national life . . . [trembled] in the balance."[16]

Despite the demands of politics and war on his off-duty hours, Hale found time to relax at cards, to attend an occasional dinner party or musical soirée.[17] Since the grey-clad armies of Stonewall Jackson, Jubal Early, and Robert E. Lee periodically menaced the safety of the national capital, Mrs. Hale and the girls usually remained in New Hampshire. Always lonely without them, Hale fretted over prolonged sessions of Congress and mailed home long letters full of love and solicitude. His womenfolk never wrote often enough to suit him and he alternately begged, demanded, and coaxed letters from them. (" 'Your wife is the handsomest lady that ever came to Washington' said a lady to me in the cars yesterday. If you have any curiosity to know who it was, I will tell you in the next letter I write after I have heard from you on the subject.") The happiest times were the summers spent together in Dover or at "the Pool" in Saco, Maine—a popular seaside resort.[18]

Whatever his unofficial wartime chores and diversions, Hale's chief duties were those of a Republican senator. At the special session of Congress which convened to the ringing of churchbells and the booming of cannons on July 4, 1861, he did much to make clear just what his conception of those duties was.

Wisconsin's Senator Timothy Howe nicely summed up the temper of Congress on the eve of its meeting:

The resolution seems to be universal to do nothing more than the special occasion demands & to do that speedily—to use few words & no palaver—to clothe the President with the utmost potentiality of this great people, and command him to see that the "Republic receives no detriment." [19]

Everything about the composition of the House and Senate indicated that Congress would give the President the legislation he needed, and give it promptly and without bickering. In both chambers empty Southern seats gave Republicans huge majorities. Except for a handful of border-state representatives of doubtful loyalty (many of whom would soon be expelled from Congress), no opposition party existed. For the time being most Northern Democrats gave the administration at least grudging support and followed the lead of Republican chieftains who for the first time held the full legislative power in their hands.[20] Unlike the House, which scattered its honors among men from all parts of the North,[21] the Senate appointed as chairmen of its most important committees chiefly New Englanders. The elegant and eloquent Charles Sumner directed the Committee on Foreign Relations. His colleague—hard-working, commonsensical Henry Wilson—presided over Military Affairs. Maine's William Pitt

Fessenden ruled the Committee on Finance, and Hale headed Naval Affairs. Uprooted Yankees chaired most of the other influential Senate committees: Ben Wade of Ohio (Territories) had once lived in western Massachusetts, James W. Grimes (District of Columbia) and Zachariah Chandler (Commerce) both had moved west from New Hampshire birthplaces, and Lyman Trumbull (Judiciary) carried a famous Connecticut name to Illinois.[22]

His contemporaries designated Hale a "Radical" Republican. By "Radical" they meant one whose hatred of slavery was deep and who favored vigorous chastisement of the South. Loosely defined, "Radical" was loosely used, in much the same way that "Liberal" is used today; but the word is useful at least in distinguishing men like Trumbull, Wade, Grimes, Chandler, Sumner, and Hale from Republican Conservatives like Orville H. Browning, Edgar Cowan, and John C. Ten Eyck, and from Moderates like James Dixon, Jacob Collamer, Lafayette Foster, and Henry B. Anthony.[23] Yet though he usually aligned himself with the Radicals on measures connected with emancipation and the conduct of the war, Hale at all times played a lone hand. He continued to display as a key member of a party in power the same distaste for caucuses and planning sessions that he had as a hopelessly outnumbered Free Soiler. It is revealing indeed that hardly any letters to or from Hale are to be found among the papers of leading Civil War politicians. He was as much a guerrillist as ever.

Hale's place as chairman of the Naval Affairs committee was an honorable one and one with which he was well pleased. It seemed eminently fitting that a son of maritime New England—a man chiefly responsible for abolishing flogging aboard American men-of-war—should represent the navy's interests in the United States Senate. In Secretary of the Navy Gideon Welles, whom he had known casually for twenty years, he would find a man in many ways like himself: a New Englander, a one-time Jacksonian Democrat who preached strict constitutionalism and economy in government, a man to whom marlinspikes and hawsepipes were a mystery, who knew of the sea at second hand. Working in tandem, the two Yankees could be expected to oversee the navy's needs with harmony and efficiency. Or so it seemed to most observers.

It came, therefore, as a shock when early in the special session Hale revealed a serious rift between himself and the Navy Department. The causes of that rift—which grew wider as the war progressed—are by no means as clearcut nor as one-sided as Welles' biographer has made them.[24] According to the Secretary of the Navy, the falling out began shortly before the Civil War Congress met. In April and May 1861 Hale had written Welles, asking that if "conducive to the public interest" contracts for gunpowder, gunboats, and steamships be given to New Hampshire firms.[25] He had even made a special trip to Washington in behalf of a New York shipowner who wished to sell two or three vessels to the Navy. Welles put Hale off with a "delicate hint" that "there was no necessity to trouble him and that it would not be expedient to employ members of Congress in these transactions." When Hale, convinced that Welles was unfairly obstructing the purchase of ships badly needed by the navy, brought the matter up again in July, the Secretary rebuffed him. By then, Welles was convinced of Hale's venality and determined to ignore his advice.[26]

Hale saw things through different glasses. It may be that he objected to the Secretary's appointment from the start, that he himself coveted the office.[27] He no doubt knew that the testy chief of the Navy Department had urged the annexation of Texas in 1845 and as a regular Democrat had willingly supported Franklin Pierce in 1852. Even after Kansas-Nebraska and his conversion to the Republican party, Welles showed none of Hale's awareness of slavery as a moral problem. Still another reason for Hale's growing distrust was Welles' unwillingness to purge his department of subordinate officers who had dirtied their hands for "fraudulent" Democratic administrations. "I felt hurt," Hale later recalled, "I felt hurt as I believe few men could be, when I saw the Secretary of the Navy retaining the same corrupt tools who had [in 1859] received the censure of the House of Representatives" for defrauding the government.[28] But what most set Hale against the Secretary was word that in May Welles had designated his brother-in-law, George D. Morgan, sole agent in New York to purchase vessels for the navy. At the same time, the Secretary had abandoned the established practice of sealed bidding, and had authorized Morgan to accept commissions from sellers, instead of paying him a salary out of Navy Department funds. It smacked to Hale of extravagance and nepotism.

In truth, there was much misunderstanding all around; the angels could have chosen neither side. Hale's interventions on behalf of shipbuilders and naval contractors may indeed have been unsavory, but hardly more so than the actions of the President, Vice-President —even Mrs. Lincoln—all of whom made "recommendations" to Welles about the purchase of ships.[29] And while it may be true, as Welles thought, that Hale collected fees for using his influence at the Navy Department, there is only sketchy, circumstantial evidence that this was so. For what is is worth, Hale repeatedly denied having any but the nation's interest to serve. As for Welles, he could and did defend his unusual system of naval purchases by pointing out that extraordinary measures were necessary to create a navy overnight.

Once begun, the quarrel continued until Hale left the Senate, albeit under the cover of an outward civility. The history of this feud reflects credit on neither man. Father Gideon, suspicious and sanctimonious, only made his task more difficult by the condescension he invariably accorded the senator, by the arbitrary way he ignored recommendations from Hale's committee, and by his open disregard of senatorial courtesy in making appointments. Hale, whose preoccupation with corruption in the Navy Department became more and more intense, not only diminished the efficiency of the naval establishment but also frittered away power and influence which might have been used much more constructively. For sixteen years a leading defender of a minority faith, a political guerrillist to whom party loyalty meant little, Hale never learned the importance of team play, never understood the ways in which power is responsibly administered. Wisconsin's James R. Doolittle was more than half right when he suggested in 1864 "that the long habit of continued denunciation against the Administration or the party in power for fifteen or twenty years in succession has had some effect upon the habits of his [Hale's] mind, both in thought and in action." [30]

It was Hale who publicized the quarrel between himself and Secretary Welles, and he wasted little time doing it. The first day of the special session was only minutes old when he submitted a resolution that the Secretary of the Navy inform the Senate regarding all contracts made by his department since March 4, 1861. [31]

There is another set of men that I desire to make war upon worse than upon the secessionists, the rebels, and the traitors [he told his colleagues a few days later]—the harpies that hang around your Departments, who want to grow fat upon the public misfortune; who want to enrich themselves upon the hard earnings of the people, which are so generously tendered to this Government. I want to guard, if it may be possible, the public treasure in all its administration, as well from being stolen by rebels as being filched by false friends; and I hope, sir, that we shall effect both these things. [32]

The allusion to Welles and Morgan was too clear to be missed. On July 20 Hale jabbed at another of the Secretary's sore spots with a resolution that the Committee on Naval Affairs investigate the circumstances surrounding the destruction and surrender of the Norfolk Navy Yard in April. [33] Although invited to appear before Hale's committee once it had begun this investigation, or to explain his department's actions during the April crisis, Welles directed that all available information should be given the committee, but himself "declined any appearance or explanation." [34] It is not surprising, then, that when Hale presented the committee's report (largely his own work), it censured the Administration's dilatoriness in defending the Norfolk Navy Yard. [35] Furious at what he labelled Hale's "distortions" and "perversions" of the truth, Welles muttered sarcastically about the senator's "military skill and intelligence" which allowed him to dissent from General Scott's earlier opinion that the yard was indefensible. [36]

In embittering the feud between the two New Englanders, the Norfolk investigation was much less important than the Morgan purchases controversy of 1861–1862. In May 1861 Morgan had written to his brother-in-law, Gideon Welles, hinting that the navy's New York purchasing agents were dishonest and suggesting that he, Morgan, take on the job of chartering and purchasing ships in that port.[37] The Secretary demurred, but after further evidence of corruption and inefficiency came to light, he decided to give to Morgan as a trial assignment the rechartering of the steamer *Quaker City,* then under hire to the Union Defense Committee at $1000 a day. Morgan managed the recharter with spectacular success, beating down the daily fee from $1000 to $600. When in June he negotiated at favorable terms the purchase of several other suitable hulls, Welles decided to make him the Department's sole agent in New York.[38] In Morgan, whose importing business had gone into eclipse with the outbreak of war, the Secretary was sure he had found an honest and competent man to do the navy's work. And it pleased him to be able to gratify Caroline Morgan, Mrs. Welles' favorite sister, at the same time he protected the nation's interest.[39]

Between May and December 1861 Morgan negotiated the purchase of 91 vessels, for which the government paid roughly $3,500,000. Morgan's own commission on these transactions, paid at Welles' insistence by the sellers, amounted to $70,000. In fairness to the Secretary and his brother-in-law it must be said that in several instances Morgan's shrewd bargaining had probably saved the government money. The very act of centralizing all purchasing authority in the hands of a single agent served to eliminate competitive bidding which would have driven prices up. And, it should be noted, Morgan's ships proved seaworthy. "Let me say that your purchased ships have turned out remarkably well," Admiral Samuel F. DuPont complimented Morgan in December 1861. "I wish I had more of them." [40] Yet the fact remained that with the assistance of his highly-placed brother-in-law, Morgan had been able to turn the national crisis to enormous personal gain. Seventy-thousand dollars was a sizable fortune, men were saying; someone should investigate the matter.

Someone already was. At the special session of Congress in July 1861 Welles had for the moment turned aside Hale's resolution of inquiry into Navy Department contracts with a curt declaration that the authority for the manner of his procurement of vessels was "to be found in the necessities and condition of the country and the times." [41] But during the late summer and fall a select committee of the House of Representatives had been busily collecting testimony relating to government war contracts of all kinds, and for two days in September it quizzed Morgan about his acquisitions.[42] Anticipating the report of these House investigators, and under heavy pressure to change his system of purchases, the Secretary of the Navy included in his annual report for 1861 a more elaborate defense of his policies. Particularly he stressed Morgan's "business capacity," his "scrupulous and unquestioned integrity," and the soundness of the flotilla he had bought.[43]

Welles' defense in no way satisfied his critics. On December 18 the House voted to print the massive report of its select committee, 112 pages of which dealt with "testimony in Relation to the Purchase of Vessels and Navy Supplies." Appended to this report was a resolution, subsequently ratified by the House, which censured such methods as Welles had used in his dealings with Morgan.[44] And all the while the senior senator from New Hampshire was preparing his own attack on the administration of the Navy Department.

The House report was a mine of information, but Hale wanted even more. On January 6, 1862, at his request, the Senate instructed the Naval Affairs Committee to investigate the system of naval purchasing in use since the beginning of the war and if necessary draft a bill "to protect the public interest." [45] That Hale's mind was anything but open on this matter, and that his feud with Welles had clouded his eyes to the nation's welfare, became painfully apparent two days later when he offered a pair of amendments to a House-sponsored bill for the construction of twenty iron-clad steam gunboats. The first amendment would have cut the number of boats from twenty to twelve, and the second would have given to the President, instead of the Secretary of the Navy, authorization to have them built. In response to questioning, Hale admitted that the amendments *were* intended "to convey a censure upon the Secretary for the manner in which he has disbursed the public funds that have been intrusted to him." He conceded that Welles was "as honest a man as there is connected with the Government," but felt that however pure his motives, there was something drastically wrong in his letting Morgan turn the navy's need into such great personal profit. By publicly chastizing Welles, the Senate could best serve warning "to everybody who has anything to do with the disbursement of public funds, that such things as this cannot go unchallenged through the Senate." [46] Connecticut's James Dixon (who privately questioned "the worldly wisdom of the arrangement with Mr. Morgan")[47] warmly defended his most celebrated constituent as "a man of spotless reputation and spotless character," and denounced the rebuke implied in the amendments. Henry Wilson, convinced of Welles' integrity yet nonetheless sure that "he committed an error in this matter," proposed a resolution directing the Secretary to report to the Senate the facts relating to Morgan's purchases. It was adopted at once. Lost in the hubbub of debate was the navy's pressing need for gunboats.[48]

Welles' report, which he laid before the Senate on January 14, was his final—and most elaborate—defense of the Morgan deals. In greater detail than ever before he discussed the reasons behind the choice of his brother-in-law as the navy's sole agent in New York and Connecticut. The experience of the first weeks of war had shown, he maintained, that naval officers, while admirable inspectors of ships, made poor purchasers. Wholly untrained in the techniques of mercantile warfare, they were easily victimized by predatory shipbrokers. Therefore the Secretary had decided in May that a board of three naval inspectors should *judge* ships in which the navy was interested, but that "a single, properly qualified, individual" should negotiate the purchases, dealing directly with the owners of vessels so as to avoid unnecessary brokerage fees. This privileged individual would receive his commission—which Welles stipulated "should in no case exceed the regular mercantile percentage fixed by the Chamber of Commerce"—from the sellers. Finally, because the emergency placed a premium on swift purchase, the Secretary had decided that the old

method of sealed bidding be scuttled. Since the success of this unusual system of purchasing turned on the honesty and commercial
sagacity of the Department's agent, Welles selected the one man in
New York of whose probity and ability he had personal knowledge.
That this man happened to be his relative had given him pause but
had not stopped him from doing what he thought best.[49] He had
picked his man and his man had bought sound ships—had bought
them quickly and at fair prices. Who but fools or knaves could ask
for more?

Such was Welles defense, and, it must be said, many found it
adequate. No less distinguished a merchant and citizen than John
Murray Forbes was convinced that "Mr. Welles was right in principle, viz: employing a business man *to do mercantile work*," and was
sure that Morgan had saved the government more than the amount
of his commissions.[50] Still, there were many who condemned the
Navy Department's commercial operations, who saw the periwigged
Secretary as anything but the white-robed defender of the Union's
interests which he pictured himself. Their leading voice was John P.
Hale.[51]

Hale's denunciation of the Morgan purchases was double-barrelled.
On January 27, 1862, he presented the seven-page report of the Naval
Affairs Committee and eleven days later he blasted Welles and his
brother-in-law in a speech to the Senate. Since the committee report
was shaped by his will and phrased in his words, these twin salvos
may be taken together as the true expression of Hale's mind. They
reveal most clearly his obsession with what he believed to be the
Secretary's extravagance and favoritism.[52]

His indictment was carefully drawn; he wasted no time assaulting
Welles' strong points. Nothing was to be gained by impugning the
fitness of Morgan for his tasks, nor would it be profitable to call into
the question the worth of the vessels he had bought. The testimony
in Morgan's favor, while not one-sided, was weighty. But where
Welles was vulnerable—and where Hale aimed his broadside—was
the arrangement by which he had permitted the New Yorker to grow
rich at public expense. For, Hale vehemently insisted, Morgan's huge
commissions *had* come from the public purse just as surely as if he

had been on the federal payroll. It was "an impeachment of common sense," he said in the committee report, "to pretend that the seller did not include . . . [Morgan's] commission in the price for which he consented to sell." [53] In permitting Morgan to demand an "exhorbitant" 2½ percent commission on all purchases (the *normal* percentage on such purchases was considerably less according to the New York Chamber of Commerce) and by adopting a mode of purchase whereby the agent's fee depended upon the price paid, Welles encouraged extravagance, collusion, and fraud. That the Secretary of the Navy had embraced such a wasteful system at a time of national peril was especially disgraceful. It was his considered opinion, Hale cried from the Senate floor, "that the liberties of this country are in greater danger to-day from the corruptions and from the profligacy practiced in the various Departments of this Government than they are from the open enemy in the field." [54]

In a limited sense, Hale won his battle: Morgan shortly left for Europe, where he remained for some time—and never made a government purchase again. But it was a pyrrhic victory, and though Hale won the battle he was to lose the war. The fury with which he attacked the Navy Department seemed to many excessive. His unfortunate declaration that Republican corruption jeopardized the nation's liberties more than did the rebel armies won immediate and widespread notoriety. No doubt uttered more for its rhetorical flavor than for the accuracy with which it expressed Hale's honest belief, that remark chilled Republicans and delighted Democrats throughout the North. Gleefully Copperhead prints pounced upon it as a testament of Republican blame.

If we were to print anything from a Democratic source reflecting seriously upon high officers of the administration for misappropriation of public funds [noted the Newport *Argus & Spectator*], we should do so with the fear of the stigma of traitor and the turnkey of Fort Warren before our eyes. But when we can get the testimony of good Republicans like that ponderous joker, Jack Hale, in the confessional, we feel on safe ground.[55]

Shocked Republican politicians looked askance at the maverick in their midst. It was all very well to expose corruption where one found it; but surely, they thought, at a time when Confederate armies kept Washington in jitters, when the disasters at Bull Run and Ball's Bluff still rankled in men's minds, when disloyal Democrats more and more brazenly obstructed the war effort—surely at such a time there were greater villains and more worthy targets than white-bearded old Gideon Welles.

It happened, then, that although he received many letters from lawyers, merchants, and other citizens congratulating him for his exposé of the Morgan purchases, and although a part of the Northern press trumpeted for Welles' removal,[56] on Capitol Hill Hale's influence and prestige declined. On February 14, a week after Hale's speech, the Senate voted 31–5 to table his resolution censuring the Morgan transactions.[57] Within his own committee even, Hale's control became increasingly insecure. Senators Solomon Foot and James W. Grimes openly clashed with their chairman and took Welles' side against him. By December 1863 feeling was so strongly against keeping as head of the Committee on Naval Affairs a man utterly at odds with the Navy Department that Hale barely averted the disgrace of deposition.[58]

But deposed he was not—until he became a lame duck—and for the war's duration he channelled the bulk of his energy into his bootless vendetta with the man whose department he represented in Congress. This is not to say that Hale opposed Welles at every turn, or that he was blind to the needs of the navy. He had the well-being of the fleet and nation too much at heart for that. To be sure, his eagerness to rebuke the Secretary for the Morgan affair had caused him spitefully to propose that Congress reduce authorized gunboat construction; but as soon as Welles made known the navy's pressing need for such vessels, Hale withdrew his proposal and urged that the administration's request be granted in full.[59] He was capable of initiating investigations in *behalf* of the navy as well as setting afoot inquiries designed to embarrass or harrass its chief. Upon occasion he facilitated legislation requested by the Navy Department.[60] All too often, however, he spent his waking hours sniffing out corruption (real and imaginary) in the navy's several branches and bureaus; bickering with Welles over the appointment of midshipmen, the removal of a clerk, or the enlargement of the Portsmouth Navy Yard; complaining to all who would listen of the incompetence and venality of the Secretary's principal advisers. As the war ground jerkily on, he developed a particular hatred of Gustavus Fox, the Assistant Secretary of the Navy—a former naval officer who had resigned his commission in 1856 to marry a daughter of Hale's onetime enemy, Levi Woodbury. Fox, he became convinced, was the real power behind Welles' throne, "a scoundrel & a copperhead" whose malign influence pervaded the Navy Department. Even after he had left the Senate, Hale strove to oust Fox.[61]

Although Hale devoted so much of his time and energy to the scrutiny of naval administration, he still voiced his opinions about other wartime issues. By his votes and speeches he helped to shape and implement the Republican program. In particular, he had the personal satisfaction of seeing to virtual completion the great task that he, and others like him, had so long ago begun: the abolition of chattel slavery in the United States.

"If . . . [the South] pushes matters to a bloody issue," Senator Doolittle had predicted not long before Sumter, "the disunion question and the slavery question may all find their solution & their end together." [62] Events were to prove Doolittle a sound prophet. Yet only gradually did the war to preserve the Union become as well a war to free the slave. Northern Democrats were quick to make clear "that we are not fighting for negro freedom or negro abolition," [63] but simply to restore the Union; and even among Republicans there were few, on the eve of First Bull Run, who advocated emancipation in the Southern states. Not until military disasters showed the North that the war would be long and bloody, and not until the loyalty of the border states was made certain, did Congress—and, even more slowly and reluctantly, the President—act to destroy slavery in the South. Thus, when in July 1861 John J. Crittenden in the House and Andrew Johnson in the Senate proposed nearly identical resolutions that Congress had no intention of tampering "with the rights or established institutions" of Southern states, Republicans endorsed them almost to a man.[64] Hale gave his unqualified support. He had contended for years, he reminded the Senate, that the federal government had no more right to interfere with slavery in the states than it had "to interfere with the condition of the serfs in Russia, or with the rights and wrongs of the laboring classes in England."[65]

During the next six months, however, Hale and most other Republican congressmen swung away from this position of strict constitutionalism and toward one more aggressively hostile to slavery. The House of Representatives tipped its hand early in the first regular session of the Thirty-Seventh Congress by refusing to reaffirm Crittenden's disclaimer resolution; the Senate never even brought it up for discussion. Timothy Howe predicted the formation of a powerful faction whose watchword was "Emancipation—the utter extinction of slavery." "The old Chiefs of Abolition," he wrote in December 1861, "are in the very midsummer of a rich revenge."[66]

There were a number of reasons for this new attitude. For one thing, although in theory one might distinguish between a struggle to preserve the Union and a war against human bondage, in practice the distinction quickly blurred. Northern field generals soon discovered that, much as they would like, they could not dodge the slavery issue. Like flies to honey, slaves in the Upper South and border states swarmed into Union lines as the Yankee armies moved South. Were these hapless bondsmen—many employed in digging trenches and erecting earthworks for rebel armies, and all at least indirectly buttressing the Confederate war effort—to be treated as contraband property and set free, or were they to be denied asylum, even returned to their masters? Some commanding officers decided one way, others decided the other. President Lincoln had had his say in September 1861, when he countermanded General John C. Frémont's proclamation freeing all slaves of Missouri masters who supported the Confederacy. It was inevitable that Congress should speak its mind as well.

Conditioning the congressional response to the problem of slavery and war were the military disasters of 1861. The bloody Union defeat at Ball's Bluff in October, coming on the heels of the rout at Bull Run established not only the incompetence of Northern generalship, but Southern determination and resourcefulness as well. If Johnny Reb were to be brought to his knees, the North would have to take drastic action. By striking hard at slavery, men like Hale felt, the foundation of the Confederate war machine might be weakened. At the same time, by giving the war a moral as well as constitutional aspect, the United States might win new support at home and abroad.[67]

I have no doubt [said Hale in 1864] that when the rebellion commenced, Mr. Lincoln and the Republican party and all those that undertook to defend the country . . . were sincere, honest, and earnest in their professions to leave existing things as they found them. But, sir, they could not do it. They found as the war progressed that slavery was the giant that stood in their way. They saw that slavery obstructed their efforts to preserve, maintain, and defend the nation's life, and they said, "If that is the alternative and it comes to this, that slavery or the nation must die, let slavery die." [68]

Beginning early in 1862, and continuing for the rest of the war, there poured from the Capitol a steady stream of legislative measures designed to crush slavery. Hale's time-consuming quarrel with the Navy Department greatly restricted his participation in the debates on antislavery bills and resolutions; yet his votes and occasional speeches helped carry the Radical program forward and enable one to reconstruct the final development of his abolitionism.

What emerges most clearly in Hale's letters and speeches during these years is his genuine concern for the Negro's welfare and his belief that the supposedly innate inferiority of the black race had yet to be proved. His egalitarian views, such as they were, derived in part from what he knew of free Negroes in the North ("industrious, patient, exhibiting very many amiable and excellent traits of character" [69]), in part from the Bible, which taught him that all men stood equal in the sight of God. Hale knew perfectly well that most Northern states discriminated against the Negro in a hundred different ways.[70] But in New Hampshire, Hale had been fond of telling slaveholders, Negroes had "the same rights with any of us. They testify in courts; they vote at the ballot-box; and they have, so far as I know, just exactly the same political rights that I have, and I hope they will always have them."[71] Nothing was more unjust, he maintained, than to heap on long-suffering blacks the burdens of slavery, and then "pronounce them as degraded, ignorant, incapable of representation, because under the crushing weight of all these disabilities they have not made such progress as to enable them to step at once on an equality into a condition which their masters have enjoyed for many years." "Take off these burdens," he pleaded, "give them a fair chance" before judging their ability "to cope and contend with their white masters."[72]

Emancipation, then, was a necessary first step toward political equality. But it was only that—a first step. It would be a mistake, Hale contended, to extend at a stroke full political privileges to "a class so long depressed & kept down under the blighting influence of slavery." In a letter to his wife, written near the end of the war, he confided:

I entirely disagree with those who hold that the right of voting is a right which belongs to the catalogue of a man's natural rights & that it is quite as wrong to withhold that from him as it is to keep him in a state of bondage. That is not so, it is not a natural right but a political one bestowed by those who frame the political institutions of a Country. If it were a natural right it would belong to women as well as to man [*sic*], & society in forming its institutions and organizations has a right to with-hold it from any person or class of persons who it believes cannot exercise it understandingly & in a manner that will subserve and promote the best interests of society.

To determine who *was* fit to vote, Hale favored a stiff literacy test, like that of Massachusetts—for whites as well as for Negroes. Those who showed themselves qualified should be entitled to vote regardless of color.[73]

Likewise, Hale saw as clearly as anyone that the freeing of Negro slaves was simply an essential preliminary act in the resolution of a much larger and more difficult problem: the peaceful social adjustment of the white and black races in America. He refused to be seduced by that will-o'-the-wisp, colonization of the Negroes outside the United States, so fervently pursued by President Lincoln and others. "The idea of removing the whole colored population from this country is one of the most absurd ideas that ever entered into the head of man or woman," he said. The records of the American Colonization Society proved the futility of such a venture. No, racial diversity was an accomplished fact, and the problems arising from it would have to be worked out within the United States.[74] But before racial adjustment could start, before the Negro could begin to participate as an equal in the development of American society, slavery had to be destroyed.

The steps by which Congress sought to liquidate slavery were many. Hale supported them all, but some caused him more soul-searching than others. About the bills abolishing slavery in the District of Columbia and nullifying the Fugitive Slave Acts of 1793 and 1850, he had no doubts. Everyone now conceded the right of Congress to enact laws on such matters. But on other legislative measures, measures such as the Second Confiscation Bill, for example, which roughly shouldered aside states' rights in order to strike at slavery, his constitutional doubts caused him no end of torment.

He was perfectly willing to confiscate the property of rebels—even to emancipate their slaves if it were done in the name of military necessity—and he denounced those moderates whom he thought too "tender-footed on this subject."[75]

I think the time has come when Congress should move [he said in a speech on the Second Confiscation Bill in April, 1862], and should show to armed rebels with arms in their hands—hands red with the blood of our brethren—that the Constitution and laws made for the protection of the rights of persons and property were made for the protection of those who were true to their allegiance, and not for the protection of those who threw it off and were fighting against it, and would subvert the Constitution and destroy the country which it was instituted to govern.

And again:

The Constitution was made for a time of peace. It was made for a civilized society, and was not framed and did not contemplate the exigencies and emergencies of an armed rebellion.[76]

But when, a week after Hale made these remarks, Henry Wilson proposed making it *mandatory* that the President set free all slaves of rebel masters whether or not he deemed it a necessary war measure, the New Hampshire maverick was at once on his feet, praising constitutional liberty as America's "great boon," and warning his fellow senators that "we must see to it that in our great zeal to put down rebellion we . . . [do] not trample on that." [77] Still, he did vote for the Confiscation Act which, in its final form, set "forever free" the slaves of rebels who came within Union lines.[78] By then (July 1862), after Shiloh and McClellan's costly and inconclusive peninsula campaign, Hale had swallowed nearly all his constitutional scruples where slavery was concerned and justified almost any attack on that institution as a necessary step in suppressing the rebellion. A year later, in fact, he introduced a bill which would have done by statute what was eventually done by the Thirteenth Amendment.[79] And during debate on the Freedmen's Bureau Bill in the summer of 1864 he argued that there were powers inherent in national sovereignty beyond those prescribed in the Constitution. To contend otherwise, he insisted, was to place oneself in the ridiculous position of the clergyman who, when called upon to pray for a man gored by a bull, answered that he could not, for his prayerbook contained no prayer appropriate for goring.[80] From time to time Hale's constitutional conscience troubled him, and once in 1863 he gloomily confessed his belief that Congress "had made a great mistake upon the slavery question, and that it would have been better both for the cause of the Country, and of emancipation if nothing had been said in regard to the negro since the war commenced." [81] Nevertheless, despite such moments of self-doubt, he went steadily ahead with the work of abolition.

For Hale, the crowning arch in a labor of twenty years was the Thirteenth Amendment, which the Senate approved in April 1864. "Mr. President," he said on the eve of its passage by the upper chamber, "permit me to say that this is a day that I and many others have long wished for, long hoped for, long striven for." Only once "the great sin and the great crime" of slavery were swept away, he declared with emotion, could men walk proudly, in step with God. "Then without shame, without reproach, and without apology, we can stand in this nineteenth century, soldiers of the new civilization and of an old Christianity, going forth to battle with every impulse of our hearts and every purpose that we entertain in full accordance with the best wishes and hopes of the good on earth and of the God in heaven." The same religious impulse which had enlisted Hale in the antislavery crusade two decades before still guided his steps.[82]

While celebrating Senate approval of the abolition amendment, Hale realized as well as anyone else that the job was not yet done. The amendment had yet to pass the House of Representatives, and after that to muster the support of three-fourths of the states before it would become a part of the Constitution. Even then it would have little meaning so long as the South remained unconquered. Never had the task of crushing the rebellion by the sword looked more discouraging and difficult than in the spring of 1864. After three years of bitter and gory warfare, the Confederates fought grimly on. Ulysses Grant in Virginia and William T. Sherman in Georgia had launched campaigns which if successful would bring at last a conquered peace; but many wondered whether the people of the North—sickened at the monstrous and ever mounting lists of dead and wounded—would wait for such success. Eighteen-sixty-four was also a Presidential election year. Rising dissatisfaction with the progress of the war strengthened the hand of Northern Democrats, and should their candidate, George B. McClellan, win in November (a possibility which deeply troubled Abraham Lincoln even after Sherman's capture of Atlanta in September), a negotiated settlement with the South appeared likely. In that event, thought Hale, all the gains of the past three years would be in jeopardy and the lives of hundreds of thousands of Union soldiers wasted. And, finally, even if the Republicans remained in power and even if the rebels were at long last whipped into submission, there remained the difficult job of reconstructing the Union and of guaranteeing to ex-slaves the rights of freemen.

At this critical moment in the nation's history, John P. Hale faced his third contest for reelection to the United States Senate. The obstacles in his path were many and formidable: the cry of rotation-in-office, raised against him in 1858, was more strident than ever in 1864; many Republicans were sharply critical of his much-publicized attacks on the Navy Department; a new breed of aggressive young politicians had largely displaced Hale's lieutenants as leaders of New Hampshire's Republican party.

In addition, Hale had to withstand the fire of those who accused him of peddling his influence as senator. Coming to Washington in December 1863 for the opening of the Thirty-Eighth Congress, Hale had looked forward to an enjoyable fortnight before returning again to New Hampshire for Christmas with his family. The first two weeks of the congressional session were altogether pleasant. As guest of Admiral Lisovski, he was piped aboard the Russian flagship then anchored off Alexandria. He made the rounds of Washington tea parties, took long walks, basked in the warm sun which sent temperatures well above 70 degrees.[83] But on Wednesday, December 16, Horace Greeley's New York *Tribune* shattered the senator's tranquility.

In an article entitled "A CASE OF BRIBERY" the *Tribune* declared:

A prominent New-England Senator is compromised by evidence going to show that he received $3000 for his influence in getting a person out of the Old Capitol prison who had been confined there on a charge of defrauding the Government, and for rendering to the same person other services of a similar nature. The affair has created the utmost astonishment among those who have heard of it. The difficulty of putting a stop to public plundering is greatly enhanced by the high influences which can so often be retained for a small percentage of the ill-gotten gains to screen the culprits from justice after their fraudulent practices have been discovered.[84]

Shortly after he read this allusive exposé, Hale received a visit from his New Hampshire colleague, Senator Clark, who brought information which left no doubt that the "prominent New-England Senator" referred to was none other than John P. Hale. Upon brief reflection, Hale decided that the charge against him being "one of a very high character," he had best lay the whole matter before the Senate. On December 17, as soon as the journal had been read, he rose "to a question of privilege."

The previous summer, Hale began, he had been asked by a Boston friend to undertake the defense of Major James M. Hunt, then locked in Washington's Old Capitol jail awaiting court martial for bilking the War Department in the sale of steamboats. The friend and his associates, a group of shipowners for whom Hunt was agent, stood to lose much should he be convicted. They offered Hale a $2000 retainer if he would take the case. It being "a large transaction," and Hale having some doubt about its "propriety and delicacy," he left matters open for the time being and sought the advice of New Hampshire friends. Only after two Strafford County lawyers independently assured Hale that he could rightfully take the case, did he at last pledge his services, collect the retainer, and set out for Washington. Once in the capital, he called upon Reverdy Johnson, United States senator from Maryland and one of the country's top lawyers, who at once laid to rest the last of Hale's doubts about the propriety of his business. There was nothing unlawful or even indelicate about the matter, Johnson assured Hale. He himself frequently took such cases. Thus reassured, Hale went to Secretary of War Edwin M. Stanton and secured Hunt's parole from Old Capitol pending trial. Since then Hale had received an additional $1000 for his services. The case had not yet come before a court martial.

Having thus explained his actions, Hale closed by asking that the Committee on the Judiciary investigate and report whether he had "been guilty of any conduct inconsistent with his duties as a Senator." [85] The request was unanimously approved and afterward several senators came to Hale's desk to express their confidence that he would be fully exonerated. "Even Fessenden," Hale bragged, "who is not very impulsive, congratulated me on the splendid manner in which I had acquitted myself." He had "not the slightest fears" that the committee would make an unfavorable report: "whatever the papers say it is all right." [86]

Not everyone was as charitable as the senators. Gideon Welles, for one, hopped with glee at Hale's embarrassment, writing in his diary:

> A charge of bribery against a Senator has resulted in John P. Hale's admission that he is the man referred to, admitting that he took the money, but that it was a *fee* not as a *bribe*. "Strange such a difference there should be twixt tweedle-dum and tweedle-dee." This loud mouthed paragon, whose boisterous professions of purity, and whose immense indignation against a corrupt world were so great that he delighted to misrepresent and belie them in order that his virtuous light might shine distinctly, is beginning to be exposed and rightly understood. But the whole is not told and never will be—he is a mass of corruption.[87]

In New Hampshire, where eyes were already on the elections of 1864, the reaction to the *Tribune's* thrust and Hale's parry was mixed. Of the Republican journals, the Dover *Enquirer* was Hale's staunchest defender. He had done nothing, it said, "which the Government itself would not and ought not to have done to further the ends of justice." Those barking at his heels were "actuated solely by partisan motives or personal enmity." [88] Other Administration prints admitted that the senator "may have acted unwisely," but not illegally.[89] Granite State Democrats, on the other hand, crowed. "That John P. Hale should prostitute his official position and influence to the purposes of private gain, will surprise no one who knows him," proclaimed the *New Hampshire Patriot*. His $3000 fee was proof enough, it said, that Hale had been hired for more than mere legal ability. Much better lawyers could have been hired at a tithe of Hale's price: "It is apparent, then, that it was Hale the Senator, politician, and Republican leader, that was bargained for and purchased at so high a price by Mr. Hunt." The Nashua *Gazette* flatly declared that the Senate had no choice but to expel Hale if it were to preserve its honor and dignity.[90]

In February, Lyman Trumbull presented the Judiciary Committee's report. As expected, it found Hale innocent of any wrong-doing. "There was not the slightest evidence before the committee that Mr. Hale undertook the defence of Hunt from any corrupt or improper motive; so far from it, he seems to have acted with peculiar caution." This much Hale had predicted. But, the report went on, Hale's very caution pointed up "the questionable propriety of the act." To prevent any such incident in the future, Trumbull's committee recommended a law (soon passed) prohibiting congressmen from accepting fees in cases "before any department of the government other than its judiciary tribunals." [91]

If the *Tribune's* disclosures—together with the Senate's left-handed criticism—were the most spectacular of the burdens Hale carried into the 1864 campaign, there were other, greater impediments in his way. The least bulky of these, and the one most easily removed, was the opposition of New Hampshire Democrats. At the March elections a united Republican party, having bought votes in critical towns [92] and strengthened by the ballots of soldiers furloughed especially for the occasion, once again won unshakable control of the state legislature. Hale himself contributed a number of rousing speeches to his party's victory and was especially pleased "that seven unconditional Hale men have been elected to the Legislature from Dover, & not one of another stripe." [93]

With the Democratic threat destroyed, there remained only an intraparty contest for the Republican nomination. But there the obstacles to Hale's selection were formidable—much more formidable than he ever realized. For the truth was that having been so long in Washington he had lost touch with New Hampshire politics, had become too much a stranger to the lawyers, farmers, and merchants on whom his future depended. His friend Aaron Young warned him of this in October 1863: "bow to a few of the new men," advised Young, "& shake hands with a few of the old ones—old ones who perhaps think they have been neglected." [94] Moreover, not only had Hale lost touch, but his closest political associates—men who had seen him safely through earlier campaigns—were no longer in positions to wage his fight for him. The reliable and politically wise

George G. Fogg, for example, was out of the country altogether, serving since 1861 as United States Minister to Switzerland. Mason Tappan, a mountain of strength to Hale in two previous senatorial campaigns, no longer possessed the influence which goes with a seat in Congress and since 1861 (after a short stint in the army) had become more and more absorbed in his own extensive law practice.

Into this power vacuum stepped a triumvirate of young, energetic, skilled politicians who by 1864 largely dominated the Republican party in New Hampshire. Variously known throughout the state as the "Concord ring," the "drugstore clique," or "the firm," these three men—William E. Chandler, Nehemiah Ordway, and Edward H. Rollins (in whose Concord pharmacy the trio sometimes met)— now led the fight against Hale's reelection. Their reasons for opposing the Dover veteran were several. For one thing they sensed New Hampshire's deep commitment to the policy of rotation-in-office and simply believed that it was time for a change. For another, party regulars and good Administration men all, they resented Hale's violent clashes with Secretary Welles which had given so much aid and comfort to the Democratic enemy. While principle had been a sufficient cement for a party out of power, political unity now depended on patronage as well; and a maverick who offended the gods of disbursement was a heavy liability. Not only did Hale stand badly with the Navy Department (which ignored his requests in making appointments at the Portsmouth Navy Yard) but because of his quarrel with Assistant Secretary Fox he had alienated as well Fox's patronage-rich brother-in-law, Postmaster General Montgomery Blair. Finally, State Republican Chairman Chandler and his associates may have given some weight to reports (which had begun circulating after Hale fell seriously ill with erysipelas the previous year) that Jack Hale was just too old for the job of senator.[95]

So strong was the Concord clique, so weighty were its arguments, and so many were the candidates, that even normally outspoken supporters of the incumbent remained mute or privately voiced a willingness to back someone new. Both the *Independent Democrat* and the Dover *Enquirer* refused to endorse any one candidate, though the *Enquirer* did print long letters to the editor pleading the case for Hale. Even Fogg confided to Tappan in April: "The election of yourself or Tuck or Cragin would not, in my judgment, be to be regretted—even in place of Hale." [96]

Still, there were many New Hampshiremen, especially among the rank-and-file, who revered "Old Jack" for his long crusade against slavery, who still chuckled with delight at the remembrance of the licking he gave the bosses in the "Hale Storm," who heartily endorsed his exposés of corruption in government. Jacob Ela remained loyal. So, too, did Mason Tappan, who once again superintended Hale's fortunes during May and June, and enough others to delude the candidate into thinking that his chances were bright. [97]

As the June meeting of the legislature drew near, the field of Republican contestants narrowed to five: Gilman Marston and Amos Tuck of Exeter; Aaron H. Cragin of Lebanon; Thomas M. Edwards of Keene, now a rickety 69; and Hale. As usual, Hale, having placed his fortunes in the hands of friends, at first refused to come home to work for his own election. He preferred instead "quietly to remain at my post of duty," leaving the wooing of legislators to others. To do otherwise, he feared, would "disgust more than it will conciliate." [98] The week before the Republican caucus was to nominate a candidate, however, in response to "earnest letters from several friends," he made a flying trip from Washington to New Hampshire in a last desperate attempt to rout his enemies. He went straight to Concord and for three days worked furiously to mend his fences, to rally the faithful and court the undecided. [99] But other seekers after the senatorship were also on the scene—as was the Clique—making deals of their own, meeting offer with counteroffer, pressing their claims to preferment. Mason Tappan saw the writing on the wall as early as June 5. The whole affair was "a scramble," he informed Hale, "and all hands seem to combine to defeat you . . . Tuck & Cragin are working together—both present—& both think that it lies between them. It may be so." [100]

On Thursday evening, June 9, Republican legislators gathered in Concord's Rumford Hall to nominate (and hence elect) a United

States senator. The first ballot rather surprisingly put Marston ahead, but his 57 votes fell far short of a majority. Cragin ran a close second, with Hale, Tuck, and Edwards strung out behind. Marston, Cragin, and Hale all increased their totals slightly on the second ballot, but thereafter Hale's support withered away. On the fifth ballot Aaron Cragin defeated Marston, 126–75, and became the successor-designate to John P. Hale. A week later the legislature formally elected Cragin, giving him twice as many votes as his Democratic opponent.[101]

News of Hale's defeat spread quickly. His enemies in the Navy Department found it highly "gratifying." "I rejoice at it," sang Welles, "for he is worthless, and a profligate politician." Others, however, were more appreciative of the beaten senator. The radical Polish emigré, Count Adam Gurowski, recalled Hale's "unrelenting attacks [on] the abuses of men in power," and feared that "his talents and . . . his sturdy courage" would not be easily replaced.[102] Hale has left no record of his own reaction to his defeat. Yet despite his repeated professions of indifference, his loss, as the victorious Cragin surmised, "must have been very mortifying." [103]

In December, the Senate added insult to injury by replacing him as chairman of the Naval Affairs Committee, appointing in his place his long-time adversary, James W. Grimes. After having loyally stumped for Lincoln in the fall of 1864, Hale had, at the request of Secretary of War Stanton, taken a steamship to Halifax "on some profess[ion]al, confidential business for the Government." [104] He was still in Halifax when Congress reconvened for what was to be Hale's last session as a senator. Greatly wishing to keep his chairmanship for the few weeks remaining in his term, he wrote Charles Sumner a long letter asking that he be retained. Sumner did what he could for his New England colleague, but at a Republican caucus on December 8, only seven senators voted to keep Hale in his post. Instead he was picked to head the Committee on the District of Columbia, a sop he promptly declined once he returned to his seat a week before Christmas.[105]

All the bitterness Hale felt he poured into a final round of vituperation against the evil spirits in the Navy Department. He was particularly incensed that the Department had the previous summer set "a board of pimps and spies" on his track to sniff out, if possible, any corruption of his own, and that it had procured the arrest and imprisonment of Franklin W. Smith, a Boston hardware merchant, ostensibly for cheating the navy in the sale of supplies, but really, Hale insisted, because Smith had provided him with evidence of corruption in the Navy Department. It also rankled him deeply that Secretary Welles had gone out of his way to appoint William E. Chandler as the navy's counsel in investigations at the Philadelphia Navy Yard. In a speech which, because of interruptions and postponements stretched over three weeks (the senators were growing tired of his harangue), he blistered Welles and Fox for ignoring the dishonesty of naval purchasing agents, for disregarding congressional instructions, for permitting favoritism and extravagance. Welles suffered in silence, happy that Hale's Senate days were numbered and that this was "his last rant and raving against the Department." [106]

While New Hampshire's lame-duck senator was "freeing his mind," he had also to plan for the future. His defeat forced him for the first time in ten years to consider means of supporting his wife and still-unmarried daughters. He could, of course, hang out his lawyer's shingle again, and it may be that he would have accepted a federal judgeship had nothing better turned up. But in December 1864 Hale set his sights on a more prestigious office: United States Minister to France. The death of William L. Dayton left that post unfilled, and upon his return from Nova Scotia, Hale, letting it be known that he was a candidate, began drumming up support among his Republican friends in the Senate. Most "signed his petition with readiness and with great pleasure" (or so he told Edwin D. Morgan), but because of objections to his lack of qualifications for so important a diplomatic position, it was finally decided, after a conference with Secretary of State Seward, that Hale be sent instead to Spain. [107] President Lincoln willingly accepted Seward's recommendation and on March 10, a week after the close of the Thirty-Eighth Congress, he appointed the New Hampshireman America's Minister at Madrid. That very day the Senate confirmed the appointment unanimously. Secretary Welles sourly declared Hale "eminently unfit" for his new office, but the senator's friends—seeing the Spanish ministership for what it was: a political prize demanding little special ability—cheered this "becoming recognition" of Hale's past services.[108]

In April Hale came to Washington to receive his instructions from the State Department and on the morning of the 14th he stopped at the White House for a last talk with the President. His relations with Lincoln, whom he had known since their days in the Thirtieth Congress, though never close had always been friendly. Although Lincoln was much more conservative on the slavery question, as well as more deeply intelligent and politically astute than Hale, the two men shared a rough good humor which dulled the edges of disagreement and kept their relations cordial. Disagreements of course there had been: from matters as important as the conduct of the war and emancipation policy to trivial differences about the election of the Secretary of the Senate or the conduct of Lincoln's friend Ward Lamon, United States Marshal for the District of Columbia. Yet Hale repeatedly praised the President as a man of unexcelled "honesty and patriotism," whose single aim was "the welfare of the country"; and not even the senator's attacks on his Secretary of the Navy kept Lincoln from receiving Hale amicably.

The two politicians chatted easily on the 14th, each mellowed by the realization that the war was nearly done. Hale requested and Lincoln granted "an act of clemency and kindness" (perhaps for a New Hampshire soldier charged with desertion). Lincoln asked that Hale keep the State Department informed of his plans and movements during the interval before his sailing. After exchanging the usual pleasantries and wishing one another well, they shook hands and Hale departed.[109] Twelve hours later, as he sat in Ford's Theater watching Laura Keene in "Our American Cousin," the President was fatally shot by John Wilkes Booth.

Hale and most Radical Republicans at first found little to complain of in Andrew Johnson's elevation to the Presidency. Although he had taken little part in wartime debates on Reconstruction policy, Hale had endorsed the position of Benjamin Wade, Henry Winter Davis, and others who favored a congressionally controlled program designed to chastise the rebel leaders and to protect the rights and liberties of Negroes in the South.[110] Johnson, whose proclamations as war governor of Tennessee revealed his bitter hatred of disloyal slaveholders, seemed likely to walk in step with the Radicals in reconstructing the Union. After a private interview with Johnson soon after Lincoln's death, Hale declared himself "highly satisfied" with the new President's views.[111] Wade felt sure that he had found a powerful ally when Lincoln's successor swore: "Treason must be made infamous and traitors must be impoverished," and Charles Sumner declared: "I am confident that our ideas will prevail.[112] Midsummer brought the first stormclouds of disillusionment, but by then Hale was thousands of miles away.

CHAPTER XII

An American in Spain

W HEN the British steamer *Africa* churned out of Boston harbor on June 21, 1865, and set course for Liverpool, she carried as passengers the United States Minister to Spain, his wife and daughters. The final weeks before their sailing had been busy and exciting for all the Hales. Mrs. Hale, Lizzie, and Lucy hastily crammed their minds with Spanish verbs and nouns much as they crammed their trunks with gowns and shoes, while the head of the family gave last-minute instructions to young John Varney, who was to manage Hale's Dover affairs during his absence. Not until the steady strokes of the *Africa's* engine put New England's shore behind them, could they relax and reflect upon the new life which lay ahead.[1]

Of his official duties, Hale had at least a rough idea what to expect, thanks to the long, informative letters of Horatio J. Perry, secretary of the American legation at Madrid. George Fogg gave him advice based on his own diplomatic experiences in Switzerland, and he received the usual briefing from State Department officials. But beyond a rather superficial understanding of recent Spanish-American relations and a rudimentary knowledge of legation affairs, all was a mystery. Never having traveled abroad, he knew next to nothing of the peoples, customs, and languages of modern Europe. Unlike his wife and daughters, he had not yet found time to acquaint himself with the Spanish tongue.[2]

Hale was seasick much of the voyage and was glad when the *Africa* finally moored at Liverpool early in July. From Liverpool the Hales went directly to London. There they put up at a fashionable hotel not far from Westminster and for two weeks traipsed about the city, guided by solicitous American diplomats, surveying the Tower of London, Westminster Abbey, the halls of Parliament, and other historic places.[3] Minister Charles Francis Adams took Mr. and Mrs. Hale to visit Lord John Russell and escorted them to an evening party at Lord Palmerston's. "I was pleased with Palmerston," Hale confided later, "not so with Russell." The latter's "shuffling, contemptible hypocritical course" toward the North during the Civil War was a sin Hale found hard to forgive.[4]

After a fortnight in London, the Hales crossed the channel to France. Letters from Perry advised Hale that since the Spanish Queen Isabella II had left Madrid for the summer, he could not expect to present his credentials before September and might as well stay until then in cooler northern Europe.[5] Accordingly, after two weeks of sightseeing in Paris, the American minister, his wife, and daughters, began a leisurely journey across the continent: from Paris to Brussels, Antwerp, Aix la Chapelle, Cologne and finally Berne. At Berne, Fogg (then in his last days as minister) welcomed them and proved himself a thoughtful and attentive host. Hale was deeply moved by the grandeur of the Alps and the mighty glaciers which descended their slopes. But best of all, he reported to a Dover friend: "We had then the only specimen of real genuine cooking after our homely fashion that we have seen, since we left home, with one exception"—and that exception at an *American* restaurant in Paris! [6]

Returning to Paris in September, Hale settled his family in a hotel and, with the understanding that they would join him in a month or two, entrained alone for Madrid. Soon after his arrival he learned that the Queen would receive him at La Granja, a mountainside palace some forty miles northwest of Madrid.[7]

The monarch to whom Hale presented his credentials, Queen Isabella II, had for twenty-two years ruled a nation in which strong currents of liberalism and industrialism relentlessly eroded the bases of a repressive and reactionary Establishment. Although her generosity and sincere devotion to the Catholic faith endeared her to many of her subjects, Isabella's rule was an amalgam of scandal, disorder, and intrigue which alienated numbers of influential Spaniards and paved the way for her downfall.[8] Throughout the past half century, revolutions had been more the rule than the exception in Spain, and, Hale soon learned, were not popular upheavals but rather the affairs of noblemen who, in league with portions of the army, sought to force their way into the Queen's cabinet.[9] Already a revolution was brewing, however, which aimed to overthrow not just an unpopular ministry but the Bourbon dynasty as well.

The presentation ceremony took place in the Queen's chambers on the afternoon of September 30. Before an audience which included the King Consort, one lady in waiting, and several high-ranking Spanish grandees, Hale, arrayed in full court dress and feeling for all the world "like a clown in the circus," [10] made his three bows to the Queen, presented his letter from the President, and exchanged with Her Highness the customary expressions of friendship and respect between nations. "I was very cool & collected and delivered what I had to say in an entirely unembarrassed manner," he later boasted to his wife. After the ceremony, the Queen expressed her pleasure at having Hale as a representative to her court. Hale then made his exit, the whole affair having taken but half an hour.[11]

During his four years in Spain, Hale had few official duties besides attendance at such ceremonial functions as this. From time to time he sent dispatches to Secretary Seward apprising him of the state of Spanish politics. He sought to use his good offices to promote a settlement of Spain's dispute with Peru, Chile, Bolivia, and Ecuador, and tactfully raised with the Spanish government the delicate subject of slavery in Cuba and Puerto Rico. In 1868 he won Seward's praise for his "diligence and discretion" in dealing with the revolutionary government which after numerous abortive attempts drove Queen Isabella from her throne. Routine diplomatic chores also took some of Hale's time: obtaining release for American sailors from Spanish jails, remonstrating against what the United States considered unduly stringent quarantine restrictions on American ships, marrying American citizens resident in Spain, entertaining visiting Americans and foreign diplomatists.[12] Yet so insignificant was his role in an era of Spanish-American good feeling that the standard account of *The Relations of the United States and Spain* omits Hale's name.[13]

Indeed, what preoccupied Hale during these years was an increasingly bitter feud with Secretary of Legation Horatio Perry, a feud which ultimately resulted in Hale's recall. Relations between the two men had at first been cordial. Perry, a tall, handsome man in his forties, had known Hale slightly since 1846 when as a Keene, New Hampshire, youth he had applauded Hale's fight against pro-Texas Democrats. Hale had been responsible for Perry's appointment as Secretary of Legation in Madrid (a post which, except for brief intervals, he had held since 1849), and when Lincoln picked Hale as Minister to Spain, Perry cheered: "The President could not have found in the whole country another minister whom it would be so agreeable to me to serve as Secretary." Hale's conduct, character, and ability, he had gushed, "make me look up to you almost as a father." [14]

Hale at first reciprocated this friendly feeling. Yet within months antagonism appeared. Perry and his Spanish wife were "so perfectly acquainted with Spanish manners, customs, & above all language," Hale presently complained, "that it renders me very dependent on them & gives them the appearance of patronizing me." Such patronizing was not displayed offensively, he admitted, but it was irritating all the same.[15] Moreover, Perry's consuming desire to rule the legation in fact if not in name soon collided with Hale's firm intention of running his own shop.

The first serious clash occurred in May 1866 when Hale insisted that his secretary cease lobbying for an American cable company in which Perry had an interest. [16] Perry's neglect of official duties, his behind-the-back letters to Seward about purely diplomatic affairs, and his connivance with Spanish revolutionaries kept the quarrel festering. By the summer of 1867 communication between the two had all but ended. There were literally months on end when Perry did not set foot in the legation. Secretary Seward, aware of Hale's shortcomings as a diplomat and bothered by rumors that he had

denounced "in a malignant manner" President Johnson's Reconstruction policies, responded to this state of affairs by asking for
Hale's resignation.[17] But Hale, stunned and hurt by what he viewed
as an act of injustice, managed to hang on a while longer. The aid
of Radical friends in the Senate, together with Seward's declining
prestige, enabled him to ride out the storm: 1868 closed with Hale
still at his post, railing more and more hysterically against the per-
fidy of his tormentors and looking forward eagerly to the inauguration of the Grant Administration and the appointment of a new
Secretary of State.[18]

His hopes were soon blighted. After Grant's election, Hale felt
strong enough to appoint Edward V. Kinsley (a young New York
businessman who had recently married Lizzie) as his *private* secretary and in December launched efforts to have Perry removed.[19]
Determined that if necessary he would pull Hale down with him,
the secretary retaliated by making public certain documents which
seemed to show that Hale had abused his franchise for the importation of goods free of duty. The disclosure had its desired effect, for
before the tempest it aroused had subsided, both minister and secretary had lost their posts.

The substance of Perry's sensational revelations, contained in a
lengthy letter to Seward on March 2, 1869, soon leaked to the newspapers. In the fall of 1866 the Spanish Collector of Customs, suspicious at the large quantities of cotton stuff, woolen felt, and carpets
imported duty free by the United States minister, had traced these
articles and found that they went not to Hale's residence but to
dry goods and home furnishing stores in Madrid. Further investigation convinced Spanish officials that this was Hale's way of squaring
accounts with merchants to whom he was in debt. At this point,
according to Perry, a Cabinet council discussed the complaints of
customs officers against the American envoy, and decided to make
no formal protest but merely to give Hale an unofficial warning.
When informed of the Cabinet's decision by Perry (whose "tactful"
intermediation was supposed to sweeten the pill!), Hale had stormed,
but at the secretary's suggestion he had acted to stop all further

imports in his name.[20] So, at least, Perry alleged. Unfortunately for Hale, the secretary's charges reached Washington just in time to be included with other Perry-Seward-Hale correspondence which the Senate had recently ordered printed by way of investigating affairs in the Spanish legation. Even the minister's staunchest supporters in the Senate found the printed correspondence damaging to him. "There are many things that reflect upon Perry," said Aaron Cragin after reading the letters from Spain, "and I am sorry to say there are some things that reflect upon Hale. I hope they can be explained."[21]

As best he could—in letters to friendly senators and influential newspapers—Hale defended his conduct. To the charge that goods imported in his name had been offered for sale in Madrid stores, he flatly answered: "I can only say if it were so it was without my knowledge or consent."[22] All applications to the Spanish government for the importation of articles for his use or for the use of the legation, he rather lamely asserted, had been made out by Perry *in Spanish*. He had blindly signed what his secretary had prepared, not knowing for sure what he was signing. Furthermore, the value of articles brought into Spain under his diplomatic privilege was less than half the permissible amount. Perry himself, Hale claimed, had imported much more, including nine carriages and sixty-seven cases of wine in the space of six years.[23]

It is difficult to know precisely where the truth lay in this matter. Perry's indictment—echoed by members of the Spanish Cortes in April 1869—seems credible enough, yet there are inaccuracies in his account which create doubts.[24] Papers like the *Independent Democrat* may have been closest to the truth when they suggested that Hale's conduct had been irregular in form but not in substance, that he had simply repaid Madrid merchants in kind for household furnishings he had bought from them earlier.[25] Nevertheless, Secretary of State Hamilton Fish appears to have accepted as true charges of Hale's "smuggling"—or he may simply have wished to clean house at Madrid. At any rate, on April 6, before Hale had had a chance to present his defense, he asked for his resignation. Angry that he should be thus condemned without a fair hearing, Hale icily replied to Fish that the accusations against him were maliciously false, stemming "from motives of vengeance," and complained of his unfair treatment. "I am sensible that mine is not the only instance in which one of the first victims of a triumphant party has been one of its earliest leaders," he remarked pointedly. But he was tired of quarrel and acrimony, he said, and if, after reading his statement, the President still wanted his resignation, he would give it effective July 1. He later regretted that he had offered this somewhat tentative resignation and on May 25 he sought to withdraw it. But by then it was too late. General Daniel E. Sickles, a swashbuckling soldier of fortune, had already been appointed to replace him. Hale's sole consolation was that Perry too had lost his post.[26]

Hale's row with Perry and his earlier feud with Welles were of a piece—the irate outbursts of a used-up man. Not that they were all of Hale's making; it takes two to quarrel. Yet so paranoic did Hale become, that one suspects that had antagonists not readily appeared he would have beat the bushes until they did. To some extent, of course, the gall of his last dozen years fed on ill health. The National Hotel sickness, followed soon after by an acute attack of erysipelas, destroyed his earlier robustness and taxed his good humor. The years in Spain brought precipitous physical decline. But illness merely heightened a combativeness, a bitterness stemming from other causes.

For all his earlier good-naturedness, Hale had won his biggest victories by fighting, by fighting alone against the "defenders of slavery." His singlehanded battles against "doughfaces" like Pierce and Southerners like Calhoun and Foote raised him to a heady prominence. Quite naturally, therefore, once the war came and the real fight against slavery switched from Congress to the battlefield, Hale sought new foes. That he found them within his own party is hardly surprising. Certainly by 1864, and probably even earlier, the feeling that Republicans had treated him shabbily nourished his willingness to attack "evil" wherever he found it. By the time

Hale reached Spain, he was a thoroughly embittered man. Accustomed to thinking in terms of conspiracy where slavery was concerned, he now discovered within the Republican party a plot to thrust aside its old leaders and ideals and put in their place self-serving scoundrels dedicated to hustle and grab. He himself had been marked for political assassination—Welles and Fox, Chandler and Ordway, Seward and Perry, had conspired to bring him down. Hence the bitterness and disillusionment that poisoned his later years.

The tragedy, of course, is not merely that Hale descended into petty squabbles with his "oppressors." More deeply tragic is that these enervating feuds prevented him from giving more than passing attention to the antislavery movement at its moment of triumph. Wartime emancipation and the supremely important task of Reconstruction proceeded without much help from Hale. For the pioneer had lost his way.

General Sickles assumed the duties of Minister to Spain on July 27, 1869, and a week later Hale, his wife, and Lucy left Madrid for Paris. August and September they spent in the French capital, where Lizzie and her husband had recently taken up residence; most of the winter of 1869–1870 found them in Rome. Hale's health had broken during his last year in Spain, and he hoped that by postponing his return to New Hampshire until spring he might, in the milder Mediterranean climate, recuperate more quickly. Lately he had suffered from a recurrence of the itchy rash which had accompanied his National Hotel illness. Neither the prescriptions of Dr. Delpeche, a Parisian physician, nor his own pet remedy—cold baths and a rough towel rub—brought lasting relief, and sleepless nights robbed him of energy. Unhappily, the winter in Rome produced no real recovery either. When in June he returned at last to America it was as an old man, "his manly form crippled and shrunken."[27]

If Hale had left Spain under a cloud, the citizens of Dover, New Hampshire betrayed no signs of knowing it. In April the city council had adopted resolutions warmly praising their famous townsman and expressing "an unabated confidence in his integrity, patriotism and unsullied honor." At the same time, the council appointed a committee to plan a gala reception for Hale, that the citizens of Dover and neighboring towns might have an occasion "to testify their respect and love for him" after his absence of five years. By Dover's standards, what followed was indeed "a reception of which kings might have been proud." A four-man welcoming committee met the ex-minister and his family upon their arrival in Boston and escorted them on the last leg of their homeward journey. As their train slowed to a stop at Dover on the afternoon of June 15, the salute of cannons and wild ringing of bells suddenly shattered the late-spring calm. Stepping gingerly from the train at the depot, Hale saw before him a swarm of friendly faces: city officials, military officers, police and firemen, benevolent societies, bands, and thousands of others. From the depot, Hale, followed by the clamorous throng of well-wishers, rode to the Kimball House where bands struck up "Hail to the Chief" and the mayor officially welcomed him "to the homes and hearts of this people." After Hale had expressed his "deep and generous gratitude," and assured his hearers of his joy at being once more in his native New Hampshire, the procession reformed and to the sprightly music of the Cocheco and Dover Cornet bands proceeded to his home. That evening there was a great testimonial meeting in the city hall at which Dover's illustrious son replied to a long string of welcoming addresses by proclaiming his delight at being again among "the green pastures and tranquil scenes of this, my old home." "Here have I returned," he said, "hoping to regain in my native air the health which has been somewhat impaired by my long residence abroad, and here amongst my old friends and neighbors, I desire to pass the remainder of my days." [28]

Instead of improving, however, Hale's health worsened. His letters during these years bear the marks of physical and mental deterioration: an increasingly shaky hand and, at times, a confused, rambling mind.[29] Shortly after his return to Dover he suffered a stroke which for a time paralyzed his right side. By 1871, however, he had recovered sufficiently to make a trip to Washington where he walked and talked with old friends and reminisced about the antislavery crusade which had so filled the best years of his life. He journeyed to Washington once again the following year, but for the most part he stuck close to home, filling long hours poking about his garden, playing backgammon with his wife, taking buggy rides with Lucy, reading, or just dozing in his rockingchair.[30]

Despite his failing health, Hale's spirits were usually high. Nor did his sense of humor fail him, as these sentences, from what may have been his last letter, show:

> Yesterday your uncle Thomas preached at the Episcopal church in this town [he informed Lizzie in the spring of 1873], but as the walking was bad, very bad indeed[,] he so far forgot the proprieties of the day & the occasion that he actually hired a carriage & two horses to take them to church, & he a minister! What kind of religion can that be, preached by a man who goes to church & back again with a hired horse? Oh tempora, Oh tempora, Oh Mores!!! Tempora Mutantur et nos cum illis.[31]

It did depress him, though, when his eye caught newspaper notices like that in the Portsmouth *Journal* which announced: "Hon. John P. Hale . . . may be seen occasionally, on pleasant days, taking short and easy drives. But it is understood that his vigor, both of body and mind, is gradually failing." The papers were "thoughtless," Mrs. Hale protested; but they were correct.[32]

In July 1873 Hale broke and dislocated his right leg at the hip in a fall from his chair. It was a shock which his already weakened system could not absorb. The leg refused to mend, his senses grew progressively more dull, and at 9 o'clock on the evening of November 19, 1873, he peacefully died, comforted to the end by his unshaken conviction that the God of his life was the God of life everlasting.[33]

Under the leaden skies of a November morn, Hale's body was placed to rest in Pine Hill cemetery, a short walk from his home. All Dover businesses closed that day and churchbells tolled steadily. On hand to assist in the funeral service was Hale's old friend and adviser, the Rev. John Parkman. And among the pallbearers who accompanied the body to the grave were George G. Fogg, Mason Tappan, Daniel Clark, Gilman Marston—faithful followers who, like Parkman, recognized the words chiseled deep into Hale's headstone:

HE WHO LIES BENEATH SURRENDERED OFFICE,
PLACE AND POWER RATHER THAN BOW DOWN AND WORSHIP SLAVERY[34]

A NOTE ON SOURCES

MANUSCRIPTS CITED

NOTES

INDEX

A NOTE ON SOURCES

By far the most valuable source for this study is the collection of John P. Hale's private papers at the New Hampshire Historical Society in Concord. Included in that collection are some 5,000 pieces of Hale's correspondence, fragmentary letterbooks covering a few, scattered years in Hale's life, a scrapbook, copies of speeches, certificates, and miscellaneous memorabilia. This collection now includes a trunkful of letters that, midway through my research, Mrs. Austin P. Palmer of Hopkinton, New Hampshire, discovered in her barn, and graciously turned over to the New Hampshire Historical Society. This windfall of letters written by Hale to his family between 1830 and 1870 enormously enriches the Hale Collection and has made this biography possible.

Besides the main collection of Hale manuscripts in Concord, there are two very minor collections. One, at Phillips Exeter Academy in Exeter, New Hampshire, contains some forty or fifty letters from Hale to other New Englanders; the other, at the Minnesota Historical Society in St. Paul, comprises a dozen or so letters to or from Hale.

Unfortunately, although at times very full, Hale's papers are occasionally sketchy. It was exasperating, for example, to find that although the manuscript record of Hale's uneventful years in Spain is amazingly complete, there exist but a handful of letters that shed any light on his conversion to antislavery or his decision to break with the New Hampshire Democrats in 1845. Moreover, the often revealing letters which Hale wrote to his wife, of course, stopped whenever she joined him at Washington or he returned to Dover. Regretfully, the Hale letters in the possession of Richard Rolfe of Concord, New Hampshire, which might have filled some of these gaps, were not open for examination.

Supplementing Hale's own papers are those of other nineteenth-century politicians and reformers. For the New Hampshire part of my story, the manuscript collections of Amos Tuck, Edmund Burke, Charles Warren Brewster, George G. Fogg, Benjamin B. French, Franklin Pierce, William Plumer, Jr., Mason W. Tappan, and Levi Woodbury were most rewarding. Manuscript "Records of the First Unitarian Society of Christians in Dover, N. H. formed September 4th, 1827" reveal Hale's defense of John Parkman's abolitionist sermons. Most helpful in reconstructing Hale's career in national politics were the papers of Charles Sumner, Charles Francis Adams, Richard Henry Dana, Jr., Joshua Giddings, Salmon P. Chase, and Gideon Welles.

Hale's impact upon his contemporaries—friends and enemies alike—is most easily discerned in the newspapers of the day. In New Hampshire, the *Independent Democrat* (published briefly at Manchester and thereafter at Concord) never swerved from its original intention "to support the candidacy of John P. Hale." Most influential of the opposition journals (after 1845) were the Concord *New Hampshire Patriot,* Dover *Gazette,* and Newport *Argus & Spectator,* while in the Exeter *News-Letter* the historian finds, *mirabile dictu,* a generally impartial antebellum newspaper. Newspapers edited at Concord provide the best accounts of debates in the New Hampshire legislature as well as official election returns and various state announcements. Of the newspapers outside the Granite State, only two need mention here. The *National Era,* published in Washington between 1847 and 1859 as an organ of the American and Foreign Anti-Slavery Society, consistently supported Hale and provided the fullest, if most partial, account of his activities on Capitol Hill. William Lloyd Garrison's *Liberator,* alternately pleased and exasperated at Hale's Senate speeches on slavery, illuminates the split between political and nonpolitical abolitionists.

Printed public records—the journals of the New Hampshire Senate and House of Representatives, state laws, the official records of Congress —all help to trace Hale's public career and to place him in the context of his times. *The Congressional Globe* provides accurate texts of Hale's remarks in Congress, since Hale, unlike most congressmen, never bothered to revise his speeches after delivery. The complete record of his official correspondence as Minister to Spain is to be found in the United States Department of State Diplomatic Correspondence (Spain, 1865–1869), National Archives. Much of that correspondence appears in *Papers Relating to Foreign Affairs, Accompanying the Annual Message of the President,* 1865–1870 (Washington, 1866–1871). Thomas H. McKee, *The National Conventions and Platforms of all Parties, 1789–1904,* 5 ed. (Baltimore, 1904) collects election statistics as well as party platforms, and James D. Richardson, comp., *A Compilation of the Messages and Papers of the Presidents,* 20 vols. (New York, 1897–1927) conveniently gathers Presidential pronouncements.

Published reminiscences of Hale's contemporaries shed light on both the man and his times. Some, for example John L. Hayes, *A Reminiscence of the Free-Soil Movement in New Hampshire, 1845* (Cambridge, 1885) and *Reunion of the Free-Soilers of 1848, at Downer Landing, Hingham, Mass., August 9, 1877* (Boston, 1877) illuminate particular events in Hale's career. Others, notably George W. Bungay, *Crayon Sketches and Off-Hand Takings* (Boston, 1852); Oliver Dyer, *Great Senators of the United States Forty Years Ago* (New York, 1889); Henry S. Foote, *Casket of Reminiscences* (Washington, 1874); George W. Julian, *Political Recollections, 1840 to 1872* (Chicago, 1883); Ben: Perley Poore, *Perley's Reminiscences of Sixty Years in the National Metropolis,* 2 vols. (Philadelphia, 1886); Frederick W. Seward, *Reminiscences of a War-Time Statesman and Diplomat, 1830–1915* (New York, 1916); Henry B. Stanton, *Random Recollections,* 3 ed. (New York, 1887); and Amos Tuck, *Autobiographical Memoirs of Amos Tuck* (n.p., 1902) speak more generally of Hale's personality and of the events which concerned him. William E. Chandler, *The Statue of John P. Hale* (Concord, N.H., 1892) contains a windy and unedifying eulogy of Hale by his Dover friend Daniel Hall, together with several reminiscences by other acquaintances, all delivered upon the occasion of the unveiling of Hale's statue at Concord in 1892.

For the work of other historians whose writing touches on the problems and events discussed in this book, I refer the reader to Oscar Handlin, *et al., The Harvard Guide to American History* (Cambridge, Mass., 1954) and to my own notes. I should add, also, that a reawakened interest in the antislavery movement has produced in the last decade new biographies of William Lloyd Garrison, Wendell Phillips, Charles Sumner, John G. Palfrey, Charles Francis Adams, Richard Henry Dana, Jr., Thomas Wentworth Higginson, Cassius M. Clay, Elijah P. Lovejoy, James G. Birney, Thaddeus Stevens, William Pitt Fessenden, and Benjamin Wade, as well as more general studies, notably Louis Filler, *The Crusade Against Slavery, 1830–1860* (New York, 1960) and Dwight L. Dumond, *Antislavery: The Crusade for Freedom in America* (Ann Arbor, 1961). These works are perhaps most conspicuous for their differences of emphasis and interpretation, yet each in its way brings us nearer to an understanding of the greatest reform movement in American history.

MANUSCRIPTS CITED

Charles Francis Adams Papers, microfilm, Widener Library, Harvard University

James Franklin Aldrich Papers, Chicago Historical Society

Antislavery Papers, American Antiquarian Society

Charles G. Atherton Papers, New Hampshire Historical Society

Bell Family Papers, New Hampshire Historical Society

Boston Vigilance Committee, Treasurers' Accounts, photostatic copy in Widener Library, Harvard University

Charles Warren Brewster Papers, New Hampshire Historical Society

Edmund Burke Papers, Library of Congress

Anson Burlingame Papers, Library of Congress

John C. Calhoun Papers, Chicago Historical Society

Simon Cameron Papers, Library of Congress

Robert Carter Papers, Houghton Library, Harvard University

William E. Chandler Papers, New Hampshire Historical Society

Salmon P. Chase Papers, Library of Congress

Salmon P. Chase Papers, New Hampshire Historical Society

Salmon P. Chase Papers, Pennsylvania Historical Society

George M. Dallas, Diary, photostatic copy in Pennsylvania Historical Society

Richard Henry Dana Papers, Massachusetts Historical Society

Moses M. Davis Papers, State Historical Society of Wisconsin

James R. Doolittle Papers, State Historical Society of Wisconsin

John Farmer Papers, New Hampshire Historical Society

Hamilton Fish Papers, Library of Congress

Azariah Flagg Papers, New York Public Library

George G. Fogg Papers, New Hampshire Historical Society

Stephen S. Foster Papers, American Antiquarian Society

Gustavus V. Fox Papers, New-York Historical Society

Benjamin Brown French Papers, Library of Congress

William Lloyd Garrison Papers, Boston Public Library

Joshua Reed Giddings Papers, Ohio Historical Society

Giddings-Julian Papers, Library of Congress
John Parker Hale Papers, Phillips Exeter Academy
John Parker Hale Papers, Minnesota Historical Society
John Parker Hale Papers, New Hampshire Historical Society
Albert R. Hatch Papers, New Hampshire Historical Society
Harry Hibbard Collection, New Hampshire Historical Society
George Frisbie Hoar Papers, Massachusetts Historical Society
Mark Howard Papers, Connecticut Historical Society
Timothy O. Howe Papers, State Historical Society of Wisconsin
Joshua Leavitt Papers, Library of Congress
Abraham Lincoln Papers, Henry E. Huntington Library and Art Gallery
Abraham Lincoln Papers, Library of Congress
Asa McFarland Papers, New Hampshire Historical Society
John McLean Papers, Library of Congress
Samuel J. May Papers, Boston Public Library
Jacob B. Moore Papers, Houghton Library, Harvard University
John Gorham Palfrey Papers, Houghton Library, Harvard University
Franklin Pierce Papers, Library of Congress
Franklin Pierce Papers, New Hampshire Historical Society
William Plumer Papers, New Hampshire State Library
Records of the First Unitarian Society of Christians in Dover, N.H.
    formed September 4th, 1827, Unitarian-Universalist Association,
    Boston, Massachusetts
William Henry Seward Collection, Rush Rhees Library, University of
    Rochester
Charles Sumner Papers, Houghton Library, Harvard University
Mason W. Tappan Papers, New Hampshire Historical Society
Amos Tuck Papers, Dartmouth College Archives
Amos Tuck Papers, New Hampshire Historical Society
United States Department of State Records, National Archives, Wash-
    ington, D.C.
Benjamin F. Wade Papers, Library of Congress
Israel Washburn Papers, Library of Congress
Elihu Washburne Papers, Library of Congress
Daniel Webster Papers, New Hampshire Historical Society
Thurlow Weed Collection, Rush Rhees Library, University of Rochester
Gideon Welles Papers, Connecticut Historical Society
Gideon Welles Papers, Library of Congress
Anne W. Weston Papers, Boston Public Library
John Greenleaf Whittier Papers, Oak Knoll Collection, Essex Institute
Levi Woodbury Papers, Library of Congress

NOTES

The following short titles have been used throughout these notes:

Cong. Globe	*The Congressional Globe*
Hale Papers	John Parker Hale Papers, New Hampshire Historical Society
N.H. House Journal	*Journal of the House of Representatives of the State of New-Hampshire*
N.H. Senate Journal	*Journal of the Honorable Senate of the State of New-Hampshire*

NOTES TO CHAPTER I: BEGINNINGS

1. [Boston] *Liberator,* May 13, 1853. The quotation is a variation on a stanza in John Greenleaf Whittier's poem, "To William Lloyd Garrison."

2. John Langdon Sibley, *Biographical Sketches of Graduates of Harvard University, in Cambridge, Massachusetts,* I (Cambridge, 1873), 509–519.

3. Charles H. Bell, *The Bench and Bar of New Hampshire* (Cambridge, Mass., 1894), pp. 419–420; Ezra S. Stearns, ed., *Genealogical and Family History of the State of New Hampshire,* 4 vols. (New York, 1908), III, 1044; John P. Hale to E. Hale, July 29, 1846, John Parker Hale Papers, Phillips Exeter Academy Library.

4. Bell, *Bench and Bar,* pp. 414–415; Hamilton D. Hurd, comp., *History of Rockingham and Strafford Counties, New Hampshire, with Biographical Sketches of Many of its Pioneers and Prominent Men* (Philadelphia, 1882), p. 602; Franklin McDuffee, *History of the Town of Rochester, New Hampshire, from 1722 to 1890,* Silvanus Hayward, ed., 2 vols. (Manchester, N.H., 1892), II, 451; John P. Hale, Sr. to William Hale, June 18, 1798, Jan. 29, 1800, Dec. 24, 1812, Dec. 13, 1814, Jan. 30, 1815, Hale Papers.

5. McDuffee, *History of Rochester,* I, 161; Hurd, *History of Rockingham and Strafford Counties,* p. 592.

6. Hale, Sr. to William Hale, Aug. 1, 1810, Hale Papers.

7. Lydia O'Brien Hale to Hale, June 27, 1822, Hale Papers.

8. Myron R. Williams, *The Story of Phillips Exeter* (Exeter, N.H., 1957), ch. iv; *Catalogue of the Officers and Students of Phillips Exeter Academy, November, 1823* (Exeter, N.H., 1823), p. 7; *General Catalogue of the Officers*

and Students of Phillips Exeter Academy, 1793–1903 (Exeter, N.H., 1903), pp. 30–31.

9. Frank H. Cunningham, *Familiar Sketches of the Phillips Exeter Academy and Surroundings* (Boston, 1883), p. 146.

10. *Catalogue of Bowdoin College, February, 1823* (Brunswick, Me.), p. 14.

11. Nehemiah Cleaveland and Alpheus S. Packard, *History of Bowdoin College* (Boston, 1882), pp. 1–14, 83–102; George A. Wheeler and Henry W. Wheeler, *History of Brunswick, Topsham, and Harpswell, Maine, Including the Ancient Territory Known as Pejepscot* (Boston, 1878), pp. 498–510; Lawrance Thompson, *Young Longfellow, 1807–1843* (New York, 1938), p. 24.

12. *General Catalogue of Bowdoin College and the Medical School of Maine, 1794–1894* (Brunswick, Me., 1894), p. lvi.

13. Cleaveland and Packard, *History of Bowdoin College,* p. 368.

14. Lewis G. Barnes to Hale, Dec. 8, 1825, Hale Papers.

15. *Catalogue of the* [Bowdoin College] *Athenaean Society, 1853* (Brunswick, Me., 1853), pp. 3–8.

16. Nathaniel Hawthorne, *The Works of Nathaniel Hawthorne,* Standard Library ed., 15 vols. (Boston, 1882–1884), XII, 357; Roy F. Nichols, *Franklin Pierce: Young Hickory of the Granite Hills,* rev. ed. (Philadelphia, 1958), p. 25; *Catalogue of the* [Bowdoin College] *Athenaean Society: to Which is Added a List of the Books Belonging to the Library, 1838* (Brunswick, Me., 1838), pp. 8–9, 14.

17. Horatio Bridge, *Personal Recollections of Nathaniel Hawthorne* (New York, 1893), pp. 39–40, 45; Nichols, *Pierce,* p. 57; Charles Choate to [Caleb Stark], Jan. 26, 1860, Dartmouth College Archives.

18. Samuel S. Boyd to Hale, May 5, 1827, Hale Papers.

19. David Barker, Jr. to Hale, May 31, 1827, Hale Papers.

20. Jeremiah H. Woodman to Hale, July 25, 1827, Hale Papers; McDuffee, *History of Rochester,* I, 332–333; II, 381–382.

21. Bell, *Bench and Bar,* pp. 258–262.

22. George Wadleigh, *Notable Events in the History of Dover, New Hampshire, from the First Settlement in 1623 to 1865* (Dover, 1913), p. 230; Bell, *Bench and Bar,* p. 417; Hale to Ichabod Bartlett, Oct. 3, 1831, Hale Papers.

23. There is no adequate history of New Hampshire politics for any part of the national period. Most helpful for the pre-Jacksonian years are William A. Robinson, *Jeffersonian Democracy in New England* (New Haven, 1916); Lynn W. Turner, *William Plumer of New Hampshire, 1759–1850* (Chapel Hill, 1962), chs. xiv–xvi; and Nichols, *Pierce,* chs. ii, iv, and v. Also useful, although less trustworthy, is volume III of Everett S. Stackpole's *History of New Hampshire,* 4 vols. (New York, 1916).

24. Jacob B. Moore to M. Carter, Oct. 5, 1821, Jacob B. Moore Papers, Houghton Library, Harvard University.

25. Stackpole, *History of New Hampshire,* III, 77–78; [Concord] *New Hampshire Patriot,* Feb. 3, 1828.

26. William Plumer, Jr. to Levi Woodbury, May 1, 1824, Levi Woodbury Papers, Library of Congress.

27. *New Hampshire Patriot,* Feb. 3, Mar. 3, 1823; Josiah Butler to Jacob B. Moore, Dec. 6, 1824, Moore Papers; William Plumer to Levi Woodbury, April 5, 1826, Woodbury Papers; Jacob B. Moore to Samuel Bell, Feb. 9, 1827, Bell Family Papers, New Hampshire Historical Society.

28. Barker to Hale, March 24, 1828, Hale Papers.

29. James Parkam to Hale, Jan. 7, April 7, 1828, Hale Papers.

30. [Dover] *Strafford Inquirer,* Oct. 7, 1828.

31. See Marvin Meyers' suggestive essay on Cooper in his *The Jacksonian Persuasion: Politics and Belief* (Stanford, Calif., 1957), pp. 42–75.

32. Cleaveland and Packard, *History of Bowdoin College,* pp. 370–371.

33. Nathaniel R. Long to Hale, Jan. 27, 1831, Hale Papers.

34. [Dover] *Enquirer,* March 20, 1832.

NOTES TO CHAPTER II: POLITICAL APPRENTICESHIP

1. Hale to Thomas Lambert, June 14, 1835, Hale Papers; Richard Henry Dana, Jr., Journal, June 1, 1851, Richard Henry Dana Papers, Massachusetts Historical Society.

2. Hale to Mrs. Hale, May 15, 1840, Hale Papers.

3. Hale to Mrs. Hale, May 27, 1840, Aug. 6, 1841, July 18, 1842, Hale Papers. One brother, Samuel Augustus, moved to Tuscaloosa, Alabama, in 1837, seeking health and fortune. There, lonely and ill, he struggled for years to "gain but a bare foothold on the thresholds of society." In time, advantageous marriages left him a rich and socially prominent slaveholder. A Democratic Unionist before the Civil War, Augustus became during Reconstruction a maverick Republican who criticised carpetbag rule. Samuel Augustus Hale to Hale, Nov. 8, 1838, July 18, 1840, Hale Papers; Hunter Dickinson Farish, "An Overlooked Personality in Southern Life," *The North Carolina Historical Review* 12: 341–353 (October 1935).

4. *New Hampshire Patriot,* March 19, 1832. The vote in the House and Senate on a joint resolution approving Jackson's antinullification proclamation of Dec. 10, 1832, and praising in dithyrambic terms his leadership and the measures of his administration provides further information about political alignments. See *N.H. House Journal,* Nov. sess. (1832), pp. 102–103 and *N.H. Senate Journal,* Nov. sess. (1832), p. 43.

5. *Ibid.* Generally speaking, National Republicans were strongest in regions where Federalists had flourished forty years before. See Jackson T. Main, *The Antifederalists: Critics of the Constitution, 1781–1788* (Chapel Hill, N.C., 1961), p. 221–222.

6. Everett S. Stackpole, *History of New Hampshire,* 4 vols. (New York, 1916), III, 72; Franklin McDuffee, *History of the Town of Rochester, New Hampshire, from 1722 to 1890,* Silvanus Hayward, ed., 2 vols. (Manchester, N.H., 1892), I, 293–302; Clifford S. Griffin, *Their Brothers' Keepers: Moral*

Stewardship in the United States, 1800–1865 (New Brunswick, N.J., 1960), p. 38; Alice Felt Tyler, *Freedom's Ferment: Phases of American Social History to 1860* (Minneapolis, 1944), pp. 322–327.

7. *Laws of New Hampshire Including Public and Private Acts, Resolves, Votes, etc.,* 10 vols. (Concord, 1904–1922), IX, 684–686; X, 29.

8. James O. Lyford, ed., *History of Concord, New Hampshire,* 2 vols. (Concord, 1903), I, 373–376.

9. [Dover] *Gazette,* June 19, 1832; *N.H. House Journal, June sess.* (1832), p. 24.

10. [Dover] *Gazette,* July 3, 1832.

11. Roy F. Nichols, *Franklin Pierce: Young Hickory of the Granite Hills,* rev. ed. (Philadelphia, 1958), p. 57; *N.H. House Journal,* June sess. (1832), p. 59.

12. [Dover] *Gazette,* March 19, 1833, March 18, 1834.

13. Henry Y. Simpson to Hale, Feb. 2, 1834, certificate dated April 8, 1834 appointing Hale "Attorney of the United States for the District of New Hampshire," Hale Papers.

14. Hale to Lucy Lambert, April 10, 1834, Hale Papers.

15. Hale to Mrs. Hale, Oct. 25, 1837, Aug. 20, 1839, Feb. 21, June 6, 1840, Hale to Samuel D. Bell, Sept. 18, 1838, Hale Papers.

16. [Epping] Committee of Arrangements to Hale, June 21, 1836, Edward B. Neally to Hale, July 8, 1836, Hale to Mrs. Hale, July 29, 1836, John L. Hayes to Hale, Sept. 21, 1840, John S. Wells to Hale, Sept. 18, 22, 1840, Thomas Marsh to Hale, Nov. 2, 1840, letter of appointment as Indian Stream Commissioner, June 17, 1836, Hale Papers.

17. Hale to Jeremiah Elkins, April 13, 1838, Hale Papers.

18. Lyford, ed., *History of Concord,* I, 408; William Plumer, Jr., Journal, Oct. 1840, William Plumer Papers, New Hampshire State Library.

19. Franklin Pierce to Edmund Burke, Oct. 15, 1840, Edmund Burke Papers, Library of Congress.

20. *New Hampshire Patriot,* Oct. 12, 1840; Nichols, *Pierce,* pp. 108–109.

21. Hale to Mrs. Hale, Oct. 14, 1840, Hale Papers; Pierce to Edmund Burke, Oct. 15, 1840, Burke Papers.

22. *N.H. House Journal,* June sess. (1835), p. 112; *N.H. Senate Journal,* June sess. (1835), p. 55; Edward E. Parker, ed., *History of the City of Nashua, N.H.* (Nashua, 1897), pp. 479–480.

23. Nichols, *Pierce,* pp. 118–122; *New Hampshire Patriot,* Dec. 9, 1841.

24. Lyford, ed., *History of Concord,* I, 409–410; II, 868.

25. [Concord] *Hill's New Hampshire Patriot,* Aug. 12, 1840, Jan. 7, 1842.

26. *Ibid.,* Feb. 18, 25, 1842; Lyford, ed., *History of Concord,* I, 409–410; Nichols, *Pierce,* p. 120.

27. Edmund Burke to Hale, Jan. 19, 1843, Hale Papers.

28. *Hill's New Hampshire Patriot,* March 11, 1842; [Dover] *Gazette,* April 2, 1842, Feb. 25, 1843; Nichols, *Pierce,* p. 119.

29. [Dover] *Gazette,* Feb. 19, 1842, Feb. 18, 1843; Matthew Bridge to Hale, Dec. 7, 1838, Hale to Mrs. Hale, Oct. 12, 1842, Hale Papers. In 1842 Hale undertook the defense of Dover merchants Andrew Pierce, Jr. and Thomas W. Pierce, charged with selling a barrel of gin without license from town selectmen. He carried the case to the United States Supreme Court in 1844, but Chief Justice Taney and his associates decided against Hale's argument that the New Hampshire licensing law was an unconstitutional abridgement of Congress' control over interstate commerce. 5 Howard 504.

30. [Exeter] *News-Letter,* March 14, 1843.

31. Hale to Mrs. Hale, Dec. 2, 1840, Samuel Augustus Hale to Hale, July 18, 1840, Hale Papers; [Dover] *Enquirer,* Nov. 15, 1842.

32. *Hill's New Hampshire Patriot,* Feb. 9, 16, 1843.

33. Hale to John T. Gibbs, Feb. 21, 1843, quoted in [Dover] *Gazette,* Feb. 25, 1843.

34. *Hill's New Hampshire Patriot,* March 9, 1843; Albert G. Allen to Hale, March 28, 1843, Hale Papers.

35. [Dover] *Gazette,* March 18, 1843; *New Hampshire Patriot,* March 23, 1843.

36. Lyford, ed., *History of Concord,* I, 413; Thomas McKee, *The National Conventions and Platforms of All Political Parties, 1789–1904,* 5 ed. (Baltimore, 1904), pp. 44, 56.

37. *First Annual Report of the New-Hampshire Anti-Slavery Society* (Concord, 1835).

38. Robert Adams, "Nathaniel Peabody Rogers: 1794–1846," *The New England Quarterly* 20: 365–376 (September 1947); Louis Filler, "Parker Pillsbury: An Anti-Slavery Apostle," *ibid.* 19: 315–337 (September 1946); Parker Pillsbury, *Acts of the Anti-Slavery Apostles* (Boston, 1884), pp. 28–46, 123–155; Hazel C. Wolf, *On Freedom's Altar: The Martyr Complex in the Abolition Movement* (Madison, Wis., 1952), pp. 69–70.

39. Lyford, ed., *History of Concord,* I, 411–413; *New Hampshire Patriot,* Sept. 7, 1835.

40. *N.H. Senate Journal,* June sess. (1836), pp. 30–31.

41. *Ibid.,* pp. 30–35; *N.H. House Journal,* June sess. (1839), pp. 414–422.

42. [Dover] *Gazette,* Aug. 4, 1835; *N.H. House Journal,* June sess. (1839), p. 300.

43. Nathan Lord et al. to Foster, Oct. 14, 1841, Stephen S. Foster Papers, American Antiquarian Society. When Foster proved unrepentent, the committee made good its threat of excommunication. E. D. Sanborn to Foster, Apr. 7, 1842, Foster Papers. The following year Foster brought out his pamphlet *The Brotherhood of Thieves, or A True Picture of the American Church and Clergy* (New London, 1843).

44. [Dover] *Gazette,* Aug. 25, 1835; [Dover] *Enquirer,* Aug. 25, 1835; [Concord] *Herald of Freedom,* Aug. 22, 1835.

45. *Cong Globe,* 31 Cong., 1 sess. (1849–1850), Appendix, pp. 800–803.

46. Hale to Mrs. Hale, Sept. 2, 1839, Oct. 12, 1842, April 18, 1843, Hale Papers.

47. Hale to Mrs. Hale, April 27, 1840, Hale Papers; Charles W. Woodbury to Levi Woodbury, Feb. 22, 1845, Woodbury Papers; Samuel J. May to J. B. Estlin, June 30, 1846, Samuel J. May Papers, Boston Public Library; "Records of the First Unitarian Society of Christians in Dover, N.H., formed September 4th, 1827," Unitarian-Universalist Association, Boston, Massachusetts.

48. Russel B. Nye, *Fettered Freedom: Civil Liberties and the Slavery Controversy, 1830–1860* (East Lansing, Mich., 1949), p. 250.

49. *N.H. House Journal,* June sess. (1835), p. 16, November sess. (1836), p. 187, June sess. (1836), pp. 147–151.

50. Unsigned letter to Charles W. Brewster, Jan. 4, 1837, Charles Warren Brewster Papers, New Hampshire Historical Society.

51. These doubts continued to plague Hale for years to come. As late as June 1848 he still questioned Congress' power to abolish slavery in the District of Columbia, and frequently as a United States senator said that the federal government might regulate but not destroy the interstate slave trade. See Hale to Salmon P. Chase, June 7, 1848, Salmon P. Chase Papers, Pennsylvania Historical Society; *Cong. Globe,* 31 Cong., 1 sess., Appendix, p. 536.

NOTES TO CHAPTER III: DEMOCRATIC CONGRESSMAN

1. Hale to Mrs. Hale, Aug. 14, 1843, Hale Papers.

2. Hale to Mrs. Hale, Feb. 22, March 2, 6, 1837, Hale Papers.

3. Hale to Mrs. Hale, Nov. 29, Dec. 15, 27, 1843, Hale Papers.

4. Hale to Mrs. Hale, Feb. 22, 1837, Dec. 1, 6, 1843, Hale Papers.

5. Hale to Elizabeth and Lucy Hale, Dec. 6, 1843, Hale to Mrs. Hale, Dec. 24, 1843, Hale Papers.

6. Hale to Mrs. Hale, Dec. 14, 21, 24, 31, 1843, Hale to Elizabeth Hale, Feb. 15, 1844, Hale to Lucy Hale, April 11, 1844, Hale to Elizabeth and Lucy Hale, April 19, 30, 1844, Hale Papers.

7. *Cong. Globe,* 28 Cong., 1 sess. (1843–1844), pp. 1, 29; Hale to Mrs. Hale, Dec. 15, 1843, Hale Papers.

8. *Cong. Globe,* 34 Cong., 1 sess. (1855–1856), p. 1476.

9. *Ibid.,* 28 Cong. 1 sess., pp. 99, 691 (U.S. Bank and Independent Treasury), pp. 102–103 (tariff), p. 592 (imprisonment for debt), p. 671 (postal rates), pp. 119, 288 (Jackson's fine), pp. 27, 229, 425 (strict construction); 28 Cong., 2 sess. (1844–1845), pp. 288, 364 (internal improvements).

10. *Ibid.,* 28 Cong., 1 sess., pp. 79, 225, 646, 670.

11. *Ibid.,* 28 Cong., 1 sess., p. 489.

12. *Ibid.,* 28 Cong., 1 sess., p. 357; 28 Cong., 2 sess., p. 290; John Hodgdon to Hale, Feb. 13, 1844, Hale Papers.

13. *Cong. Globe,* 28 Cong., 1 sess., pp. 71, 75, 78–79, 81; "Report of the Secretary of the Navy," 1843–1845, House Executive Documents, No. 2, 28 Cong., 1 sess. (p. 482), 28 Cong., 2 sess. (p. 513), 29 Cong., 1 sess. (1845–

1846), (p. 646). There is no evidence that Hale shared the belief of Giddings and others that the home squadron existed to protect the slave trade. He seems to have objected to it solely on grounds of economy.

14. John Quincy Adams, *Memoirs of John Quincy Adams, Comprising Portions of His Diary from 1795 to 1848,* Charles Francis Adams, ed., 12 vols. (Philadelphia, 1874–1877), XI, 501; *Cong. Globe,* 28 Cong., 1 sess., pp. 610–611, 671.

15. Russel B. Nye, *Fettered Freedom: Civil Liberties and the Slavery Controversy, 1830–1860* (East Lansing, Mich., 1949) pp. 41–42; G. H. Barnes, *The Antislavery Impulse, 1830–1844* (New York, 1933), pp. 110–118.

16. Nye, *Fettered Freedom,* pp. 41–42; Barnes, *Antislavery Impulse,* pp. 181, 189; Samuel F. Bemis, *John Quincy Adams and the Union* (New York, 1956), pp. 420–437.

17. *N.H. House Journal,* June sess. (1839), pp. 419–421; Hale to Mrs. Hale, Dec. 3, 1843, Hale Papers.

18. Hale to Mrs. Hale, Dec. 21, 1843, Hale Papers.

19. *Cong. Globe,* 28 Cong., 1 sess., p. 4; Adams, *Memoirs,* XI, 462; Austin Willey, *The History of the Antislavery Cause in State and Nation* (Portland, Me., 1886), p. 233.

20. John Parkman to Hale, Dec. 12, 1843, William Claggett to Hale, Jan. 3, 1844, Albert R. Hatch to Hale, Feb. 9, 1844, Obed Hall to Hale, Jan. 4, 1844, J.W. James to Hale, Jan. 8, 1844, William Plumer, Jr. to Hale, Jan. 17, 1844, Hale Papers; Amos Tuck to Hale, Jan. 5, 1844, Amos Tuck Papers, New Hampshire Historical Society.

21. John H. Wiggins to Hale, Jan. 5, 1844, Hale Papers; [Dover] *Gazette,* Jan. 6, 1844; *Hill's New Hampshire Patriot,* Dec. 14, 1843; *New Hampshire Patriot,* Dec. 28, 1843; [Newport] *Argus & Spectator,* Jan. 12, 1844.

22. Hale to John H. Wiggins, Dec. 14, 1843, Hale to Mrs. Hale, Dec. 20, 21, 23, 1843, Hale Papers.

23. Hale to J. B. Wiggin, Jan. 2, 28, 1844, John P. Hale Papers, Minnesota Historical Society.

24. C. L. McCurdy to Hale, Dec. 26, 1843, Samuel P. Clusley to Hale, March 12, 1844, Samuel Downing to Hale, Jan. 4, 1844, Timothy Muncey to Hale, March 25, 1844, Hale Papers; [Exeter] *News-Letter,* Jan. 8, Feb. 19, 1844.

25. Ezekial Hurd to Hale, March 25, 1844, Hale Papers; [Newport] *Argus & Spectator,* Jan. 12, 1844.

26. G. A. Grant to Hale, March 20, 1844, G. McDaniel to Hale, Mar. 22, 1844, Hale Papers; Moses A. Cartland to John G. Whittier, Mar. 24, 1844, John G. Whittier Papers, Oak Knoll Collection, Essex Institute.

27. *Cong. Globe,* 28 Cong., 2 sess., p. 7; John Quincy Adams, *The Diary of John Quincy Adams, 1794–1845,* Allan Nevins, ed., (New York, 1951), p. 573.

28. Isaac Hill to John Farmer, Jan. 10, 1838, John Farmer Papers, New Hampshire Historical Society; *N.H. House Journal,* June sess. (1839), p. 419;

New Hampshire Patriot, Nov. 23, 1843; [Nashua] *Gazette*, Nov. 16, 1843, quoted in [Concord] *Independent Democrat*, May 15, 1845.

29. Adams, *Diary of John Quincy Adams*, pp. 570–571; Hale to William Horten, March 25, 1844, Hale Papers.

30. *Cong. Globe*, 28 Cong., 1 sess., p. 611.

31. [Dover] *Gazette*, March 30, 1844; *New Hampshire Patriot*, March 28, 1844; *Hill's New Hampshire Patriot*, April 4, 1844.

32. Although Senator Atherton voted against the Texas treaty on June 8, he apparently was expressing anti-Tyler, not anti-Texas feeling. His colleague, Levi Woodbury, was among the minority favoring its ratification. *Journal of the Executive Proceedings of the Senate of the United States of America*, vols. VI–VIII (Washington, 1887), VI, 312.

33. *Cong. Globe*, 31 Cong., 1 sess. (1849–1850), Appendix, p. 801.

34. Oliver P. Chitwood, *John Tyler: Champion of the Old South* (New York, 1939), 355–357; *Cong. Globe*, 28 Cong., 2 sess., pp. 2–6.

35. *Ibid.*, 28 Cong., 2 sess., pp. 26, 65–66, 76.

36. *Ibid.*, 28 Cong., 2 sess., pp. 85–88.

37. *Ibid.*, 28 Cong., 2 sess., pp. 94–95.

38. *N.H. Senate Journal*, Nov. sess. (1844), pp. 91–92; *N.H. House Journal*, Nov. sess. (1844), pp. 346–356, 362; *Cong. Globe*, 28 Cong., 2 sess., p. 100.

39. *Ibid.*, 28 Cong., 2 sess., pp. 120–121.

40. *Ibid.*, 34 Cong., 1 sess., Appendix, p. 849; *New Hampshire Patriot*, Jan. 23, 1845.

NOTES TO CHAPTER IV: THE "HALE STORM"

1. *Letter from John P. Hale, of New Hampshire, to His Constituents, on the Proposed Annexation of Texas* (Washington, 1845), pp. 2, 8; *New Hampshire Patriot*, Jan. 23, 1845. Whether, as his enemies later charged, Whig senators Rufus Choate of Massachusetts and George Evans of Maine collaborated with him in drafting the letter, remains a mystery. If so they, the printers, and a few antislavery representatives (Preston King, for one) were the only persons who knew of its existence before Hale made it public on the 11th. See Preston King to Azariah Flagg, Jan. 8, 1845, Azariah Flagg Papers, New York Public Library.

2. *Letter from John P. Hale to His Constituents*, pp. 3-4.

3. *Ibid.*, pp. 4–8.

4. Amos Tuck, *Autobiographical Memoir of Amos Tuck* (n.p., 1902), p. 66; William Claggett to Hale, Jan. 4, 1845, Hale Papers.

5. Levi Woodbury to Pierce, Jan. 11, 1845, Franklin Pierce Papers, New Hampshire Historical Society; Charles G. Atherton to Pierce, Jan. 13, 15, 1845, Pierce Papers, Library of Congress; Roy F. Nichols, *Franklin Pierce: Young Hickory of the Granite Hills*, rev. ed. (Philadelphia, 1958), p. 133.

6. Pierce to Edmund Burke, Jan. 16, 1845, Burke Papers.

7. Hale to Pierce, Nov. 19, 1843, Pierce Papers, New Hampshire Historical

Society; Hale to Pierce, Dec. 3, 1844, Pierce Papers, Library of Congress. "I have always been a personal friend of Mr. Hale," Pierce wrote to Edmund Burke on Jan. 16, 1845, "but in a case like this I know no personal friendships." Burke Papers.

8. Pierce to William Butterfield [Jan. 1845], Pierce Papers, New Hampshire Historical Society.

9. E. Hurd to Hale, Jan. 22, 1845, Jacob Ela to Hale, Jan. 29, 1845, Hale Papers.

10. Pierce to William Butterfield [Jan. 1845], Pierce Papers, New Hampshire Historical Society; Nichols, *Pierce,* pp. 133, 135.

11. Pierce to Edmund Burke, Jan. 16, 1845, Burke Papers; *New Hampshire Patriot,* Jan. 16, 1845.

12. Nichols, *Pierce,* pp. 133–134.

13. Pierce to Hale, Jan. 24, 1845, Pierce Papers, Library of Congress.

14. Nathaniel S. Berry to Hale, May 31, 1848, Hale Papers; [Dover] *Enquirer,* Jan. 21, 1845.

15. Hayes to Hale, Jan. 16, 1845, William Claggett to Hale, Jan. 21, 1845, Hale Papers; Amos Tuck, "Biographical memoranda (Washington, July, 1848)," Tuck Papers, Dartmouth College Archives, pp. 88–90; Henry F. French to Benjamin B. French, Jan. 16, 19, 1845, Benjamin B. French Papers, Library of Congress; John L. Hayes, *A Reminiscence of the Free-Soil Movement in New Hampshire, 1845* (Cambridge, Mass., 1885), p. 13; Nichols, *Pierce,* pp. 133–134.

16. Pierce to Woodbury, Jan. 20, 1845, Woodbury Papers; Atherton to Pierce, Jan. 25, 1845, Pierce Papers, Library of Congress; [Dover] *Gazette,* Jan. 25, 1845.

17. Pierce to Woodbury, Jan. 20, 1845, Woodbury Papers.

18. James W. James to Hale, Jan. 8, 1844, Hale Papers.

19. [Portsmouth] *New Hampshire Gazette,* Jan. 21, 1845; *Hill's New Hampshire Patriot,* Jan. 23, Feb. 6, 1845; *New Hampshire Patriot,* Jan. 23, 1845.

20. [Dover] *Gazette,* Feb. 22, 1845; Henry Wilson, *History of the Rise and Fall of the Slave Power in America,* 7 ed., 3 vols. (Boston, 1872–1877), I, 625.

21. Abraham Emerson to Hale, Feb. 14, 1845, Hale Papers.

22. Hale to Pierce, Jan. 18, 1845, Pierce Papers, Library of Congress.

23. There are two drafts of Pierce's reply to Hale (each dated Jan. 24, 1845), one in the Pierce Papers, New Hampshire Historical Society, the other in the Pierce Papers, Library of Congress. Neither appears to have been mailed.

24. *Cong. Globe,* 28 Cong., 2 sess. (1844–1845), p. 194. Reding's vote "surprised and mortified" the Clique, but created little stir because he was not a candidate for reelection and did not, as Hale had done, "beard the lion in his den." See J. A. Eastman to Charles G. Atherton, Jan. 30, 1845, Charles G. Atherton Papers, New Hampshire Historical Society.

25. *Cong. Globe,* 31 Cong., 1 sess. (1849–1850), Appendix, p. 801; Tuck, *Autobiographical Memoir,* p. 75. Hale spent a few days in New York early in

February, and it may have been then that he reached an informal agreement with Sedgwick. See [New York] *Morning Express,* Feb. 1, 3, 1845.

26. See, for example, N. P. Cram to Hale, Jan. 18, 1845, William Claggett to Hale, Jan. 21, 1845, N. F. Barnes to Hale, Jan. 29, 1845, John Brown to Hale, Feb. 1, 1845, Hale Papers.

27. J. P. Brody to Hale, Feb. 13, 1845, Hale Papers; *Democracy and Patriotism* (pamphlet account of the Coos County meeting, bound between March 1 and March 8 issues of the [Dover] *Gazette* in the New Hampshire Historical Society).

28. *Independent Democrat,* June 19, 1845; N. F. Barnes to Hale, Feb. 14, 1845, Hale Papers.

29. Peverly to Hale, Jan. 16, 1845, Hale Papers. See also Henry F. French to Benjamin B. French, Jan. 16, 1845, French Papers.

30. *Independent Democrat,* June 12, 1845.

31. N. F. Barnes to Hale, Jan. 29, 1845, Josiah Butler to Hale, Feb. 10, 1845, Hale Papers.

32. Tuck to Hale, Jan. 15, 1845, Hale Papers.

33. Tuck to Hale, Jan. 5, 1844, Tuck Papers; *New Hampshire Patriot,* Feb. 27, 1845.

34. *Laws of the State of New Hampshire, Passed November Session, 1844* (Concord, 1845), pp. 121–126; Ela to Hale, Jan. 15, 29, 1845, David Gilchrist to Hale, Jan. 20, 1845, Hale Papers.

35. Hayes to Hale, Feb. 15, 1845, Hale Papers; Hayes, *Free-Soil Movement in New Hampshire,* pp. 14–15. William Claggett reported that Hayes had made his speech "amid some occasional noise." Either Hayes was being overly dramatic or Claggett was trying to belittle his efforts out of jealousy. See Claggett to Hale, Feb. 11, 1845, Hale Papers.

36. Hayes, *Free-Soil Movement in New Hampshire,* pp. 13–14, 32–35. In his manuscript autobiography, Tuck claimed that the idea for the Exeter meeting was his alone. See Tuck, "Biographical memoranda," Tuck Papers, Dartmouth College Archives, p. 91.

37. Hayes, *Free-Soil Movement in New Hampshire,* pp. 14, 35–37, 37n; [Exeter] *News-Letter,* Feb. 24, 1845; Claggett to Hale, Feb. 20, 1845, Hale Papers.

38. *Proceedings of a Democratic Meeting, At Rochester, Strafford County, New Hampshire, March 1st, 1845, in opposition to the present scheme for the annexation of Texas and in favor of the re-election of the Hon. John P. Hale a member of Congress.* Broadside, bound with the [Dover] *Gazette,* before March 8, 1845 issue, New Hampshire Historical Society.

39. J. H. Fuller to Hale, Feb. 24, 1845, Hale Papers. Henry F. French believed that Hale's "supineness" had "extinguished a great portion of the zeal in his support." French to Benjamin B. French, Feb. 16, 1845, French Papers.

40. [Dover] *Gazette,* March 8, 1845.

41. Claggett to Hale, Jan. 21, 1845, Barnes to Hale, Feb. 14, 1845, Hale Papers.

42. *Liberator,* Jan. 24, 1845; Anne Weston to Caroline and Deborah Weston [Jan. 25, 1845?], Anne Weston Papers, Boston Public Library.

43. Whittier to Hale, Jan. 24, 1845, quoted in Samuel T. Pickard, *Life and Letters of John Greenleaf Whittier,* 2 vols. (Boston, 1894), I, 306–307.

44. John Greenleaf Whittier, *The Writings of John Greenleaf Whittier,* Riverside ed., 7 vols. (Boston, 1892), III, 101–102.

45. Whittier to Elizur Wright, Jr., Oct. 19, 1845, quoted in Samuel T. Pickard, *Whittier as a Politician* (Boston, 1900), pp. 38–39.

46. [Concord] *New Hampshire Statesman,* Jan. 17, Feb. 21, 1845; [Dover] *Enquirer,* Jan. 28, 1845.

47. McFarland to Charles W. Brewster, Feb. 17, 1845, Asa McFarland Papers, New Hampshire Historical Society.

48. Salma Hale to Brewster, Feb. 28, 1845, Miscellaneous Manuscripts, Massachusetts Historical Society; Claggett to Hale, Jan. 29, 1845, Hale Papers.

49. [Newport] *Argus & Spectator,* Jan. 31, Feb. 14, March 7, 1845; *New Hampshire Patriot,* Jan. 30, March 6, 1845; [Dover] *Gazette,* March 8, 1845; Charles W. Woodbury to Levi Woodbury, Feb. 22, 1845, Woodbury Papers.

50. William Claggett to Hale, Jan. 21, 29, 1845, Tuck to Hale, Feb. 5, 1845, Ela to Hale, Feb. 21, 1845, C. Robbins to Hale, March 5, 1845, Hale Papers; Charles W. Woodbury to Levi Woodbury, Feb. 22, 1845, Woodbury Papers.

51. Each party presented a full slate, each candidate running at large. Democratic and Independent Democratic tickets were identical except that on the latter Hale's name replaced Woodbury's.

52. *New Hampshire Patriot,* March 20, 1845; Ela to Hale, March 20, 1845, Tuck to Hale, March 14, 1845, Hale Papers.

Notes to Chapter V: Fruits of Coalition

1. *New Hampshire Patriot,* March 20, 1845; [Newport] *Argus & Spectator,* March 28, 1845. Available evidence indicates that the Independent Democrats *were* guilty of distributing spurious ballots. The practice was not uncommon at the time, most voters were on the alert for them, and it is doubtful that the ruse deceived many.

2. Henry F. French to Benjamin B. French, March 20, 1845, French Papers; Hayes to Hale, March 31, 1845, Hale Papers.

3. John R. St. John to Hale, Oct. 22, 1847, Hale Papers.

4. Hale to Mrs. Hale, March 12, 1845, Hayes to Hale, March 20, 1845, Hale Papers; John L. Hayes, *A Reminiscence of the Free-Soil Movement in New Hampshire, 1845* (Cambridge, Mass., 1885), p. 40.

5. Amos Tuck, *Autobiographical Memoir of Amos Tuck* (n.p., 1902), p. 75; Hayes, *Free-Soil Movement in New Hampshire,* p. 16; William Claggett to Hale, March 27, 1845, Hale Papers.

6. *Prospectus for Publishing a Paper to be Called "The Independent Demo-*

crat" (Manchester, April 1, 1845). Bound at the beginning of the first volume of the *Independent Democrat* in the New Hampshire Historical Society.

7. *Independent Democrat, passim;* [Dover] *Gazette,* April 19, May 10, 1845.

8. Peverly to Hale, April 12, 1845, Robert C. Wetmore to Hale, June 28, 1845, Hale Papers; Franklin McDuffee, *History of the Town of Rochester, New Hampshire, from 1722–1890,* Silvanus Hayward, ed., 2 vols. (Manchester, N.H., 1892), II, 411; *Independent Democrat,* July 3, 1845.

9. Robert C. Wetmore to Hale, July 25, 1845, Hale Papers.

10. Robert C. Wetmore to Hale, June 24, 1845, Hale Papers; Tuck, *Autobiographical Memoir,* p. 75; *New Hampshire Patriot,* Aug. 7, 1845.

11. James O. Lyford, ed., *History of Concord, New Hampshire,* 2 vols. (Concord, 1903), I, 416.

12. Tuck to Hale, April 17, 1845, Hale Papers; *Liberator,* May 9, 1845, correspondence from the [Boston] *Post.*

13. George Santayana, *Character & Opinion in the United States* (New York, 1920), p. 3; Hale to Elizabeth Hale, Dec. 11, 1843, Hale to Mrs. Hale, Dec. 12, 1843, Hale Papers; Daniel Hall to William E. Chandler, Sept. 9, 1890, William E. Chandler Papers, New Hampshire Historical Society.

14. [Dover] *Gazette,* May 10, 1845; James Peverly et al. to Hale, May 15, 1845, Hale Papers; Roy F. Nichols, *Franklin Pierce: Young Hickory of the Granite Hills,* rev. ed. (Philadelphia, 1958), pp. 135–136.

15. William E. Chandler, *The Statue of John P. Hale* (Concord, N.H., 1892), pp. 169–170. The evidence here is admittedly shaky, being Henry P. Rolfe's recollection in 1892 of a conversation with Hale in 1872 about events in 1845.

16. *Independent Democrat,* June 12, 1845; [Concord] *Granite Freeman,* June 12, 1845.

17. *Independent Democrat,* June 12, 1845.

18. Peverly to Hale, June 9, 1845, Fogg to Hale, June 17, 1845, Hale Papers; [Dover] *Gazette,* June 14, 1845.

19. Albert R. Hatch to Moses G. Hoit, July 20, 1845, Albert R. Hatch Papers, New Hampshire Historical Society.

20. *Independent Democrat,* Aug. 21, Sept. 18, 1845.

21. *Ibid.,* Sept. 11, 1845.

22. *New Hampshire Patriot,* Sept. 4, 1845.

23. [Dover] *Gazette,* Sept. 6, 1845.

24. Henry F. French to Benjamin B. French, Sept. 5, 1845, French Papers; Atherton to Woodbury, Sept. 23, 1845, Woodbury Papers; [Dover] *Gazette,* Oct. 18, 1845.

25. [Dover] *Gazette,* Dec. 27, 1845; *Independent Democrat,* Dec. 4, 1845.

26. James Peverly to Hale, May 12, 26, 1845, Hale Papers; Asa McFarland to Charles W. Brewster, Oct. 1, 1845, McFarland Papers; *New Hampshire Patriot,* Nov. 6, 1845.

27. The shadowy workings of this alliance during 1845 are best revealed in

Whig correspondence. See, for example, Asa McFarland to Charles W. Brewster, July 12, Aug. 20, Oct. 1, Nov. 21, 1845, McFarland Papers; William Plumer, Jr. to Stephen C. Phillips et al., June 28, 1845, Journal, Plumer Papers.

28. Jacob Ela to Hale, Feb. 2, 1845, Hale Papers; [Dover] *Gazette,* Jan. 10, 1846.

29. Hale to Mrs. Hale, Feb. 27, 1846, Hale Papers.

30. Hale to Fogg, Oct. 21, 1845, Fogg to Hale, Jan. 22, 1846, Robert C. Wetmore to Hale, Jan. 9, 1846, Hale Papers; *Independent Democrat,* Feb. 5, 1846.

31. Asa McFarland to Charles W. Brewster, Dec. 18, 1845, Jan. 16, 1846, McFarland Papers.

32. John L. Carlton to Hale, March 14, 1846, James Peverly to Hale, March 15, 1846, Hale Papers; Dudley S. Palmer to Charles W. Brewster, Feb. 16, 1846, Brewster Papers.

33. Peverly to Hale, March 15, 1846, Hale Papers.

34. [Dover] *Gazette,* March 14, 28, April 4, May 23, 1846; *Independent Democrat,* March 26, 1846.

35. Whittier to "Dear Cousin," March 7, [1846] (typed copy), Moses A. Cartland Papers, Houghton Library, Harvard University.

36. John G. Whittier, *The Writings of John Greenleaf Whittier,* Riverside ed., 7 vols. (Boston, 1892), III, 117–122.

37. George T. Clark to Hale, March 13, 1846, Hale Papers.

38. S. B. Parsons to Hale, May 30, 1846, Hale Papers.

39. Hale to Joshua Giddings, April 5, 1846, Joshua Reed Giddings Papers, Ohio Historical Society.

40. David Murray to Hale, March 21, 1846, Samuel Webster to Hale, April 17, 1846, Austin Cass to Hale, April 23, 1846, Hale Papers; Amos Tuck to George G. Fogg, May 3, 1846, Tuck Papers; *Independent Democrat,* May 14, 1846.

41. Hale to Joshua Giddings, April 5, 1846, Giddings Papers; Tuck to Fogg, May 3, 1846, Tuck Papers; *Independent Democrat,* May 14, 1846.

42. *N.H. House Journal,* June sess. (1846), pp. 10, 13–15, 22; Hale to Mrs. Hale, June 5, 1846, Hale Papers.

43. Washington Hunt to Hale, June 3, 1846, Hale Papers.

44. *New Hampshire Patriot,* June 11, 1846; Hale to Mrs. Hale, June 7, 1846, Hale Papers.

45. *N.H. House Journal,* June sess. (1846), p. 73; *N.H. Senate Journal,* June sess. (1846), p. 32; Lyford, ed., *History of Concord,* I, 416; *New Hampshire Patriot,* June 11, 1846.

46. *N.H. House Journal,* June sess. (1846), pp. 101–103.

47. *Ibid.,* pp. 34–39.

48. *Ibid.,* pp. 74–75, 146–148.

49. *Speech of Hon. John P. Hale, Upon the Slavery Resolutions, in the* [New

Hampshire] *House of Representatives, June 25th, 1846* (Boston, [1846]); Hale to Mrs. Hale, June 26, 1846, Hale Papers.

50. *N.H. House Journal,* June sess. (1846), pp. 283–307, 418; *N.H. Senate Journal,* June sess. (1846), p. 153; Hale to Mrs. Hale, July 3, 1846, Hale Papers.

51. *N.H. House Journal,* June sess. (1846), pp. 238–239, 376–379, 407.

52. *Ibid.,* pp. 17, 223–224, 376.

53. *Laws of the State of New Hampshire, Passed June Session, 1846* (Concord, 1846), p. 295. This act, said William Plumer, Jr., had been passed "rather to please the abolitionists than from any urgent need of it. We are so far north that few slaves reach this state. It was however proper in itself & goes to increase the growing mass of public opinion which is every day accumulating against slavery." William Plumer, Jr., Journal, Feb. 6, 1847, Plumer Papers.

54. Hale to Salmon P. Chase, April 3, 1846, Chase Papers, Pennsylvania Historical Society.

55. Arthur B. Darling, *Political Changes in Massachusetts, 1824–1848: A Study of Liberal Movements in Politics* (New Haven, 1925), ch. vii; Charles E. Hamlin, *The Life and Times of Hannibal Hamlin* (Cambridge, Mass., 1899), pp. 147–152, 176–179; Albert B. Hart, *Salmon Portland Chase* (Boston, 1899), pp. 104–112; Charles B. Going, *David Wilmot: Free-Soiler* (New York, 1924), ch. vii; Arthur M. Schlesinger, Jr., *The Age of Jackson* (Boston, 1945), ch. xxxiv. Two states followed New Hampshire's example by electing anti-slavery Democrats to the United States Senate. Maine chose Hamlin in 1847 and Ohio elected Chase in 1848.

56. Adams to D. P. King, Jan. 27, 1847, Letterbooks, Charles Francis Adams Papers, microfilm, Widener Library, Harvard University.

NOTES TO CHAPTER VI: A RELUCTANT CANDIDATE

1. Hale to Anne Weston, Sept. 11, 1846, Weston Papers.

2. Ellis Gray Loring to Hale, Sept. 9, 1846, Hale Papers.

3. Hale to Mrs. Hale, Sept. 19, 1846, Hale Papers; David Donald, *Charles Sumner and the Coming of the Civil War* (New York, 1960), p. 148.

4. Hale to Mrs. Hale, Feb. 11, 1847, Hale Papers; Hale to Salma Hale, Oct. 16, 1847, Harry Hibbard Collection, New Hampshire Historical Society; William Plumer, Jr., Journal, Mar. 15, 20, 1847, Plumer Papers.

5. Hale to Giddings, June 28, 1847, Giddings Papers; George G. Fogg to Hale, July 2, 1847, Hale Papers. The Whigs reluctantly agreed to support Tuck in the first district in return for the promises of Independent Democrats to vote for Wilson in the third. See William Plumer, Jr., Journal, May 5, June 2, 3, 19, 1847, Plumer Papers.

6. Charles Sumner to Salmon P. Chase, Dec. 12, 1846, Chase Papers, Library of Congress.

7. Hale to Salma Hale, Oct. 16, 1847, Hibbard Collection.

8. Hale to Henry I. Bowditch, Oct. 9, 1846, quoted in Vincent Y. Bowditch,

Life and Correspondence of Henry Ingersoll Bowditch, 2 vols. (Boston, 1902), I, 184–187.

9. Zebina Eastman to Hale, May 25, 1847, Hale Papers. See also Bowditch, *Bowditch,* I, 183.

10. Theodore C. Smith, *The Liberty and Free Soil Parties in the Northwest* (New York, 1897), p. 98; Theodore Foster to James G. Birney, Aug. 1, 1846, James G. Birney, *Letters of James Gillespie Birney,* Dwight L. Dumond, ed., 2 vols. (New York, 1938), II, 1026.

11. Hale to Henry I. Bowditch, Oct. 9, 1846, quoted in Bowditch, *Bowditch,* I, 184–187.

12. Zebina Eastman to Hale, June 29, 1847, Hale Papers; *Independent Democrat,* Jan. 14, 1847; Smith, *Liberty and Free Soil Parties,* pp. 117–118.

13. Stanton to Hale, July 6, 1847, Hale Papers.

14. Charles F. Adams, Diary, July 22, 1847, Adams Papers; Charles Sumner to Joshua Giddings, July 28, 1847, Giddings Papers. For an able discussion of the Conscience Whig movement, see Frank Otto Gatell, " 'Conscience and Judgment'; the Bolt of the Massachusetts Conscience Whigs," *The Historian* 21: 18–45 (November 1958).

15. Stanton to Chase, Aug. 6, 1847, Chase Papers, Library of Congress.

16. Tuck to Hale, Aug. 2, 1847, Fogg to Hale, Aug. 3, 1847, Hale Papers.

17. Sumner to Giddings, July 28, 1847, Giddings Papers; Adams, Diary, July 29, 1847, Adams Papers.

18. Chase to Hale, May 12, 1847, Hale Papers; Chase to Preston King, July 15 [1847], Salmon P. Chase, *Diary and Correspondence,* published in the American Historical Association, *Annual Report for the Year 1902,* II (Washington, 1903), 120–122.

19. Chase to Hale, Sept. 23, 1847, Chase Papers, New Hampshire Historical Society; Chase to Joshua Leavitt, June 16, 1847, Letterbooks, Chase Papers, Library of Congress. Chase had no really strong preference for any one candidate, shifting his favor almost daily. The reason was simple enough. "I care nothing for names," he wrote Sumner. "All that I ask for is a platform and an issue, not buried out of sight, but palpable and paramount." Chase to Sumner, Sept. 22, 1847, *Diary and Correspondence,* p. 123.

20. Chase to Hale, Sept. 23, 1847, Chase Papers, New Hampshire Historical Society; Chase to Hale, June 15, 1848, *Diary and Correspondence,* pp. 134–136.

21. Whittier to Hale, July 30, 1847, quoted in Samuel T. Pickard, *Life and Letters of John Greenleaf Whittier,* 2 vols. (Boston, 1894), I, 319–321.

22. Stanton to Hale, Sept. 10, 1847, Tuck to Hale, Sept. 11, 1847, Hale to Lewis Tappan (copy), Oct. 12, 1847, Hale Papers. See also Hale to Zebina Eastman, Sept. 1, 1847, James Franklin Aldrich Papers, Chicago Historical Society.

23. Smith, *Liberty and Free Soil Parties,* pp. 118–119; Ralph V. Harlow, *Gerrit Smith: Philanthropist and Reformer* (New York, 1939), pp. 177–180; *Liberator,* Nov. 19, 1847.

24. Smith, *Liberty and Free Soil Parties,* p. 119; Harlow, *Smith,* p. 181.

25. Smith, *Liberty and Free Soil Parties,* p. 119.

26. William Day to Hale, Feb. 27, 1851, Hale Papers; William Goodell, *Slavery and Anti-Slavery: A History of the Great Struggle in Both Hemispheres, with a View of the Slavery Question in the United States* (New York, 1852), p. 478.

27. Austin Willey to Hale, Nov. 5, 1847, Hale Papers. The Liberty Leaguers opposed Hale, Gerrit Smith explained, not because they doubted his antislavery sentiments, but "for the sufficient reason that, whatever respect might be due him from the Liberty party, it was quite too much to admit a stranger into the very sanctuary of their confidence;—quite too much to make a man of another name and another creed their presidential candidate." See Smith's letter to New Hampshire Liberty party leaders, quoted in the *New Hampshire Patriot,* Apr. 20, 1848.

28. Joshua Leavitt to Hale, Nov. 9, 1847, Hale Papers. "The chief reason, given in the Convention of Liberty men at Buffalo for nominating Hale at this time was, that, if they did not nominate him, a National Wilmot-Proviso Convention would, and 'swallow up' . . . the Liberty party." E. S. Hamlin to Charles Sumner, Oct. 26, 1847, Charles Sumner Papers, Houghton Library, Harvard University.

29. Smith, *Liberty and Free Soil Parties,* p. 120; Whittier to Hale, Nov. 8, 1847, quoted in Pickard, *Whittier,* I, 323–324; *Liberator,* Dec. 17, 1847; Wendell Phillips to Elizabeth Pease, Aug. 29, 1847, William Lloyd Garrison Papers, Boston Public Library. For opinion adverse to Hale's nomination, see William L. Chaplin to James G. Birney, Feb. 10, 1848, James G. Birney to Lewis Tappan, July 10, 1848, Birney, *Letters,* II, 1091, 1108–1109.

30. See, for example, Charles Sumner to Thomas Corwin, Sept. 7, 1847, Sumner Papers.

31. Donald, *Sumner,* pp. 157–159.

32. William Plumer, Jr. to James Wilson, March 24, 1848, Plumer Papers.

33. Hale to Mrs. Hale, Dec. 5, 1847, Hale Papers.

34. E. S. Hamlin to Sumner, Oct. 26, 1847, Sumner Papers; Sumner to Giddings, Nov. 1, 1847, Giddings Papers; Chase to Sumner, Dec. 2, 1847, *Diary and Correspondence,* pp. 124–127; Albert B. Hart, *Salmon Portland Chase* (Boston, 1899), p. 96; Charles F. Adams, Diary, Aug. 3, 9, Oct. 21, 1847, Adams Papers; Arthur M. Schlesinger, Jr., *The Age of Jackson* (Boston, 1945), p. 464.

35. William Plumer, Jr., Journal, Nov. 18, 1847, Plumer Papers; *Massachusetts Liberty Convention and Speech of Hon. John P. Hale, Together with his Letter Accepting his Nomination for the Presidency* [Boston, 1848], p. 8.

36. Distressed at Hale's low spirits, Whittier asked Sumner to "write to John P. Hale, an encouraging, & at the same time suggestive letter." "It would do him good," Whittier felt. "He needs the support & counsel of all who

love freedom. He is fearless, & willing to do his duty: but his position is a very difficult one." Whittier to Sumner, Jan. 7, 1848, Sumner Papers.

37. Sumner to Chase, June 12, 1848, Chase Papers, Library of Congress; Smith, *Liberty and Free Soil Parties,* pp. 125–131. Some Northern Whigs objected to Taylor as much for being an unreliable party man as for his suspected proslavery views. Wrote one Massachusetts Whig in 1848: "General Taylor!—I have been Tylerized once, & I will be *paralyzed* before I will consent to vote for a candidate whose political doctrines are unknown, or for one who covets territory for increasing the slave power either by the increase of slaves or the addition of slave states to the Union." Myron Lawrence to Charles Allen, April 1, 1848, George Frisbie Hoar Papers, Massachusetts Historical Society. Richard Henry Dana, Jr. complained that Taylor had "always refused to be the candidate of a party." Richard Henry Dana, Jr. to Richard Henry Dana, July 11, 1848, Dana Papers.

38. Joshua Leavitt to Hale, July 1, 1848, Hale Papers.

39. Leavitt to Joshua Giddings, July 6, 1848, Giddings Papers; Whittier to William F. Channing, July 1, 1848, quoted in Pickard, *Whittier,* I, 333–334.

40. Bailey to Charles Sumner, May 31, 1848, Sumner Papers; Amos Tuck to George G. Fogg, June 1, 1848, Tuck Papers; Adams to John G. Palfrey, July 16, 1848, Letterbooks, Adams Papers. Chase never altered his opinion that Hale should withdraw his name prior to the Buffalo convention, but he repeatedly changed his mind about which candidate he most favored. Hale, McLean, and Van Buren all engaged his fancy at one time or another. See Chase to Hale, June 15, 1848, Chase to Sumner, June 20, 1848, *Diary and Correspondence,* pp. 136, 137–138; Chase to Hale, June 24, 1848, Chase Papers, New Hampshire Historical Society; Chase to John McLean, Aug. 2, 12, 1848, John McLean Papers, Library of Congress.

41. Lewis Tappan to Hale, July 8, 1848, L.D. Catell to Hale, July 24, 1848, T. Gilbert to Hale, July 27, 1848, Hale Papers.

42. Amos Tuck to Hale, June 21, 1848, Rufus Elmer to Hale, July 7, 1848, Hale Papers.

43. Hale to Lewis Tappan, July 6, 1848 (copy), Hale Papers.

44. Tappan to Hale, July 8, 1848, Lewis to Hale, July 10, 1848, Hale Papers.

45. Tappan to Hale, July 14, 1848, Lewis to Hale, July 29, 1848, Hale Papers.

46. [Washington] *Union,* Aug. 12, 1848, correspondence from the [New York] *Herald; Liberator,* Sept. 8, 1848; *Independent Democrat,* Aug. 17, 1848; George W. Julian, *Political Recollections, 1840–1872* (Chicago, 1883), pp. 56–57; Philip S. Foner, *The Life and Writings of Frederick Douglass,* 4 vols. (New York, 1950–1955), II, 70–71.

47. Richard Henry Dana, Jr., *Speeches in Stirring Times and Letters to a Son,* Richard H. Dana, III, ed., (Boston, 1910), pp. 150–152.

48. Oliver Dyer, *Great Senators of the United States Forty Years Ago (1848 and 1849), with Personal Recollections and Delineations of Calhoun, Benton, Clay, Webster, General Houston, Jefferson Davis, and other Distinguished Statesmen of that Period* (New York, 1889), p. 95.

49. After conversations with Barnburners William Cullen Bryant and B. F. Butler, who insisted on Van Buren and expressed reluctance to go beyond the anti-extension principle, Tappan had decided to remain in New York. He did, however, help pay the expenses of two or three pro-Hale delegates to the Buffalo convention. Tappan to Hale, Aug. 2, 11, 1848, Hale Papers. See Stanton to Salmon P. Chase, June 6, 1848, Chase Papers, Library of Congress.

50. Stanton to Hale, Aug. 20, 1848, Hale Papers. See also Leavitt to Hale, Aug. 22, 1848, Hale Papers.

51. Oliver Dyer, *Phonographic Report of the Proceedings of the National Free Soil Convention at Buffalo, N.Y., August 9th and 10th, 1848* (Buffalo, 1848), pp. 19–20; Dana, Jr., *Speeches in Stirring Times,* pp. 153–154; Adams, Diary, Aug. 10, 1848, Adams Papers.

52. Dana, Jr., *Speeches in Stirring Times,* p. 154.

53. Dana, Jr., *Speeches in Stirring Times,* pp. 154–156; Dyer, *Great Senators,* pp. 99–102; Martin B. Duberman, *Charles Francis Adams, 1807–1886* (Boston, 1960), p. 150 n39. Van Buren's nomination came *before* Hale's, not *after* as Dana recorded at the time and others have said since. Dana, Jr., Journal, Aug. 10, 1848, Dana Papers; Duberman, *Adams,* p. 150. Adams and Leavitt both describe the order of nomination correctly, each reporting that impatient calls for the roll cut Stanton's remarks short. Adams, Diary, Aug. 10, 1848, Adams Papers; Leavitt to Hale, Aug. 22, 23, 1848, Hale Papers.

54. Dana, Jr., *Speeches in Stirring Times,* p. 156.

55. Charles F. Adams, Diary, Aug. 10, 1848, Adams Papers.

56. Henry B. Stanton to Hale, Aug. 20, 1848, Hale Papers. See also Richard Henry Dana, Jr., Journal, Aug. 10, 1848, Dana Papers; Dana, Jr., *Speeches in Stirring Times,* pp. 156–158.

57. Leavitt to Hale, Aug. 22, 1848, Hale Papers; Adams, Diary, Aug. 10, 1848, Adams Papers; Julian, *Political Recollections,* pp. 60–61; Dana, Jr., Journal, Aug. 10, 1848, Dana Papers; Dyer, *Phonographic Report,* p. 31; *Reunion of the Free-Soilers of 1848 at Downer Landing, Hingham, Mass., August 9, 1877* (Boston, 1877), pp. 58–59.

58. Hart, *Chase,* pp. 99–101; Smith, *Liberty and Free Soil Parties,* p. 143.

59. George G. Fogg to Hale, Aug. 21, 1848, Hale Papers.

60. James Russell Lowell, *The Writings of James Russell Lowell,* Riverside ed., 10 vols. (Boston, 1890), VIII, 141.

61. Louis Filler, *The Crusade Against Slavery, 1830–1860* (New York, 1960), p. 189; unsigned letter to Hale, Aug. 19, 1848, Stanton to Hale, Aug. 20, 1848, Leavitt to Hale, Aug. 22, 23, 1848, Hale Papers.

62. Hale to Samuel Lewis, Aug. 28, 1848, quoted in the *Independent Democrat,* Sept. 7, 1848.

63. Hale to [Ohio Free Soil Convention] Oct. 18, 1848, quoted in the *Independent Democrat,* Nov. 30, 1848.

NOTES TO CHAPTER VII: "THE PLACE OF AN ISHMAELITE"

1. Hale to Mrs. Hale, Dec. 5, 6, 1847, Hale Papers; John G. Palfrey to Mrs.

Palfrey, Dec. 4, 1847, John G. Palfrey Papers, Houghton Library, Harvard University.

2. Frederick W. Seward, *Reminiscences of a War-Time Statesman and Diplomat, 1830–1915* (New York, 1916), pp. 68–69; Allan Nevins, *Ordeal of the Union,* 2 vols. (New York, 1947), I, 39–41; Constance M. Green, *Washington: Village and Capital, 1800–1878* (Princeton, 1962), chs. vi–viii.

3. *Cong. Globe,* 30 Cong., 1 sess. (1847–1848), p. 1.

4. Hale to Mrs. Hale, Dec. 6, 1847, Hale Papers.

5. Nathan Sargent, *Public Men and Events, from the Commencement of Mr. Monroe's Administration, in 1817, to the close of Mr. Fillmore's Administration, in 1853,* 2 vols. (Philadelphia, 1875), II, 208; [Washington] *National Era,* June 13, 1850, Aug. 14, 1851; George W. Bungay, *Crayon Sketches and Off-Hand Takings* (Boston, 1852), pp. 13–15; Oliver Dyer, *Great Senators of the United States Forty Years Ago . . .* (New York, 1889), pp. 126–129; Ben: Perley Poore, *Perley's Reminiscences of Sixty Years in the National Metropolis,* 2 vols. (Philadelphia, 1886), I, 458; George W. Julian to Isaac Julian, Jan. 25, 1850, Giddings-Julian Papers, Library of Congress; William Plumer, Jr., Journal, Feb. 2, 1850, Plumer Papers.

6. At his own request Hale was at first excused from committee service because of his maverick status. Later he was appointed as a junior member of such insignificant committees as those on Enrolled Bills, Pensions, Engrossed Bills. In the second session of the Thirty-Second Congress he again received no committee assignment because, as Jesse D. Bright explained, "we considered him outside of any healthy political organization in this country." Eventually, however, he was named to fill a vacancy on the Committee on Agriculture. See *Cong. Globe,* 30 Cong., 1 sess., p. 21; 30 Cong., 2 sess. (1848–1849), p. 28; 31 Cong., 1 sess. (1849–1850), p. 1028; 31 Cong., 2 sess. (1850–1851), p. 6; 32 Cong., 1 sess. (1851–1852), p. 32; 32 Cong., 2 sess. (1852–1853), pp. 40, 53.

7. Henry B. Stanton, *Random Recollections,* 3 ed. (New York, 1887), p. 127.

8. James D. Richardson, comp., *A Compilation of the Messages and Papers of the Presidents,* 20 vols. (New York, 1897–1927), IV, 533–549, especially pp. 544, 549.

9. *Cong. Globe,* 30 Cong., 1 sess., pp. 78–81.

10. Hale to Mrs. Hale, Dec. 30, 1847, Hale Papers; Sumner to Whittier, Jan. 5, 1848, quoted in Edward L. Pierce, *Memoir and Letters of Charles Sumner,* 4 vols. (London, 1877–1893), III, 157.

11. *Cong. Globe,* 30 Cong., 1 sess., 26; Charles M. Wiltse, *John C. Calhoun: Sectionalist, 1840–1850* (Indianapolis, 1951), p. 326; Nevins, *Ordeal of the Union,* I, 8.

12. *Cong. Globe,* 30 Cong., 1 sess., pp. 96–100.

13. *Ibid.,* 30 Cong., 1 sess., pp. 122–126.

14. "Nichols & Co." to Hale, Jan. 11, 1848, Hale Papers; Sumner to Salmon P. Chase, Feb. 7, 1848, Chase Papers, Library of Congress.

15. Plumer to Hale., Feb. 23, 1848, Hale Papers.

16. Quoted in the *Independent Democrat,* Jan. 13, 1848.

17. *Cong. Globe,* 30 Cong., 1 sess., pp. 341–342, 368; Sumner to Palfrey, Jan. 11, 1848, Palfrey Papers. For Giddings' vote see George W. Julian, *The Life of Joshua Giddings* (Chicago, 1892), p. 238.

18. *Journal of the Executive Proceedings of the Senate of the United States,* VII, 326–327, 330.

19. *Cong. Globe,* 31 Cong., 1 sess., p. 591.

20. *Slavery at Washington* (London, 1848), pp. 5–7. This pamphlet, an account of the *Pearl* affair, contains a contemporary if partisan report by Samuel Gridley Howe. See also Daniel Drayton, *Personal Memoir of Daniel Drayton, for Four Years and Four Months a Prisoner (for Charity's Sake) in Washington Jail. Including a Narrative of the Voyage and Capture of the Schooner Pearl* (Boston, 1855), pp. 23–32; [Washington] *Union,* April 22, 1848.

21. *Slavery at Washington,* pp. 8–9; Drayton, *Personal Memoir,* pp. 32–35.

22. *Ibid.,* 39–53; [Washington] *Daily National Intelligencer,* April 19, 1848; Hale to Elizabeth Hale, April 19, 1848, Hale Papers.

23. Joshua R. Giddings, *History of the Rebellion: Its Authors and Causes* (New York, 1864), pp. 272–276; *Cong. Globe,* 30 Cong., 1 sess., p. 648.

24. Hale to Elizabeth Hale, April 18, 19, 1848, Hale Papers.

25. The debates of April 20, 1848 on Hale's Riot Bill, described in the following paragraphs, are reported in *Cong. Globe,* 30 Cong., 1 sess., Appendix, pp. 500–510.

26. Henry S. Foote, *Casket of Reminiscences* (Washington, 1874), p. 76.

27. [Washington] *Union,* April 29, 1848. See also John C. Calhoun to Wilson Lumpkin, April 21, 1848, John C. Calhoun Papers, Chicago Historical Society.

28. Hamlin to Hale, May 20, 1848, Hale Papers.

29. Chase to Hale, April 29, 1848, Chase Papers, New Hampshire Historical Society; Giddings to J. A. Giddings, April 26, 1848, Sumner to Giddings, May 6, 1848, Giddings Papers; Adams to Hale, May 23, 1848, Letterbooks, Adams Papers.

30. George S. Riley to Hale, Jan. 13, 1850, Hale Papers.

31. Parkman to Hale, July 10, 1848, Hale Papers.

32. Hale to Elizabeth Hale, April 26, 1848, C. D. Cleveland to Hale, May 1, 1848, Hale Papers; Sumner to Joshua Giddings, May 6, 1848, Giddings Papers; Chase to Hale, April 29, 1848, Chase Papers, New Hampshire Historical Society.

33. [Salmon P. Chase] *Slavery in the District Unconstitutional* (n.p., n.d.). See also the speech of John Crowell of Ohio in the U.S. House of Representatives on July 26, 1848, *Cong. Globe,* 30 Cong., 1 sess., Appendix, pp. 956–961.

34. Hale to Chase, June 7, 1848, Chase Papers, Pennsylvania Historical Society.

35. Chase to Hale, June 15, 1848, Salmon P. Chase, *Diary and Correspond-*

ence, published in the American Historical Association, *Annual Report for the Year 1902,* II (Washington, 1903), 134–136.

36. *Cong. Globe,* 30 Cong., 1 sess., pp. 870, 872. The seven were Hale and Whigs Roger S. Baldwin (Conn.), John H. Clarke (R.I.), Thomas Corwin (Ohio), John Davis (Mass.), Jacob W. Miller (N.J.), and William Upham (Vt.).

37. Hale to Mrs. Hale, June 25, 1848, Hale Papers; John G. Palfrey to Charles Sumner, June 24, 1848, Palfrey Papers.

38. *Cong. Globe,* 30 Cong., 1 sess., p. 871. See also Wiltse, *Calhoun,* p. 345ff.; Nevins, *Ordeal of the Union,* I, 21, 24.

39. Even with the fiery Henry Foote, Hale maintained amicable relations. Soon after the Riot Bill debates, freesoiler John G. Palfrey was astonished to find Hale and the Mississippian cordial friends. And Foote himself later recalled that it was not long before "the jolly and kind-hearted Senator from New Hampshire and myself had gotten on good terms, and I had even taken a decided liking for him on account of his genial disposition, his natural amiableness of temper, and his sparkling vivacity, either in debate or in conversation." Palfrey to Anna R. Palfrey, July 7, 1848, Palfrey Papers; Foote, *Reminiscences,* pp. 76–77.

40. Hale to Mrs. Hale, July 4, 1848, Hale Papers.

41. *Cong. Globe,* 30 Cong., 1 sess., pp. 927–928.

42. *Ibid.,* 30 Cong., 1 sess., p. 950; Wiltse, *Calhoun,* pp. 350–351.

43. *Cong. Globe,* 30 Cong., 1 sess., pp. 988–989, 992, 1001.

44. Nevins, *Ordeal of the Union,* I, 24.

45. *Cong. Globe,* 30 Cong., 1 sess., Appendix, p. 692.

46. Hale to Mrs. Hale, July 27, 1848, Hale Papers; *Cong. Globe,* 30 Cong., 1 sess., p. 1002.

47. *Ibid.,* 30 Cong., 1 sess., pp. 1006–1007, 1074–1078. For a copy of the bill see pp. 1078–1080.

48. Wiltse, *Calhoun,* ch. xxvi, especially p. 384. By no means all Southern congressmen signed Calhoun's memorial. Benton, Houston, John M. Berrien, Thomas S. Rusk, and Alexander Stephens clamored against it. And James Westcott confided to Vice President Dallas "that Florida was ⅔ds for the [Wilmot] Proviso, as it might induce planters to come with their slaves into her territory." George M. Dallas, Diary, Jan. 13, 16, 1849, photostatic copy in Pennsylvania Historical Society.

49. *Cong. Globe,* 30 Cong., 2 sess., p. 36; Hale to Mrs. Hale, Dec. 17, 1848, Hale Papers.

NOTES TO CHAPTER VIII: CRISIS AND COMPROMISE

1. Hale to Moses M. Davis, Aug. 25, 1849, Moses M. Davis Papers, State Historical Society of Wisconsin.

2. Albert B. Hart, *Salmon Portland Chase* (Boston, 1899), pp. 103–112.

3. Hale to Mrs. Hale, Feb. 23, 1849, Hale Papers.

4. Chase to Mrs. Chase, March 6, 1849, Chase Papers, Library of Congress.

5. Hart, *Chase, passim*. There is, unhappily, no good modern biography of Chase. Hart's volume is still the best, but see also Robert B. Warden, *An Account of the Private Life and Public Services of Salmon Portland Chase* (Cincinnati, 1874) and J. W. Schuckers, *The Life and Public Services of Salmon Portland Chase, United States Senator and Governor of Ohio, Secretary of the Treasury and Chief-Justice of the United States* (New York, 1874).

6. Hart, *Chase,* pp. 113, 115.

7. George W. Julian, *Political Recollections, 1840 to 1872* (Chicago, 1883), p. 107; Chase to Mrs. Chase, Jan. 7, 1850, Chase Papers, Library of Congress.

8. Hale to Mrs. Hale, Dec. 3, 1849, Hale Papers; *Cong. Globe,* 31 Cong., 1 sess. (1849–1850), p. 1.

9. Hale to Mrs. Hale, Dec. 20, 1849, Hale Papers.

10. James D. Richardson, comp., *A Compilation of the Messages and Papers of the Presidents,* 20 vols. (New York, 1897–1927), V, 9–24; Holman Hamilton, *Zachary Taylor: Soldier in the White House* (Indianapolis, 1951), pp. 256–259.

11. *Cong. Globe,* 31 Cong., 1 sess., pp. 87, 99–100.

12. *Ibid.,* 31 Cong., 1 sess., pp. 244–247. The definitive history of the Compromise of 1850 is Holman Hamilton, *Prologue to Conflict: The Crisis and Compromise of 1850* (University of Kentucky, 1964).

13. "Mr. Clay's speech is regarded here as a sensible performance," reported Daniel Webster. "With some fooleries, such as he always commits, his view of the matter was rather statesmanlike." Webster to ?, Jan. 29, 1850, Daniel Webster Papers, New Hampshire Historical Society.

14. E. Plone to Hale, Feb. 19, 1850, Hale Papers; *National Era,* Feb. 7, 1850; Allan Nevins, *Ordeal of the Union,* 2 vols. (New York, 1947), I, 267–275, especially p. 268.

15. William N. Chambers, *Old Bullion Benton: Senator from the New West* (Boston, 1956), pp. 359–360; Hamilton, *Taylor,* pp. 285–286. "What a singular political conjunction is that of Cass, Clay & Webster?" Salmon Chase wrote E. S. Hamlin. "What a curious spike team they make with Foote for a driver!" May 27, 1850, *Diary and Correspondence,* published in The American Historical Association, *Annual Report for the Year 1902,* II (Washington, 1903), 212.

16. Hale to Elizabeth Hale, Feb. 5, 1850, Hale Papers.

17. *Cong. Globe,* 31 Cong., 1 sess., Appendix, pp. 115–127.

18. *Ibid.,* pp. 149–157.

19. *Ibid.,* pp. 451–455; Nevins, *Ordeal of the Union,* I, 283–285.

20. *Cong. Globe,* 31 Cong., 1 sess., Appendix, pp. 269–276; Frederick W. Seward, *Reminiscences of a War-Time Statesman and Diplomat, 1830–1915* (New York, 1916), p. 76.

21. A. Merrill to Hale, March 18, 1850, Isaac Knight to Hale, April 18, 1850, Theodore Parker to Hale, March 8, 1850, Hale Papers.

22. Hale to Parker, March 6, 1850, Parker to Hale, March 8, 1850, Tappan to Hale, March 11, 1850, Phillips to Hale, March 13, 1850, Hale Papers.

23. *Cong. Globe,* 31 Cong., 1 sess., Appendix, pp. 260–269.

24. *Ibid.,* 31 Cong., 1 sess., Appendix, pp. 1054–1065.

25. *Cong. Globe,* 31 Cong., 1 sess., p. 774. Members of the committee, besides chairman Clay, were Whigs Webster, Samuel S. Phelps, James Cooper, Willie P. Mangum, John Bell, and John Berrien; Democrats Cass, Daniel S. Dickinson, Jesse D. Bright, William R. King, James M. Mason, and Solomon W. Downs. See *ibid.,* p. 780.

26. *Ibid.,* 31 Cong., 1 sess., pp. 663, 758.

27. *Ibid.,* 31 Cong., 1 sess., pp. 944–948.

28. *Ibid.,* 31 Cong., 1 sess., pp. 954–955, 1004–1005.

29. Hale to Parker, May 15, 1850, Hale Papers.

30. Chase to [Speaker, Ohio House of Representatives] Dec. 3, 1850, Chase Papers, Library of Congress; Hale to Lucy Hale, May 30, 1850, Hale Papers.

31. Hale to Mrs. Hale, June 8, 9, 1850, Hale Papers. See also Hale to Theodore Parker, April 12, 1850, Hale Papers.

32. *Cong. Globe,* 31 Cong., 1 sess., Appendix, pp. 798–800; *National Era,* June 13, 1850.

33. *Cong. Globe,* 31 Cong., 1 sess., Appendix, pp. 800–803; Hale to Mrs. Hale, June 11, 1850, Hale Papers.

34. Sumner to Hale, June 15, 1850, Hale Papers. See also Gerrit Smith to Hale, June 25, 1850, Asa Fowler to Hale, June 27, 1850, Henry I. Bowditch to Hale, Aug. 3, 1850, Hale Papers.

35. Hale to Mrs. Hale, July 16, 1850, Hale Papers.

36. Bailey to Charles Sumner, July 9, 1850, Sumner Papers; Hale to Mrs. Hale, July 10, 1850, Hale Papers. See also Nevins, *Ordeal of the Union,* I, 327–336; *Independent Democrat,* July 18, 1850.

37. Hale to Mrs. Hale, July 22, 26, 1850, Hale Papers.

38. *Cong. Globe,* 31 Cong., 1 sess., pp. 1490–1491; Nevins, *Ordeal of the Union,* I, 340.

39. *Cong. Globe,* 31 Cong., 1 sess., pp. 1504, 1573, 1589, 1647, 1764, 1772, 1807, 1830, 1837.

40. Hale to Mrs. Hale, Sept. 25, 1850, Hale Papers.

41. Hale to Mrs. Hale, June 7, 1844, Hale Papers; *Cong. Globe,* 28 Cong., 1 sess. (1843–1844), pp. 681–682.

42. *Ibid.,* 28 Cong., 2 sess. (1844–1845), p. 373, 30 Cong., 1 sess. (1847–1848), pp. 954, 982, 983.

43. John Woods to Hale, Feb. 19, 1849, James Norris to Hale, April 16, 1849, Jonathan A. Lockwood to Hale, Feb. 14, 1849, Hale Papers; *National Era,* Feb. 15, 1849. Of the navy men, Captain Uriah P. Levy most boldly condemned flogging. His strictures upon the lash, published in the New York *Globe,* the *Democratic Review* and elsewhere, were a great help to Hale. See

Donovan Fitzpatrick and Saul Saphire, *Navy Maverick: Uriah Phillips Levy* (New York, 1963), pp. 185–189.

44. "Report of the Secretary of the Navy, with Returns of Punishments in the Navy," *Senate Executive Report No. 23,* 30 Cong., 2 sess. (1848–1849).

45. *Cong. Globe,* 30 Cong., 2 sess., p. 489.

46. *Ibid.,* 30 Cong., 2 sess., p. 507; Hale to Lucy Hale, May 30, 1850, Hale Papers.

47. *Cong. Globe,* 30 Cong., 2 sess., pp. 506–507.

48. *Ibid.,* 30 Cong., 1 sess., p. 983, 30 Cong., 2 sess., pp. 512–513.

49. *Ibid.,* 31 Cong., 1 sess., pp. 2057–2061; Hale to Mrs. Hale, Sept. 30, 1850, Hale Papers. The spirit ration was not abolished until 1862.

50. William Chester et al. to Hale, Nov. 15, 1850, Hale Papers; *Independent Democrat,* April 28, 1853.

51. J. C. Long to Hale, Jan. 23, 1851 (typed copy), Hale Papers; Charles Francis Adams, *Richard Henry Dana,* 2 vols., (Boston, 1890), I, 231.

52. *Cong. Globe,* 31 Cong., 1 sess., pp. 1858, 1860; Richardson, comp., *Messages and Papers of the Presidents,* V, 93, 138–139.

53. *Cong. Globe,* 32 Cong., 1 sess., pp. 34–35 and *passim,* 31 Cong., 2 sess., pp. 304–309.

54. Henry Steele Commager, *Theodore Parker* (Boston, 1936), p. 219.

55. *Cong. Globe,* 31 Cong., 2 sess., pp. 596–600.

56. Dana, Journal, June 1, 1851, Dana Papers.

57. Adams, *Dana,* I, 198.

58. John L. Hayes, *A Reminiscence of the Free-Soil Movement in New Hampshire, 1845* (Cambridge, Mass., 1885), p. 43.

59. The stubborn juror, Francis E. Bigelow, had for a time concealed Shadrach in his Concord home, later sneaking him to a hiding place in Sudbury. T. J. Damon, "Inside history of Shadrach fugitive slave case," unpublished MSS (May 25, 1905) in Antislavery Papers, American Antiquarian Society. Damon's source on this point was his interview with Bigelow's widow, Mrs. Ann H. Bigelow. See also Adams, *Dana,* I, 216–217.

60. Adams, *Dana,* I, 195–199, 210, 212, 220–222; Boston Vigilance Committee, Treasurers' Accounts (photostatic copy in Widener Library, Harvard University), entries for May 27, June 19, Nov. 10, 1851; Robert Morris to Hale, Jan. 1, 1852, Hale to Morris, Jan. 18, 1852, quoted in *Liberator,* March 19, 1852.

61. As late as January 1851 Hale was putting out feelers for a position with a New York law firm. See William Hoppin to John H. Clark, Jan. 15, 1851, Hale Papers.

62. See N. G. Upham to Levi Woodbury, March 5, 1848, Woodbury Papers; Nathaniel S. Berry to Hale, May 31, 1848, Hale Papers. See also the antislavery resolutions of the Democratic-controlled state legislature, for example, *N.H. House Journal,* June sess. (1848), pp. 287, 310–311, Nov. sess. (1848), pp. 258–259, 406–407, 425, 437, June sess. (1849), pp. 249, 350; *N.H. Senate Journal,* Nov. sess. (1848), pp. 162, 171, June sess. (1849), p. 180.

63. *Independent Democrat,* Dec. 19, 26, 1850, Jan. 23, Feb. 13, 1851.

64. [Dover] *Gazette,* March 6, 13, 1852.

65. *N.H. House Journal,* Nov. sess. (1852), pp. 55–56; *N.H. Senate Journal* (1852), pp. 37–38. In the House the vote was Atherton 148, Ira Perley 81, John Preston 27, Hale 4, John S. Wells 4, scattering 5. In the Senate Atherton had 10 votes, Perley and Preston one each.

NOTES TO CHAPTER IX: LAW, LYCEUMS, AND FREE SOIL

1. Theodore C. Smith, *The Liberty and Free Soil Parties of the Northwest* (New York, 1897), pp. 220–225, 239.

2. Hale to Sumner, Feb. 17, 1850, Sumner Papers.

3. Hale to George G. Fogg, Aug. 4, 1852, quoted in *Independent Democrat,* Aug. 12, 1852.

4. Charles W. Elliott, *Winfield Scott: The Soldier and the Man* (New York, 1937), p. 634; Chase to E. S. Hamlin, June 28, 1852, Chase Papers, Library of Congress.

5. *National Era,* June 24, 1852. Free Democratic replaced Free Soil as the party's official designation, although the two were used interchangeably during the 1852 campaign (and are so used here). The feeling that without New York's Barnburners the party was substantially different from the coalition of 1848, and the desire to suggest a broader platform than mere free soil were most responsible for the change. See Smith, *Liberty and Free Soil Parties,* p. 244; Salmon P. Chase to Charles Sumner, Feb. 26, 1851, Sumner Papers.

6. William G. W. Lewis, *Biography of Samuel Lewis, First Superintendant of Common Schools for the State of Ohio* (Cincinnati, 1857), pp. 392, 399.

7. Estes Howe to Hale, July 7, 1852, Hale Papers; Chase to E. S. Hamlin, July 19, 1852, Chase Papers, Library of Congress; Charles F. Adams, Diary, July 28, 1852, Adams Papers.

8. Hale to Fogg, Aug. 4, 1852, quoted in *Independent Democrat,* Aug. 12, 1852. There is a manuscript fragment of this letter in the Hale Papers.

9. Adams, Diary, Aug. 6, 7, 1852, Adams Papers.

10. Chase to Hale, Aug. 7, 1852, Hale Papers.

11. Tuck to Hale, Aug. 5, 1852, Hale Papers.

12. Adams, Diary, Aug. 9, 10, 1852, Adams Papers.

13. Adams, Diary, Aug. 11, 12, 1852, Adams Papers; *National Era,* Aug. 26, 1852.

14. Adams, Diary, Aug. 13, 1852, Adams Papers; Adams to Sumner, Aug. 15, 1852, quoted in Edward L. Pierce, *Memoir and Letters of Charles Sumner,* 4 vols. (London, 1877–1893), III, 316; David Donald, *Charles Sumner and the Coming of the Civil War* (New York, 1960), pp. 239–240; Chase to E. S. Hamlin, Aug. 13, 1852, Chase Papers, Library of Congress; Samuel Lewis to George W. Julian, Aug. 19, 1852, Giddings-Julian Papers.

15. Wilson to Giddings, Aug. 21, 1852, Giddings Papers; Thurlow Weed to Hamilton Fish, Aug. 22, 23, 1852, Hamilton Fish Papers, Library of Congress;

Walter Whitman to Hale, Aug. 14, 1852, Hale Papers; Hale to Wilson, Sept. 6, 1852, quoted in *Liberator,* Sept. 17, 1852.

16. Hale to Mrs. Hale, Sept. 13, 1852, Hale Papers; Ralph V. Harlow, *Gerrit Smith: Philanthropist and Reformer* (New York, 1939), pp. 190–191.

17. Hale to O. B. Matteson, Sept. 27, 1852, William Henry Seward Collection, Rush Rhees Library, University of Rochester. In New England, also, Free Democrats sought to undermine Pierce. W. B. Greene, stumping for Hale in Massachusetts, reported to Robert Carter: "I *endeavour* to avoid all but Democratic towns." Oct. 1, 1852, Robert Carter Papers, Houghton Library, Harvard University.

18. Hale to Mrs. Hale, Oct. 2, 1852, Hale Papers.

19. *National Era,* Sept. 30, Oct. 7, 14, 21, Nov. 11, 1852; *Independent Democrat,* Oct. 7, 14, 1852; Hale to Mrs. Hale, Oct. 15, 19, 24 (misdated 14), 1852, Hale to Lucy Hale, Oct. 17, 1852, Hale Papers.

20. Smith, *Liberty and Free Soil Parties,* p. 255; *National Era,* Sept. 16, 1852; [Washington] *Union,* Aug.–Nov. 1852; Robert H. Morris to Hamilton Fish, Sept. 10, 1852, Fish Papers.

21. Arthur C. Cole, *The Irrepressible Conflict, 1850–1865* (New York, 1934), p. 270; *National Era,* Nov. 11, 1852; George W. Julian, *Political Recollections, 1840 to 1872* (Chicago, 1883), pp. 129–132. "The abolition of the Whig party is hopeful to the cause of freedom, here & elsewhere," opined Joshua Leavitt. "Unless prevented by a strife about the Tariff, which I hope may not be the case, the Free Democracy now comes to the position of the radical party, & will carry the country in eight years, if not in four: So I prophesy." Leavitt to R. H. Leavitt, Nov. 12, 1852, Joshua Leavitt Papers, Library of Congress.

22. Chase to Mrs. Chase, Feb. 8, 1850, Chase Papers, Library of Congress; Hale to Mrs. Hale, Feb. 11, 1849, Samuel A. Hale to [Lucy Hale] March 21, 1853, Hale Papers.

23. Hale to Mrs. Hale, May 11, 1853, Hale Papers; Hale to James Morse, June 6, 1853, Hale Papers, Phillips Exeter Academy Library; Hale to Charles Sumner, March 31, 1854, Sumner Papers. See also the description of the testimonial banquet in Chapter I, pp. 1–2.

24. Hale to Mrs. Hale, May 11, 1853, Hale to Elizabeth Hale, May 12, 14, 1853, Hale Papers.

25. Hale to Mrs. Hale, May 14, 16, 22, June 23, 25, Sept. 8, 12, 1853, Hale to Elizabeth Hale, May 18, 22, 1853, June 4, 1854, Hale to Lucy Hale, June 4, 1853, Hale Papers.

26. Hale to Elizabeth Hale, April 13, Nov. 25, 1854, Hale Papers.

27. The [New York] *Evening Post* accused Hale of having been in the pay of "borers" seeking to get private appropriations through Congress. Hale denied that he had "ever made a corrupt proposition, or whispered a personal motive to any member of the House or Senate." Still, he admitted that while out of Congress he had used his influence in favor of "honest" measures. See Hale to Charles Sumner, March 31, 1854, Sumner Papers.

28. For a scholarly account of the Burns episode, see Samuel Shapiro, "The Rendition of Anthony Burns," *The Journal of Negro History,* 44: 34–51 (January 1959).

29. Mary T. Higginson, ed., *Letters and Journals of Thomas Wentworth Higginson, 1846–1906* (Boston, 1921), p. 70.

30. Henry B. Stanton, *Random Recollections,* 3 ed. (New York, 1887), p. 128; Hale to Elizabeth Hale, April 13, 1855, Hale Papers.

31. Henry Steele Commager, *Theodore Parker* (Boston, 1936), p. 245; Theodore Parker, *The Trial of Theodore Parker, for the "Misdemeanor" of a Speech in Faneuil Hall against Kidnapping, before the Circuit Court of the United States at Boston, April 3, 1855* (Boston, 1855); Boston Vigilance Committee, Treasurers' Accounts, entry for May 18, 1855.

32. Hale to Charles Sumner, Oct. 22, 1850, Sumner Papers; Hale to Elizabeth Hale, Dec. 20, 1851, Hale Papers.

33. The 1853–1854 box of the Hale Papers is largely filled with correspondence about lecture arrangements. See especially H. C. Goodwin et al. to Hale, Jan. 16, 27, 1854, C. H. Parkhurst to Hale, Nov. 8, 1853, E. Paulk to Hale, Nov. 1, 1853, O. Johnson to Hale, Nov. 5, 1853, Isaiah Stetson to Hale, Oct. 28, 1853, Hale to Mrs. Hale, Jan. 26, March 17, 30, 1855, Hale Papers.

34. Brigs Arnold to Hale, Dec. 23, 1853, Hale Papers.

35. Hale to Mrs. Hale, Jan. 6, 1854, Hale Papers.

36. Hale to Mrs. Hale, Nov. 27, 1854, Hale Papers. See also Hale to Mrs. Hale, Oct. 2, 1854, Hale Papers.

37. Allan Nevins, *Ordeal of the Union,* 2 vols. (New York, 1947), II, 94–159, 316–346, especially pp. 96, 125.

38. *Independent Democrat,* March 2, 9, 1854, Hale to S. L. Howe, April 29, 1854, Hale to the Rev. H. Adams, April 29, 1854, Hale to the Rev. Asa Truman, April 29, 1854, Letterbooks, Hale Papers.

39. Hale to Charles Sumner, March 17, 1854, Sumner Papers; Mason W. Tappan to Hale, March 25, 1854, Hale Papers; Henry F. French to Benjamin B. French, Feb. 19, May 30, June 16, 1854, French Papers; Amos Tuck to Israel Washburn, March 18, 1854, Israel Washburn Papers, Library of Congress.

40. George G. Fogg to Hale, Feb. 10, April 21, 1854, Hale to Fogg, June 14, 1854, Hale Papers.

41. Mason W. Tappan to Hale, June 19, 1854, Hale Papers.

42. Tappan to Hale, May 1, 1854, Hale Papers.

43. *New Hampshire Patriot,* June 14, 1854.

44. These resolutions, proposed by George M. Flanders of Manchester, condemned the Kansas-Nebraska Act as "unnecessary, impolitic, a breach of faith with the North, dangerous and wrong," and censured Hibbard, Norris, and Williams for voting for it. The House adopted the Flanders resolutions on July 5, 1854. See *N.H. House Journal,* June sess. (1854), pp. 34–35, 283–298.

45. Tappan to Hale, June 19, 1854, Hale Papers; *N.H. House Journal,* June sess. (1854), pp. 89, 107–108, 222, 225, 313–314, 316–317. The Senate elected John S. Wells to serve out Atherton's term and Harry Hibbard to serve the

full term, but without the House's concurrence its action was without effect. See *N.H. Senate Journal*, June sess. (1854), pp. 159, 220.

46. *Independent Democrat*, Sept. 7, 28, 1854.

47. For general accounts of the Know-Nothing movement see Ray A. Billington, *The Protestant Crusade, 1800–1860: A Study of the Origins of American Nativism* (New York, 1938), pp. 380–397; Nevins, *Ordeal of the Union*, II, 323–346, 397–404. See also Carroll John Noonan, *Nativism in Connecticut, 1829–1860* (Washington, 1938) and Charles Stickney, "Know-Nothingism in Rhode Island," *Publications of the Rhode Island Historical Society*, new series, vol. I, no. 4 (January 1894), pp. 243–257.

48. James O. Lyford, *Life of Edward H. Rollins: A Political Biography* (Boston, 1906), pp. 39–40; Everett S. Stackpole, *History of New Hampshire*, 4 vols. (New York, 1916), III, 154ff.; Billington, *Protestant Crusade*, pp. 425–427; Hale to Thurlow Weed, Feb. 2, 1855, Thurlow Weed Collection, Rush Rhees Library, University of Rochester.

49. Hale to Tappan, Nov. 19, 1854, Letterbooks, Hale to Mrs. Hale, Nov. 27, 1854, Hale Papers.

50. *Independent Democrat*, Nov. 2, 1854, Jan. 25, Feb. 1, March 1, 1855; *New Hampshire Patriot*, Jan. 24, 1855; Tappan to Hale, Jan. 20, 26, 1855, Hale Papers.

51. Tappan to Hale, Jan. 26, 1855, Hale Papers.

52. Tappan to Hale, Jan. 20, 26, Feb. 19, 1855, Hale Papers.

53. Tappan to Hale, Jan. 20, 1855, Hale Papers; Hale to Thurlow Weed, Feb. 2, 1855, Weed Collection.

54. Hale to Mrs. Hale, March 1, 1855, Hale Papers.

55. *Independent Democrat*, Dec. 14, 1854, Jan. 11, March 8, 1855.

56. *Independent Democrat*, March 15, 1855; Tappan to Hale, March 19, 1855, Hale Papers.

57. Tappan to Hale, March 19, 1855, Hale Papers.

58. W. Darrell Overdyke, *The Know-Nothing Party in the South* (Louisiana State University, 1950), pp. 40–43; Tappan to Hale, May 2, 1855, Hale Papers.

59. Tappan to Hale, June 2, 1855, Hale Papers.

60. Hale to Tappan, June 9, 1855, Letterbooks, Hale Papers.

61. Fragment of a letter to Mrs. Hale written sometime during the spring of 1855, Hale Papers.

62. Tappan to Hale, June 11, 1855, Hale Papers.

63. Tappan to Hale, June 12, 1855, Hale Papers.

64. Tappan to Hale, June 15, 1855, George O. Odlin to Hale, June 13, 1855, Hale Papers; *New Hampshire Statesman*, June 16, 1855.

65. *N.H. House Journal*, June sess. (1855), pp. 71–72; *N.H. Senate Journal*, June sess. (1855), p. 68; Tappan to Hale, June 14, 1855, Hale Papers.

NOTES TO CHAPTER X: THE COMING OF THE CIVIL WAR

1. Allan Nevins, *Ordeal of the Union*, 2 vols. (New York, 1947), II, 301–311, 380–393, 408–411.

2. *Cong. Globe,* 34 Cong., 1 sess. (1855–1856), p. 1.

3. Hale to Parker, Dec. 16, 1855, Hale Papers; Nevins, *Ordeal of the Union,* II, 412–416.

4. James D. Richardson, comp., *A Compilation of the Messages and Papers of the Presidents,* 20 vols. (New York, 1897–1927), V, 327–350.

5. *Cong. Globe,* 34 Cong., 1 sess., pp. 134–135.

6. Ben: Perley Poore, *Perley's Reminiscences of Sixty Years in the National Metropolis,* 2 vols. (Philadelphia, 1886), I, 458–459; Roy F. Nichols, *Franklin Pierce: Young Hickory of the Granite Hills,* rev. ed. (Philadelphia, 1958), p. 440.

7. [Washington] *Union,* Jan. 5, 1856; Louis M. Sears, *John Slidell* (Durham, N.C., 1925), p. 119.

8. Hale to Mrs. Hale, July 3, 1856, Hale Papers.

9. *Cong. Globe,* 34 Cong., 1 sess., pp. 495–497; C. H. Crane to Hale, Feb. 20, 1856, Hale Papers.

10. *Cong. Globe,* 34 Cong., 1 sess., Appendix. pp. 102–109.

11. John Jay to Hale, March 3, 1856, Hale Papers; *Liberator,* March 21, 1856; *Independent Democrat,* March 13, 1856.

12. David Donald, *Charles Sumner and the Coming of the Civil War* (New York, 1960), pp. 281–297.

13. Hale to Elizabeth Hale, May 25, 1856, Hale Papers.

14. Hale to Parker, May 25, 1856, Hale Papers.

15. *Cong. Globe,* 34 Cong., 1 sess., pp. 1480–1481.

16. Hale to Mrs. Hale, June 28, 1856, Hale Papers.

17. Hale thought Burlingame's retaliatory address had "killed Sumner's speech out and out." "Nobody talks of anything else here just now but Burlingame and Massachusetts," he wrote Burlingame's wife. Hale to [Jennie] Burlingame, June 24, 1856, Anson Burlingame Papers, Library of Congress. See also Hale to Mrs. Hale, July 22, 1856, Hale Papers.

18. Donald, *Sumner,* p. 323.

19. Hale to Mrs. Hale, July 3, 1856, Hale Papers. See also Hale to Theodore Parker, Aug. 12, 1856, Hale Papers.

20. Hale to Mrs. Hale, July 3, 1856, Hale to Elizabeth Hale, July 6, 1856, Hale Papers.

21. *Cong. Globe,* 34 Cong., 1 sess., Appendix, pp. 844–849. Senator Douglas and Charles E. Stuart of Michigan scored Hale for his inconsistency in opposing the repeal of a measure—the Missouri Compromise—whose principle he had so often attacked. "Sir," Hale returned, "the free States complained of the Missouri compromise because they got so little by it in 1820. In 1854 they objected to its abrogation because they lost what little they had got. That is it." *Ibid.*

22. John Tweedy, *A History of the Republican National Conventions from 1856 to 1908* (Danbury, Conn., 1910), p. 28; Francis Curtis, *The Republican Party,* 2 vols. (New York, 1904), I, 261; Henry Wilson, *History of the Rise*

and Fall of the Slave Power in America, 7 ed., 3 vols. (Boston, 1872–1877), II, 514. Chase, who desired the nomination himself and who thought it wrong to go outside the party for a candidate, later scolded Hale and Sumner for giving in "too readily to the availability idea" at Philadelphia. But since neither was a delegate there was really little they might have done. See Chase to Sumner, Jan. 18, 1858, Sumner Papers.

23. William E. Smith, *The Francis Preston Blair Family in Politics,* 2 vols. (New York, 1933), I, 359; Henry Wilson to Charles Sumner, Aug. 3, 1856, William H. Seward to Sumner, Aug. 13, 1856, Sumner Papers; Hale to Mrs. Hale, Sept. 13, 18, 28, Oct. 2, 6, 1856, Hale to Elizabeth Hale, Sept. 17, 20, 1856, Hale Papers.

24. Hale to Washburne, Oct. 24, 1856, Elihu Washburne Papers, Library of Congress.

25. Hale to Salmon P. Chase, May 15, 1857, Chase Papers, Pennsylvania Historical Society; Hale to Mason W. Tappan, March 21, 1857, Hale to Theodore Parker, April 3, 1857, Hale Papers.

26. Allan Nevins, *The Emergence of Lincoln,* 2 vols. (New York, 1950), I, 90–118. See also Vincent C. Hopkins, *Dred Scott's Case* (New York, 1951).

27. *Cong. Globe,* 35 Cong., 1 sess. (1857–1858), pp. 315–321, 341–345. For an earlier expression of Hale's lack of confidence in the Supreme Court, see *ibid.,* 31 Cong., 1 sess. (1849–1850), Appendix, p. 1453. For the New Hampshire legislature's resolution regarding the Dred Scott decision, see *N.H. House Journal,* June sess. (1857), pp. 161–162, 304, 350–352, 376.

28. Chase to Hale, March 19, 1858, Herndon to Hale, Feb. 10, 1858, Hale Papers; Fogg to Tappan, Jan. 31, 1858, Mason Weare Tappan Papers, New Hampshire Historical Society; *Independent Democrat,* Jan. 28, 1858.

29. Nevins, *Emergence of Lincoln,* I, 275–279, 295–301; *Cong. Globe,* 35 Cong., 1 sess., pp. 1264–1265, 1437–1438, 1821–1822, 1899.

30. *N.H. House Journal,* June sess. (1857), p. 128, (1858), p. 228.

31. John Preston to Hale, June 23, 1858, Hale Papers; James O. Lyford, *Life of Edward H. Rollins: A Political Biography* (Boston, 1906), pp. 88–90.

32. John J. Prentiss to Hale, Feb. 26, 1858, Hale Papers; Mason W. Tappan to George G. Fogg, May 15, 29, 1858, Tappan Papers.

33. John L. Carlton to Hale, April 24, 1858, Hale Papers.

34. E. Thompson to Hale, Feb. 10, 1858, Hale Papers.

35. John L. Carlton to Hale, April 24, 1858, Hale Papers.

36. Tappan to George G. Fogg, May 15, 1858, Tappan Papers; John J. Prentiss to Hale, Feb. 26, 1858, Hale Papers.

37. Hale to Fogg, May 9, 1858, Hale Papers.

38. Fogg to Tappan, April 25, 1858, Tappan Papers.

39. Tuck to Fogg, April 26, 1858, Tuck Papers; Thomas L. Tullock to Hale, May 14, 1858, Hale Papers.

40. John R. Varney to Hale, May 12, 1858, W. H. Gove to Hale, June 3, 1858, Hale Papers; *Independent Democrat,* May 20, 1858.

41. Fogg to Tappan, June 6, 1858, Tappan Papers; *Independent Democrat,* June 10, 1858; *N.H. House Journal,* June sess. (1858), p. 66.

42. Hale to Fogg, June 9, 13, 1858, Hale Papers.

43. Richardson, comp., *Messages and Papers of the Presidents,* V, 511; *Cong. Globe,* 35 Cong., 2 sess., (1858–1859), pp. 277, 538.

44. *Ibid.,* 35 Cong., 2 sess., pp. 543–544; Fogg to Hale, Feb. 6, 1859, Hale Papers; Tappan to Fogg, Feb. 13, 1859, Tappan Papers.

45. *Cong. Globe,* 35 Cong., 2 sess., Appendix, pp. 160–166.

46. *Ibid.,* 35 Cong., 2 sess., p. 1354.

47. C. Vann Woodward, *The Burden of Southern History* (Baton Rouge, 1960), pp. 61–67.

48. [New York] *Herald,* Oct. 27, 28, 1859.

49. Wilson, *Rise and Fall of the Slave Power,* II, 592; Woodward, *Burden of Southern History,* pp. 49–51. Franklin B. Sanborn, knowing only that Forbes had been seen talking to Hale in May 1858, mistakenly concluded that Hale, as well as Seward and Wilson, had heard about Brown's projects. See Sanborn to Thomas W. Higginson, May 18, 1858, quoted in Oswald Garrison Villard, *John Brown, 1850–1859: A Biography Fifty Years After,* rev. ed. (New York, 1943), p. 339.

50. Hale to editors of [Chicago] *Press and Tribune,* Oct. 29, 1859, quoted in *Independent Democrat,* Nov. 10, 1859; [New York] *Herald,* Oct. 27, 1859.

51. Woodward, *Burden of Southern History,* pp. 61–68.

52. *Cong. Globe,* 36 Cong., 1 sess. (1859–1860), pp. 7–9, 15.

53. Fragment of a letter from Hale to Mrs. Hale, written in mid-March, 1860, Hale Papers.

54. *Cong. Globe,* 36 Cong., 1 sess., pp. 2213–2215, 2351–2352.

55. *Ibid.,* 36 Cong., 1 sess., pp. 126–127, 760–768; *Independent Democrat,* Jan. 5, 1860.

56. M. O. C. Vaughan et al. to Simon Cameron, Feb. 8, 1859, Simon Cameron Papers, Library of Congress; William Baringer, *Lincoln's Rise to Power* (Boston, 1937), pp. 122, 189. On April 26, 1860, the *Independent Democrat* listed in order these "Republicans mentioned in connection with the Chicago nomination": Seward, Chase, Frémont, Hale, Lincoln, Fessenden, Banks, Cameron, Bates, McLean, Wade, and Wilson.

57. Charles Francis Adams, Diary, April 19, 1860, Adams Papers; Henry B. Stanton, *Random Recollections,* 3 ed. (New York, 1887), p. 213.

58. Hale to Mrs. Hale, Aug. 13, 26, Sept. 15, Oct. 21, 22, 27, 1860, Hale to George G. Fogg, Aug. 25, Oct. 16, 1860, Horace White to Hale, Oct. 9, 1860, Hale Papers; Hale to N. B. Judd, Oct. 2, 1860, Washburne Papers; *Independent Democrat,* Oct. 25, 1860.

59. Arthur C. Cole, "Lincoln's Election an Immediate Menace to Slavery in the States?" *The American Historical Review* 36:740–767 (July 1931). But see also J. G. de Roulhac Hamilton, "Lincoln's Election an Immediate Menace to Slavery in the States?" *ibid.,* 37:700–711 (July 1932).

60. Hale to Mrs. Hale, Dec. 3, 1860, Hale Papers. While in New York, Hale posed for photographer Mathew Brady. See the frontispiece to this book.

61. Kenneth M. Stampp, *And the War Came: The North and the Secession Crisis, 1860–1861* (Louisiana State University, 1950), pp. 63–66.

62. *Cong. Globe,* 36 Cong., 2 sess. (1860–1861), 9–10.

63. Stampp, *And the War Came,* pp. 66–67. William Seward and Charles Francis Adams were two Republicans who urged moderation and were willing to make slight concessions. Seward proposed a constitutional amendment protecting slavery in the states, and Adams, though he later reneged, at first agreed to sponsor a bill for the admission of New Mexico, perhaps as a slave state (*ibid.,* p. 138); Martin B. Duberman, *Charles Francis Adams, 1807–1886* (Boston, 1961), pp. 223–255.

64. Lucien H. Adams to Hale, Jan. 5, 1861, Robert Carter to Hale, Dec. 6, 1860, David Root to Hale, Feb. 4, 1861, Hale Papers.

65. *Cong. Globe,* 36 Cong., 2 sess., pp. 112–116.

66. Hale to Mrs. Hale, Dec. 14, 1860, Hale Papers. Other Republicans shared Hale's opinion of Buchanan. "Would to Heaven we had a President equal to the emergency," Chase moaned. "Imbecility, now, works as treason." Chase to Benjamin F. Wade, Benjamin F. Wade Papers, Library of Congress. For a highly sympathetic view of Buchanan's actions during the secession crisis see Philip S. Klein, *President James Buchanan: A Biography* (University Park, Pa., 1962), chs. xxvii–xxix.

67. Hale to Chase, Jan. 11, 1861, Chase Papers, Pennsylvania Historical Society; Chase to Hale, Jan. 14, 1861, Chase Papers, New Hampshire Historical Society; Hale to Lincoln, Jan. 19, 1861, Abraham Lincoln Papers, Library of Congress.

68. Ichabod Goodwin to Hale, Jan. 31, 1861, Hale Papers. Hale also urged Representative Charles Francis Adams to recommend to Governor John Andrew that Massachusetts send commissioners to the peace conference. Adams and other Massachusetts congressmen complied, not realizing that the day before Sumner had advised Andrew *not* to send commissioners. "Sumner is said to be hurt with Hale's behavior, which was certainly not open, for though Hale says he did not know that Sumner would oppose it, he probably believed he would, and ought at any rate to have consulted him." Henry Adams to Charles Francis Adams, Jr., Feb. 5, 1861, in Henry Adams, *Letters of Henry Adams,* Worthington C. Ford, ed., 2 vols. (Boston, 1930–1938), I, 85.

69. *Cong. Globe,* 36 Cong., 2 sess., pp. 662–664.

70. New Hampshire's delegates—Amos Tuck, Asa Fowler, and Levi Chamberlain—voted against five of the seven sections of the constitutional amendment proposed by the Washington Conference. Only section 5, which prohibited the foreign slave trade forever, and section 7, which called upon Congress to compensate slaveholders in certain cases for fugitives, received their approval. Tuck, the only Granite State delegate to take part in debate, generally echoed Hale's remarks of January 31, although he went farther in

proposing a national constitutional convention. L. H. Chittenden, *A Report of the Debates and Proceedings in the Secret Sessions of the Conference Convention . . . Held at Washington, D. C. in February, A.D. 1861* (New York, 1864), pp. 311–312, 425–426. For the history of the conference see Robert Gray Gunderson, *Old Gentlemen's Convention: The Washington Peace Conference of 1861* (Madison, 1961).

71. *Cong. Globe*, 36 Cong., 2 sess., p. 664.

NOTES TO CHAPTER XI: RADICAL REPUBLICAN

1. [Dover] *Enquirer,* April 18, 1861.

2. In June 1861 Hale was enrolled as Judge Advocate in Company C, Governor's Horse Guards—an honorary group which paraded once a year at Concord.

3. Otis F. R. Waite, *New Hampshire in the Great Rebellion* (Norwich, Conn., and Concord, N.H., 1870), pp. 49–57; *Independent Democrat,* April 25, 1861.

4. *Ibid.,* April 18, 1861; [Dover] *Gazette,* April 27, 1861. See also *New Hampshire Patriot,* April 17, May 1, 1861.

5. Hale to Welles, April 24, 1861, Gideon Welles Papers, Library of Congress.

6. [Dover]*Gazette,* June 1, 1861.

7. James G. Randall and David Donald, *The Civil War and Reconstruction,* 2 ed. (Boston, 1961), pp. 275–276.

8. Welles to Hale, June 10, 1861, Hale to Mrs. Hale, June 30, 1861, Hale Papers; Hale to Welles, June 17, 1861, Welles Papers, Library of Congress. Welles' biographer mistakenly says that in June Hale "failed to reply" to Welles' letters and that Hale did not reach Washington until the 1st or 2nd of July. Richard S. West, Jr., *Gideon Welles: Lincoln's Navy Department* (Indianapolis, 1943), pp. 121–122.

9. William H. Russell, *My Civil War Diary,* Fletcher Pratt, ed. (London, 1954), p. 17; Margaret Leech, *Reveille in Washington, 1860–1865* (New York, 1941), ch. v; Constance M. Green, *Washington: Village and Capital, 1800–1878* (Princeton, 1962), chs. ix–xi.

10. Hale to Lucy Hale, July 1, 1861, Hale Papers.

11. [Dover] *Gazette,* Oct. 26, 1861; Hale to Lucy Hale, June 10, 1862, Hale to Mrs. Hale, Dec. 15, 1861, July 14, Sept. 22, 1862, Elizabeth Hale to Hale, Dec. 17, 1861, Hale Papers.

12. Hale to Mrs. Hale, Oct. 16, 1862, Hale to Elizabeth Hale, May 23, 1864, Hale Papers. In December 1862 Hale introduced "a bill to abolish the rank and grade of medical officers in the United States service, and to provide that hereafter no medical officer shall have or exercise any military authority whatever." *Cong. Globe,* 37 Cong., 3 sess. (1862–1863), pp. 25–26.

13. Hale to Mrs. Hale, Sept. 20, 1862, Hale Papers.

14. Recommendation for Belle Garcia, Sept. 24, 1863, Abraham Lincoln

Papers, Henry E. Huntington Library and Art Gallery.

15. John Jay to Hale, Aug. 13, 22, 1861, Hale Papers; Hale to Charles Sumner, Nov. 19, 1861, Sumner Papers. Jay was appointed Minister to Austria, but not until 1869, after Hale had left the Senate.

16. *Cong. Globe,* 37 Cong., 2 sess. (1861–1862), pp. 8, 26–27, 37 Cong., 3 sess., pp. 270–271.

17. Mrs. Hale to Mrs. Lambert, May 2, 1862, Hale to Elizabeth Hale, May 21, 1864, Hale Papers; Orville H. Browning, *The Diary of Orville Hickman Browning,* T. C. Pease and J. G. Randall, ed., 2 vols., Collections of the Illinois State Historical Library (Springfield, 1927, 1933), XX, 548 (June 3, 1862); Amos Tuck French, ed., *From the Diary and Correspondence of Benjamin Brown French* (New York, 1904), p. 129 (Jan. 26, 1865). For a fine discussion of society in Civil War Washington, see John Y. Simon, "Congress Under Lincoln, 1861–1863," unpub. diss., Harvard University, 1960, pp. 15–18.

18. Hale to Mrs. Hale, Dec. 11, 1862, Aug. 12, 1864, Hale Papers.

19. Howe to Horace Rublee, July 3, 1861, Timothy O. Howe Papers, State Historical Society of Wisconsin.

20. For the composition and political complexion of the Thirty-Seventh Congress, see Simon, "Congress Under Lincoln," chs. ii–v. Of the 49 senators who attended the special session in July 1861, 32 were Republicans; in the House there were 109 Republicans and 65 Democrats.

21. Galusha A. Grow of Pennsylvania was Speaker. Other House leaders were: John J. Crittenden (Kentucky), Francis P. Blair (Missouri), Thaddeus Stevens (Pennsylvania), Charles B. Sedgwick (New York), Owen Lovejoy (Illinois), John A. Bingham (Ohio), Elihu Washburne (Illinois), Justin S. Morrill (Vermont).

22. *Cong. Globe.,* 37 Cong., 1 sess. (1861), p. 17.

23. For a more elaborate and somewhat different classification see Simon, "Congress Under Lincoln," pp. 37–64. For contemporary references to Hale as a Radical see Adam Gurowski, *Diary,* 3 vols. (Boston, 1862–1866), I, 106, 139, 210; *Liberator,* Aug. 22, 1862.

24. West, Jr., *Welles,* pp. 115, 121–123.

25. Hale to Welles, April 24, May 29, 1861, Welles Papers, Library of Congress.

26. Welles, "Narrative of Events, 1861," Welles Papers, Library of Congress.

27. Reinhard H. Luthin, *The Real Abraham Lincoln* (Englewood Cliffs, N.J., 1960), pp. 248, 552. Welles himself was convinced that Hale felt "somewhat mortified" at not being appointed Secretary of the Navy. See Welles, "Narrative of Events, 1861," Welles Papers, Library of Congress.

28. *Cong. Globe,* 38 Cong., 2 sess. (1864–1865), p. 855.

29. Hannibal Hamlin to Welles, June 8, 1861 (confidential), Mary Lincoln to Welles, Sept. 16, 1861, Gideon Welles Papers, Connecticut Historical Society.

30. *Cong. Globe,* 38 Cong., 1 sess. (1863–1864), p. 437.

31. *Ibid.,* 37 Cong., 1 sess., p. 1.

32. *Ibid.,* p. 42.

33. *Ibid.,* p. 216.

34. Gideon Welles, *Diary of Gideon Welles, Secretary of the Navy under Lincoln and Johnson,* Howard K. Beale, ed., 3 vols. (New York, 1960), I, 48–49.

35. "Report of the Surrender and Destruction of Navy Yards, etc.," [U.S.] *Senate Report No. 37* (April 18, 1862), 37 Cong., 2 sess.

36. Welles, *Diary,* I, 49–50.

37. Morgan to Welles, May 2, [1861] Welles Papers, Library of Congress.

38. West, Jr., *Welles,* pp. 121, 138–139; Richard S. West, Jr., "The Morgan Purchases," *United States Naval Institute Proceedings,* vol. LXVI, no. 443 (January 1940), pp. 73–77.

39. West, Jr., *Welles,* p. 138.

40. S. F. DuPont to George D. Morgan, Dec. 24, 1861, newspaper clipping in Welles Papers, Library of Congress.

41. "Report of the Secretary of the Navy," [U.S.] *Senate Ex. Doc. No. 1* (July 4, 1861), 37 Cong., 1 sess., pp. 85–111.

42. "Government Contracts," [U.S.] *House Report No. 2* (Dec. 17, 1861), 37 Cong., 2 sess., pt. I, pp. 249–361. For Morgan's testimony, see pt. I, pp. 260–288, 299–305.

43. "Report of the Secretary of the Navy," [U.S.] *Senate Ex. Doc. No. 1* (Dec. 2, 1861), 37 Cong., 2 sess., pp. 14–16.

44. "Government Contracts," pt. I, p. 136.

45. *Cong. Globe,* 37 Cong., 2 sess., p. 199.

46. *Ibid.,* p. 219.

47. James Dixon to Mark Howard, Jan. 11, 1862, Mark Howard Papers, Connecticut Historical Society.

48. *Cong. Globe,* 37 Cong., 2 sess., pp. 245–249.

49. "Letter of the Secretary of the Navy . . . ," [U.S.] *Senate Ex. Doc. No. 15* (Jan. 14, 1862), 37 Cong., 2 sess.

50. Forbes to Charles B. Sedgwick, Jan. 18, 1862 (copy), Welles Papers, Library of Congress.

51. *Independent Democrat,* Jan. 23, 1862; Robert L. Taylor to Capt. J. Riley, Jan. 24, 1862, Hale Papers. Even Forbes had grave reservations about the Welles-Morgan arrangement. "As compared with buying through a naval officer, I have no question that M. saved five or ten times his commission," he wrote George Ripley of the New York *Tribune* on Feb. 17, 1862. But, he went on, "There is no sort of question, either, that the commission was too high, and that Gideon blundered! and that M. deserves some scorching for not disgorging the surplus on the whole." John Murray Forbes, *Letters from Recollections of John Murray Forbes,* Sarah Forbes Hughes, ed., 2 vols. (Boston, 1899), I, 289. See also *ibid.,* I, 230, 231.

52. "George D. Morgan," [U.S.] *Senate Report No. 9* (Jan. 27, 1862), 37 Cong., 2 sess.; *Cong. Globe,* 37 Cong., 2 sess., pp. 698–701.

53. Morgan's own testimony was damaging. On Sept. 5, 1861, he had ad-

mitted to the House committee investigating war contracts that "in some cases of the purchase of vessels by me, where the owner has asked what I thought to be a large price, and where the negotiation was a close one, I have, for the purpose of buying the vessel cheap, given up my commissions to him." "Government Contracts," pt. I, 274.

54. *Cong. Globe,* 37 Cong., 2 sess., p. 700.

55. [Newport] *Argus & Spectator,* Feb. 21, 1862.

56. See, for example, Amasa Walker to Hale, Jan. 28, 1862, W. O. Bartlett to Hale, Jan. 29, 1862, Samuel D. Bell to Hale, March 14, 1862, Moody Hobbs to Hale, June 24, 1862, Hale Papers; *Harper's Weekly* 6:80 (Feb. 1, 1862); *Frank Leslie's Illustrated Newspaper* 13:162 (Feb. 1, 1862); 13:227 (March 1, 1862); 13:242 (March 8, 1862).

57. *Cong. Globe,* 37 Cong., 2 sess., p. 821. James Harlan, John Sherman, Morton Wilkinson, Robert Wilson, and Hale made up the five votes.

58. *Ibid.,* 37 Cong., 2 sess., pp. 817–819, 1155; Welles, *Diary,* I, 54, 227, 482–483, 490–491, 507–508; James W. Grimes to Gustavus V. Fox, Oct. 6, 1862, Gustavus V. Fox Papers, New-York Historical Society; Hale to Mrs. Hale, Dec. 11, 1863, Hale Papers; Gideon Welles to Edgar T. Welles, Dec. 13, 1863, Welles Papers, Library of Congress.

59. Welles to Hale, Feb. 3, 1863, Welles Papers, Library of Congress; *Cong. Globe,* 37 Cong., 2 sess., p. 619.

60. See, for example, *ibid.,* pp. 697, 1390, 1394–1395, 1689. After 1862 Welles and Fox worked almost exclusively through Senator Grimes, so that by the last years of the war Hale was in no position to offer assistance even had he wished to do so.

61. Hale to Charles Sumner, April 28, 1865, Sumner Papers. See also Hale to George G. Fogg, April 27, 1863, Hale Papers.

62. Doolittle to Henry Doolittle, Jan. 7, 1861, James R. Doolittle Papers, State Historical Society of Wisconsin.

63. [Dover] *Gazette,* April 27, 1861.

64. *Cong. Globe,* 37 Cong., 1 sess., p. 257. In his inaugural address of March 4, 1861, Lincoln had similarly disclaimed any intention of interfering with slavery in the states. See James D. Richardson, comp., *A Compilation of the Messages and Papers of the Presidents,* 20 vols. (New York, 1897–1927), VI, 5. In the Senate the vote was 30-5; in the House Thad Stevens alone dissented.

65. *Cong. Globe,* 37 Cong., 1 sess., p. 260.

66. Howe to Grace T. Howe, Dec. 13, 1861, Howe Papers.

67. George Perkins Marsh, United States Minister to Italy, advised Sumner in July 1861 that the Italian government "in all its branches" was "most warmly inclined to sympathize with us of the North in our great struggle, but this sympathy is founded on the belief that it is not a question of territory, not of mere re-union, but emphatically of light and darkmen, liberty and slavery." Marsh to Sumner, July 26, 1861, Sumner Papers.

68. *Cong. Globe,* 38 Cong., 1 sess., p. 754.

69. *Ibid.*, 35 Cong., 1 sess. (1857–1858), p. 1970.
70. See Leon Litwack's able and comprehensive *North of Slavery: The Negro in the Free States, 1790–1860* (Chicago, 1961).
71. *Cong. Globe*, 36 Cong., 1 sess. (1859–1860), p. 761.
72. *Ibid.*, 37 Cong., 2 sess., pp. 1266–1268.
73. Hale to Mrs. Hale, May 29, 1864, Hale Papers.
74. *Cong. Globe*, 37 Cong., 2 sess., pp. 1605–1606.
75. *Ibid.*, p. 1785.
76. *Ibid.*, pp. 1881–1882.
77. *Ibid.*, p. 1957.
78. *Ibid.*, pp. 3274–3276.
79. *Ibid.*, 38 Cong., 1 sess., p. 17.
80. *Ibid.*, pp. 3308–3309.
81. Browning, *Diary*, I, 612.
82. *Cong. Globe*, 38 Cong., 1 sess., p. 1443.
83. Hale to Mrs. Hale, Dec. 8, 13, 1863, Hale to Lucy Hale, Dec. 16, 1863, Hale Papers.
84. [New York] *Tribune*, Dec. 16, 1863.
85. *Cong. Globe*, 38 Cong., 1 sess., pp. 40–41.
86. Hale to Mrs. Hale, Dec. 17, 1863, Hale to Elizabeth Hale, Dec. 17, 1863, Hale Papers.
87. Welles, *Diary*, I, 489 (Dec. 18, 1863).
88. [Dover] *Enquirer*, Jan. 7, 1864.
89. [Portsmouth] *Journal*, Jan. 2, 1864. See also *Independent Democrat*, Dec. 24, 1863; [Lancaster] *Coos Republican*, Jan. 5, 1864.
90. *New Hampshire Patriot*, Dec. 23, 1863; [Nashua] *Gazette*, Dec. 31, 1863.
91. "Hon. John P. Hale," [U.S.] *Senate Report No. 5* (Feb. 1, 1864), 38 Cong., 1 sess.; *Cong. Globe*, 38 Cong., 1 sess., pp. 93, 420, 555–562; [Dover] *Enquirer*, Feb. 4, 1864.
92. J. D. Moulton to Hale, Feb. 22, 1864, Hale Papers.
93. Hale to Mrs. Hale, March 3, 1864, Hale to Elizabeth Hale, March 4, 1864, Hale to Lucy Hale, March 8, 1864, Hale Papers.
94. Young to Hale, Oct. 30, 1863, Hale Papers.
95. Leon B. Richardson, *William E. Chandler: Republican* (New York, 1940), pp. 29–46; James O. Lyford, *Life of Edward H. Rollins: A Political Biography* (Boston, 1906), pp. 74–75, 164–165; Larkin D. Mason to Mason W. Tappan, May 9, 1864, Tappan Papers; Andrew H. Young to Hale, June 22, 1864, Hale Papers.
96. Fogg to Tappan, April 12, 1864, Tappan Papers.
97. Ela to Hale, Feb. 3, 1864, Oliver Wyatt to Hale, May 10, 1864, John Preston to Hale, March 20, 1864, Daniel Smith to Hale, May 30, 1864, Hale Papers; Hale to Charles W. Brewster, May 13, 1864, Misc. MSS, Massachusetts Historical Society; Hale to Elizabeth Hale, May 2, 1864, Hale Papers.
98. Hale to Mason W. Tappan, June 2, 1864, Hale Papers.

99. Hale to Mrs. Hale, June 7, 1864, Hale Papers.

100. Tappan to Hale, June 5, 1864, Hale Papers.

101. *Independent Democrat,* June 16, 1864. The results of the first ballot were: Marston 57, Cragin 49, Hale 35, Tuck 32, Edwards 24, and five votes scattered.

102. Welles to Edgar T. Welles, June 12, 1864, Welles Papers, Library of Congress; Welles, *Diary,* II, 51–52 (June 10, 1864); Gurowski, *Diary,* III, 255–256 (June 12, 1864).

103. Cragin to Tappan, July 22, 1864, Tappan Papers.

104. Hale to Mrs. Hale, Oct. 9, 1864, Hale Papers.

105. Welles, *Diary,* II, 193–194 (Dec. 8, 1864); *Cong. Globe,* 38 Cong., 2 sess., pp. 8, 56. Timothy Howe recalled later that Hale had been replaced by Grimes "for the reason that he had criticised from his place in the Senate, the Secretary of the Navy, for some transactions, very sharply, and as some Senators felt needlessly." Howe to Hamilton Fish, Dec. 22, 1877, Fish Papers.

106. *Cong. Globe,* 38 Cong., 2 sess., pp. 468–469, 489–491, 512–513, 851–855; Welles, *Diary,* II, 231 (Jan. 28, 1865).

107. Edwin D. Morgan to John Bigelow, Dec. 23, 1864, quoted in John Bigelow, *Retrospections of an Active Life,* 3 vols. (New York, 1909), II, 248; Welles, *Diary,* II, 255 (March 11, 1865).

108. *Ibid.; Independent Democrat,* March 16, 1865.

109. [Dover] *Enquirer,* April 27, 1865.

110. *Cong. Globe,* 38 Cong., 1 sess., pp. 3449–3460, 3461.

111. [Dover] *Enquirer,* April 27, 1865.

112. Eric L. McKitrick, *Andrew Johnson and Reconstruction* (Chicago, 1960), p. 137; Sumner to F. W. Bird, April 25, 1865, Sumner Papers.

NOTES TO CHAPTER XII: AN AMERICAN IN SPAIN

1. Elizabeth Hale to Mrs. Hale, March 30, 1865, Hale to Mrs. Botta (?), June 10, 1865, Hale to John R. Varney, June 22, 1865, Hale Papers. During his five-year absence, Hale kept in close touch with Varney, asking about "that little pet pear tree of mine immediately behind the barn," inquiring about his "money affairs, bank stock &c," giving instructions about the upkeep of the house, the care of livestock, and so on. Hale to Varney, Sept. 5, Oct. 29, 1865, April 16, 1867, Hale Papers.

2. Perry to Hale, May 20, 27, 1865, Fogg to Hale, April 19, 1865, Hale Papers; W. Hunter to Hale, May 10, 1865, U.S. Department of State, "Diplomatic Instructions, Spain," National Archives.

3. Hale to John R. Varney, July 8, 1865, Hale Papers.

4. Hale to Mason W. Tappan, Aug. 31, 1865, Letterbooks, Hale Papers.

5. Perry to Hale, July 12, 19, 26, Aug. 19, Sept. 10, 16, 1865, Hale Papers.

6. Mrs. Hale to Mrs. A. Lambert, Aug. 6, 1865, Hale to John R. Varney, Aug. 3, Sept. 5, 1865, Hale Papers.

7. Hale to Mrs. Hale, Sept. 20, 25, 1865, Hale Papers.

8. Joseph A. Brandt, *Toward the New Spain* (Chicago, 1932), pp. 33–83; H. Butler Clarke, *Modern Spain, 1815–1898* (Cambridge, Eng., 1906), chs. viii–xii.

9. Hale to Elizabeth Hale, Jan. 12, 1866, Hale Papers.

10. Hale to Charles Sumner, April 9, 1867, Letterbooks, Hale Papers.

11. Hale to Mrs. Hale, Sept. 30, 1865, Hale Papers. Although Hale remained *persona grata* at Isabella's court, a careful examination of all the available materials pertaining to his years in Spain reveals not a shred of evidence to support the allegation in the *Dictionary of American Biography* (VIII, 106) that "the minister was charged with serious moral delinquencies involving the Queen of Spain."

12. Hale to William H. Seward and Hamilton Fish, U.S. Department of State, "Despatches, Spain," 1865–1869, National Archives.

13. French Ensor Chadwick, *The Relations of the United States and Spain: Diplomacy* (New York, 1909).

14. Perry to Hale, Jan. 15, 1861, March 24, 1865, Hale Papers.

15. Hale to Mrs. Hale, Oct. 25, 1865, Hale Papers.

16. Hale to Perry, May 20, 1866 (copy), Perry to Hale, May 20, 1866, Hale Papers.

17. Seward to Hale, Despacho Telegrafico, Dec. 1867, Hale Papers.

18. Hale to Elihu Washburne, March 17, 1868, Hale to James W. Patterson, March 26, 1868, Letterbooks, Hale Papers; Hale to Charles Sumner, Dec. 26, 1867, Feb. 10, 1868, Sumner Papers.

19. Hale to Kinsley, Dec. 10, 1868, Hale to Jacob Ela, Dec. 30, 1868 (copy), Hale to Zachariah Chandler, Feb. 3, 1869, Letterbooks, Hale Papers.

20. Perry to Seward, March 2, 1869, quoted in the *New York Times,* April 10, 1869.

21. Cragin to George G. Fogg, April 4, 1869, Fogg Papers.

22. Hale to T. J. Ryan, March 2, 1869 (copy), Hale Papers. Ryan was the *New York Times'* correspondent in Spain.

23. Hale to [Spanish] Minister of State, April 3, 1869 (copy), Hale to George G. Fogg, April 6, 1869 (copy), Hale Papers. For Hale's letters to the press see his scrapbook of clippings, 1869–1873, Hale Papers.

24. For example, it appears that there had never been a cabinet council, such as Perry described, which discussed Hale's importations. See Hale to Count Nava de Tajo, April 27, 1869 (copy), [Spanish] Minister of State to Hale, April 29, 1869, Hale Papers.

25. *Independent Democrat,* April 15, 1869.

26. Fish to Hale, April 6, May 25, 1869, U.S. Department of State, "Diplomatic Instructions, Spain," Hale to Fish, April 7, May 25 (telegram), 1869, U.S. Department of State, "Despatches, Spain," National Archives. John Hay, once Lincoln's private secretary, replaced Perry as secretary of legation in July 1869.

27. Lucy Hale Chandler, Journal, 1869, Chandler Papers; Franklin McDuffie,

History of Rochester, New Hampshire, from 1722 to 1890, Silvanus Hayward, ed., 2 vols. (Manchester, N.H., 1892), II, 389. The Dover *Morning Star* of June 22, 1870, noted: "Mr. Hale has grown old during his absence. The round, rubicund, radiant face is thin, furrowed and careworn; the once portly form is now spare; the step lacks the old elasticity; there is less humor lurking in the eye and at the corners of the mouth; one observes a slight stoop in the shoulders, as though the added years were beginning to press like a burden."

28. [Dover] *Enquirer,* May 5, June 16, 1870; [Boston] *Journal,* June 16, 1870.

29. See, for example, Hale to Elizabeth Hale Kinsley, Feb. 26, 1871 [misdated 1870], June 17, 1871, Jan. 24, 1872, Hale Papers.

30. Hale to Lucy Hale, Feb. 13, 14, March 26, 1871, Memoranda Book, Jan. 23, 1872, Mrs. Hale to Elizabeth Hale Kinsley, Dec. 31, 1871, June 18, Dec. 24, 1872, Hale to Elizabeth Hale Kinsley, June 17, 1871, Hale Papers.

31. Hale to Elizabeth Hale Kinsley, March 31, 1873, Hale Papers.

32. Mrs. Hale to Elizabeth Hale Kinsley, March 2, 1873, Hale Papers.

33. Mrs. Hale to Elizabeth Hale Kinsley, Aug. 7, 8, 11, 1873, Hale Papers.

34. [Dover] *Enquirer,* Nov. 27, 1873.

INDEX

Abbot, Benjamin, 4
Abolition movement, 84, 105, 130; in
  N.H., 27–35, 59, 64–65; and right of
  petition, 42–47; during Civil War,
  207–213
Adams, Charles Francis, 1, 89–90, 96,
  100, 118, 274; hopes much from Hale,
  85; doubts Hale should accept Liberty
  nomination, 90–91; and Free Soil
  party, 98, 101–104; and Free Demo-
  cratic party, 145–148; guides Hale
  about London, 225; in secession crisis,
  274
Adams, John Quincy, 8, 10–11, 39, 106–
  107; opposes "federal ratio," 40; calls
  Hale's speeches "demagogical," 42; on
  right of petition, 43–44, 47; on annexation of Texas, 48
Adams-Onís Treaty, 47
Allen, Charles B., 157
American Colonization Society, 211
American Society for the Promotion of
  Temperance, 15
Andrew, John, 274
Anthony, Henry B., 197
Atchison, David R., 167
Athenaean Society, 6–7, 12
Atherton, Charles G., 25, 37, 76, 143,
  155, 269; sponsors gag rule, 44; op-
  poses Hale's Texas stand, 54–56, 75
Atwood, John, 143

Badger, George E., 133, 138
Bailey, Gamaliel, 98–99; on Liberty
  party, 88–89; threatened by proslavery mob, 114; lauds Zachary Taylor, 135; and John Brown's raid, 182
Banks, Nathaniel P., 165
Barker, David, Jr., 7, 11

Barnburners, 95–104, 145, 260, 267
Barnes, N. F., 64
Bartlett, Ichabod, 8–9
Beecher, Henry Ward, 151
Bell, James, 158, 160–162
Bell, John, 11, 106
Bell, S. M., 148
Bell, Samuel, 15
Belser, James E., 53
Benjamin, Judah P., 164, 168
Bennett, James G., 183
Benton, Thomas, Hart, 106–108, 125,
  127, 136, 263
Berrien, John M., 263
Berry, Nathaniel, 80–81
Biddle, Nicholas, 21
Bigelow, Francis E., 266
Bird, Francis W., 100
Birney, James G., 28, 88, 104, 150
Blair, Francis P., 170
Blair, Montgomery, 218
Booth, John Wilkes, 222
Borden, Nathaniel, 43
Borland, Solon, 124
Boston Vigilance Committee, 141–142,
  153
Bowdoin College, 5–7
Breckinridge, John, 185
Bright, Jesse, 164, 261
Brinkerhoff, Jacob, 102
Brooks, Preston S., 168–170
Brown, John, raid on Harper's Ferry,
  182–184, 273
Browning, Orville H., 197
Bryant, William C., 260
Buchanan, James, 166, 172–173; favors
  Lecompton Constitution, 174; seeks
  annexation of Cuba, 180; in secession
  crisis, 186; timidity enrages Hale, 187

Bullitt, Alexander C., 125
Burke, Edmund, 24, 26, 44–46; opposes Hale's Texas stand, 51, 54–55
Burlingame, Anson, 169–170, 172, 271
Burns, Anthony, 152, 167
Butler, Andrew P., 124, 139, 164, 168
Butler, Benjamin F., 97, 100–102, 260

Calhoun, John C., 24, 91, 106, 110, 125, 230, 263; on annexation of Texas, 48–50, 53; on Ten Regiment Bill, 109; on Riot Bill, 115–117; and "Southern Address," 122; on Compromise of 1850, 127–130; views attacked by Hale, 129–130
California, statehood for, 121, 125–127, 132, 136
Carr, Samuel W., 12
Carter, Robert, 146
Cartland, Moses, 46–47, 70, 100
Cass, Lewis, 97, 104, 106, 109, 125, 127, 132–133, 158, 164, 264
Chamberlain, Levi, 274
Chandler, William E., 218, 221, 231
Chandler, Zachariah, 164, 197
Chase, Salmon P., 108, 144, 150, 164, 172, 185, 192; and Liberty party, 89, 91, 93, 257; and Free Soil party, 95–98, 100–102, 259; on abolition in the District of Columbia, 118–119; relations with Hale in Senate, 124, 132–133; and Compromise of 1850, 127, 136, 264; and Free Democratic party, 145–148; applauds Hale's speech on Kansas, 176; and John Brown's raid, 182; appointment to cabinet urged by Hale, 188; on Frémont's nomination, 272; on Buchanan's "imbecility," 274
Choate, Rufus, 55, 58, 73, 250
Christie, Daniel, 8–9, 11
Cilley, Joseph, 82
Claggett, William, 54, 63–64, 66, 252
Clark, Daniel, 82, 161, 186, 214–215, 234
Clay, Cassius M., 1–2, 145
Clay, Henry, 21, 49, 125, 133, 139–140, 264; and annexation of Texas, 50; on Compromise of 1850, 126–128, 131–132, 135–136; Shadrach rescue, 141
Clayton, John M., 106–107, 109, 120–121, 125

Cleveland, Charles D., 90
Clingman, Thomas L., 186
Clinton, Henry, 111
Cobb, Howell, 39, 125, 174
Colby, Anthony, 76, 78, 80–84, 158, 179
Collamer, Jacob, 197
Compromise of 1850, 125–136, 140, 143, 145–147
Concord Railroad, 22
Confiscation Act, 211–212
Conscience Whigs, 86, 89–90, 94–95, 98, 100, 155
Constitutional Union Party, 185
Cooper, James, 127
Cooper, James Fenimore, 11
Cornwallis, Charles, 2nd Earl Cornwallis, 111
Corwin, Thomas, 95, 106, 121
Cowan, Edgar, 197
Cragin, Aaron H., 158, 160, 177, 219–220, 229
Crittenden, John J., 106–107, 207–208; compromise plan, 187
Crittenden Compromise, 187
Cram, N. Porter, 61
Creole resolutions, 43
Crawford, William H., 10
Cuba, attempts to annex, 180–181
Curtis, Benjamin R., 173

Dallas, George M., 106, 263
Dana, Richard Henry, Jr., 1, 100, 153; Shadrach rescue trials, 141–142; opposes nomination of Zachary Taylor, 259
Davis, Henry W., 223
Davis, Jefferson, 106, 125, 164; and Riot Bill, 116; on slavery in the territories, 119–120; on Compromise of 1850, 127–128, 132, 136; flogging in navy, 139; Shadrach rescue, 141
Davis, John, 159
Dawson, William C., 133–134, 139
Dayton, William L., 221
Debree, John, 142
Democratic party: splits in N.H., 21–27, 54–82; attacks abolitionism, 31; and right of petition, 42–46; and annexation of Texas, 47–49, 55; ostracizes Hale, 54–57, 66; splits over slavery, 94–97; 1852 campaign, 144–146, 148–

149; split over Kansas-Nebraska Act, 155–157; declines in N.H., 177; breaks up in *1860*, 185; in Civil War Congress, 196; exploits Hale's attacks on Welles, 205; opposes wartime emancipation, 207; *1864* campaign, 213

Dinsmoor, Samuel, 10

District of Columbia: abolition of slavery in, 42, 83–84, 88, 93, 115, 118–119, 211; slave trade in, 88, 122, 126–127, 132, 136; and fugitive slaves, 113–114; during Civil War, 193; *see also* Washington, D.C.

Dix, Dorothea, 194

Dix, John A., 121

Dixon, James, 197, 203

Doolittle, James R., 199–200, 207

Douglas, Stephen A., 39, 106–107, 117, 125, 164, 174, 271; on annexation of Texas, 49; and Compromise of *1850*, 127, 132, 136; drafts Kansas-Nebraska Bill, 154; denounces Lecompton Constitution, 174; and slavery crisis in Kansas, 171, 174–175; Freeport Doctrine, 180; nominated for President, 185

Douglass, Frederick, 100, 148

Dover, N.H., 8, 192, 231–232

Dow, Charles, 163

Downing, Andrew J., 106

Drayton, Daniel, 113–114

Dred Scott decision, 173–176

DuPont, Samuel F., 201

Dyer, Oliver, 100

Early, Jubal, 195

Eastman, Joel, 161

Edwards, Thomas M., 178–179, 219–220

Ela, Jacob, 61, 67, 70–71, 219

Ellis, Charles M., 153

Emerson, Ralph Waldo, 1

English, Chester, 114

English Bill, 176, 179

Erskine, Thomas, 153

Evans, George, 250

Ewing, Thomas, 125

Exeter Academy, 4–5

Fessenden, William P., 196–197, 215

Field, David D., 100, 151

Fillmore, Millard, 133, 135, 139–140, 150

Finney, Charles G., 149

Fish, Hamilton, 39, 229–230

Flanders, George M., 269

Fletcher, Ryland, 182

Fogg, George G., 72, 80–81, 100, 146–147, 161, 176, 218, 224, 234; on Hale-Pierce debate, 74; as editor of *Independent Democrat*, 77, 159–160, 178; elected N.H. Secretary of State, 82; warns Hale against Liberty nomination, 90; friendly to Know-Nothingism, 159–160; elected state printer, 177; promotes Hale's candidacy in *1858*, 178–179; on Cuban annexation, 180; willing to drop Hale, 219; hosts Hale in Switzerland, 225

Foot, Solomon, 206

Foote, Henry S., 124, 230; clashes with Hale on Riot Bill, 116–118; on Compromise of *1850*, 125–126, 127, 132; cordial relations with Hale, 263

Forbes, Hugh, 182–183

Forbes, John M., 204, 277

Forrest, Edwin, 19

Foster, Lafayette, 197

Foster, Stephen S., 29, 31, 35, 57, 247

Fowler, Asa, 274

Fox, Charles James, 111

Fox, Gustavus V., 207, 218, 221, 231, 278

Free Democratic party, 145–150, 267–268

Freedmen's Bureau Bill, 212

Free Soil party, 143, 155; organized, 94–97; Buffalo convention of *1848*, 97–103; decline of, 144; changes name, 267

Free Will Baptists, 31, 34

Frémont, John C., 171–173, 208

French, Henry F., 56, 68, 252

Fugitive Slave Acts, 93, 126, 128, 130, 132, 136, 140–142, 147, 152, 174, 184, 211

"Gag" rule, *see* Right of petition

Garcia, Belle, 195

Gardner, C. K., 26

Garrison, William L., 1–2, 31, 64, 168

Gates, Seth, 43

Gibbs, John T., 27, 56
Giddings, Joshua, 39, 81, 95, 100, 102, 106–107, 118, 172, 249; on right of petition, 43–44; aids N.H. Alliance, 87; on Mexican War, 111; and *Pearl* affair, 114; and Free Democratic party, 145–148; and John Brown's raid, 182
Goodell, William, 93, 148
Goodwin, Ichabod, 67–68, 75, 191
Gove, Charles F., 24
Grant, Ulysses, 213, 228
Gregg, David A., 56
Greeley, Horace, 151, 153, 157, 214
Greene, W. B., 268
Greenough, Horatio, 37
Grimes, James W., 197, 206, 220, 278, 280
Guadalupe Hidalgo, Treaty of, 111–112
Gurowski, Adam, 220

Hale, Elizabeth, 13, 36, 114, 118, 150–152, 224, 228, 231, 233
Hale, John, 3
Hale, Rev. John, 2
Hale, John P., Sr., 3–4
Hale, John Parker: early years, 3–11; in N.H. legislature, 12, 14–17, 78, 81–84; advocates temperance, 15–17, 25; as U.S. District Attorney, 18–19; elected to Congress, 25–27; as U.S. representative, 36–51, 59; breaks from Democratic party, 52–82; first election to U.S. Senate, 82; and Liberty party nomination, 88–96; loses Free Soil nomination to Van Buren, 100–104; second election to U.S. Senate, 158–162; on Sumner-Brooks affair, 168–170; on Kansas crisis, 165–168; 171, 174–176; third election to U.S. Senate, 177–179; opposes Fugitive Slave Act, 140, 184, 211; and secession crisis, 184–190, 274; feuds with Welles, 197–207, 218, 220–221; and wartime emancipation, 207–213; loses Senate seat, 214, 217–220; Minister to Spain, 221–222, 224–230
  appearance, 17, 282; character, 107, 124, 141–142, 159, 230–231; law practice, 7–9, 18–19, 141–142, 150–153; oratorical skill, 17, 71–72, 74,

142, 149, 153–154; political style, 132–133, 181, 195, 197; private life, 13–14, 37–39, 136, 150, 195–196; antislavery beliefs, 28–35, 87–88; relations with slaveholders, 120, 263; attitude toward Negroes, 209–211; on Reconstruction, 223
Hale, Lucy L. (Hale's daughter), 13, 36, 119, 150, 151, 224, 231, 233
Hale, Lucy Lambert (Hale's wife), 13, 36, 38, 82, 112, 127, 134, 136, 150–151, 195, 224–225, 231, 233
Hale, Lydia (Hale's grandmother), 3
Hale, Lydia O'Brien (Hale's mother), 3–4
Hale, Robert, 2
Hale, Salma, 66
Hale, Samuel, 2–3
Hale, Samuel A., 26, 245
Hale, William, 5, 7
Hamlin, E. S., 95, 118, 258
Hamlin, Hannibal, 39, 86, 121, 127, 139, 164, 199
Harrison, William H., 20, 21
Hart, Albert G., 103
Hawthorne, Nathaniel, 6–7, 17
Hayden, Lewis, 141
Hayes, John L., 56, 62, 68–69, 80, 252
Herndon, William, 176
Hibbard, Harry, 61, 82, 155, 156, 269
Higginson, Thomas W., 1, 152
Hill, Isaac, 10, 18, 19, 23, 60, 74, 75–76; leads Conservative Democrats, 22; attacks Hale, 24–27; defends slavery, 30; on annexation of Texas, 47
Hodgdon, John, 6, 12, 41
Hoit, Daniel, 27–28
Holt, John, 153
Houston, Samuel, 125, 263
Howe, Samuel G., 1, 86, 182
Howe, Timothy, 196, 208, 280
Hoyt, Joseph G., 62, 71, 100
Hubbard, Henry, 23–24, 27
Hunt, James M., 215–217
Hunter, Robert M. T., 106, 164

Independent Democrat, establishment of, 69–71
Independent Democratic party (in N.H.): organized, 62–63; efforts to elect Hale, 63–82; alliance with Whigs

and Liberty men, 76–78, 80–87, 92, 142–143
Indian Stream dispute, 19
Ingersoll, Charles J., 49
Isabella II, Queen of Spain, 225–226, 281
Iverson, Alfred, 186

Jackson, Andrew, 10, 11, 18, 39–40, 47–48
Jackson, Thomas J. "Stonewall," 195
Jackson, William, 103
James, Francis, 43
Jay, John, 151, 195
Jenness, Benning W., 82
Johnson, Andrew, 107, 207, 223, 228
Johnson, James H., 57, 67
Johnson, Reverdy, 106, 215
Julian, George W., 124, 147–148, 150

Kansas: slavery crisis in, 163–176; rejects Lecompton Constitution, 176
Kansas-Nebraska Act, 154–160, 163, 174
Keene, Laura, 222
King, Leicester, 94
King, Preston, 39, 97, 100, 186, 250
King, William R., 127
Kinsley, Edward V., 228
Kittredge, George W., 18, 155
Know-Nothing party, 157–162, 164, 177

LaBranche, Alcee, 39
Lamon, Ward, 222
Lane, Charles, 26
Lane, James H., 163
Latham, Milton S., 158
Leavitt, Joshua, 1, 89–90, 100, 111; and right of petition, 43; presses for Hale's nomination, 92–93; objections to Van Buren, 97; and Free Soil party, 101, 103–104; on Free Democratic party, 268
Lecompton Constitution, 173–176, 179
Lee, Robert E., 182, 195
Lemoyne, Francis J., 147
Levy, Uriah P., 151, 265
Lewis, Samuel, 89, 95, 99–100, 103–104, 145, 147
Liberty League, 92–93, 98, 100, 258

Liberty party, 104, 145, 148; in N.H., 27–28, 35, 81–82; backs Hale's Texas stand, 64, 67, 76; prefers Hale as Presidential candidate, 88–92; Buffalo convention of 1847, 92–94; merges with Free Soil party, 98–103
Lincoln, Abraham, 107, 176, 188, 191, 194–195, 199, 220; nominated for President, 185; initial war measures, 191–192; and emancipation, 208; favors colonization of Negroes, 211; relations with Hale, 221–222
Lincoln, Mary, 199
Lisovski, Admiral, 214
Long, J. C., 139
Longfellow, Henry W., 6
Lord, Nathan, 19
Loring, Ellis Gray, 86
Louis-Philippe, King of France, 113
Lovejoy, Elijah P., 114
Lovejoy, Owen, 103
Lyceums, 153–154

McClellan, George B., 212–213
McClelland, Robert, 37–38
McFarland, Asa, 65, 82
Mackintosh, James, 153
McLean, John, 95, 102, 173
Madison, Dolly, 115
Maine Liquor Law, 143
Mangum, Willie P., 106–107, 109
Mann, Horace, 2
Marsh, George P., 278
Marston, Gilman, 193, 219–220, 234
Marston, W. A., 100
Mason, James M., 128, 132, 138–139, 164
Mason, Jeremiah, 3, 8
Mason, John Y., 137
Massachusetts Anti-Slavery Society, 64
Metcalf, Ralph, 158, 160
Mexican War, 83–85, 87–88, 90, 108–109
Morgan, Caroline, 201
Morgan, Edwin D., 221
Morgan, George D., 199–206, 277–278
Morris, Thomas, 108
Missouri Compromise, 154, 159, 171, 173, 189, 271
Morrison, George W., 155–156
Moulton, Mace, 57–67

Nashua & Concord Railroad, 22
Nashua & Lowell Railroad, 21
National Era, 114
Native American party, *see* Know-Nothing party
Navy, United States: home squadron, 41; abolition of flogging in, 137–139; controversy over purchase of Civil War vessels, 199–206
Negroes: N.H. attitude toward, 30; during Civil War, 208; Hale's attitude toward, 209–211
Nesmith, George W., 66, 179
New England Emigrant Aid Company, 167
New Hampshire Anti-Slavery Society, 28
New Hampshire Soldiers' Aid Society, 194
Nicholas, Commodore, 139
Norfolk Navy Yard, surrender of, 200
Norris, Moses, Jr., 26, 44, 46, 51, 55, 57, 67, 78, 155, 269
Noyes, Jefferson, 72

Ordway, Nehemiah, 218, 231
Oregon Bill, 119–121, 123, 130

Packard, Alpheus S., 6
Palfrey, John G., 1, 89, 99, 106, 108, 111, 114, 144, 148, 263
Palmerston, Lord, Hale's opinion of, 225
Panama Conference of *1826,* 52
Parker, John, 3
Parker, Theodore, 1, 86, 108, 132, 153, 168–169, 183; condemns Webster, 129; fugitive slaves, 141; Anthony Burns case, 152–153
Parkman, John, 33–34, 44, 118, 151, 234
Pearl affair, 113–118
Perkins, Jared, 156
Perry, Horatio J., 224, 227–231
Personal Liberty Law, in N.H., 83–84
Peucinian Society, 6–7
Peverly, James, 60, 70, 72, 74, 82
Phillips, Stephen C., 100
Phillips, Wendell, 94, 129, 152
Phillips Exeter Academy, 4–5
Pierce, Andrew, Jr., 247

Pierce, Franklin, 10, 16, 25, 26, 61, 68, 75, 150, 155–156, 164, 198, 230; at Bowdoin College, 6–7; exposes Hale to Jacksonianism, 12; and election of *1840,* 20–21; leads Radical Democrats, 22; on right of petition, 46; punishes Hale's "insubordination," 55–57, 59, 251; debates Hale, 72–73; drags drunks to polls, 77–78; and election of *1852,* 144–145, 148–149; Kansas policy attacked by Hale, 165–168; snubs Hale, 166
Pierce, Thomas W., 247
Pike, James, 158, 160
Pillsbury, Parker, 29, 35
Plumer, William, Jr., 111, 256
Polk, James K., 50, 54, 68–69, 73, 84; *1844* campaign, 48–49; on Mexican War, 109–110

Quincy, Josiah, 153

Railroad issue in N.H., 20–23, 61
Randolph, John, 129
Reding, John R., 26, 44, 46, 51, 59, 251
Reeder, Andrew H., 163, 167
Republican party: organized in N.H., 156–157; *1856* campaign, 172–173; wins control in N.H., 177; victories in *1858* elections, 179; *1860* campaign, 184–185; in secession crisis, 186–187; controls Civil War Congress, 196–197; and emancipation, 207–213; *1864* campaign, 213
Rhett, Robert B., 180
Right of petition, 42–47, 54
Riley, Patrick, 141
Riot Bill, 114–117
Robinson, Charles, 163
Rochester (N.H.) Society for the Suppression of Intemperance, 15
Rollins, Edward H., 218
Romilly, Samuel, 153
Roosevelt, James J., 151
Rogers, Nathaniel P., 29, 35
Ruffin, Edmund, 180
Rusk, Thomas S., 263
Russell, Lord John, 225

Sanborn, Franklin B., 182, 273

Sayres, Edward, 113–114

Scott, Winfield, 108, 111, 144, 148–149, 200

Secession crisis, 185–190

Secret Six, 182

Sedgwick, Theodore, 59, 252

Seward, William H., 125, 135, 139, 164, 170, 172, 185, 188, 221, 226–229, 231, 273; on Compromise of *1850*, 127, 129, 136; and John Brown's raid, 182; in secession crisis, 274

Sherman, William T., 213

Sickles, Daniel E., 230–231

Simpson, Henry Y., 18

Slade, William, 43

Slavery: and the Slave trade, 42, 84, 88, 122, 126–127, 132, 136, 140; in the territories, 83, 93, 112, 119–123, 125–132, 135–136, 154, 163, 167, 169, 173–176, 184; in the District of Columbia, 42, 83–84, 93, 115, 118–119, 211

Slidell, John, 164, 166, 174, 180

Smith, Caleb, 107

Smith, Franklin W., 221

Smith, Gerrit, 98, 147–148; and Liberty party, 92–94, 258

Soulé, Pierre, 136

"Southern Address," 122, 263

Spooner, Lysander, 93

Stanton, Edwin M., 215, 220

Stanton, Henry B., 89, 100, 108; and Liberty party, 92–93; and Free Soil party, 101–104

Starr, Peter, Jr., 150–152

Steele, John, 56–57, 61, 75, 82

Stephens, Alexander, 39, 107, 263

Storrs, George, 32, 133

Stuart, Charles E., 271

Sturge, Joseph, 85

Sumner, Charles, 1, 86, 89, 96, 111, 118, 144, 164, 169, 197, 220; opposes Liberty nomination of Hale, 90; opposes Taylor, 97; praises Hale, 109, 111, 134; and Free Democratic party, 145, 147; caned by Brooks, 168–170; and John Brown's raid, 182; criticized by Hale for vituperation, 184; heads Foreign Relations Committee, 196; on

Reconstruction, 223; on Washington Peace Conference, 274

Taney, Roger B., 173, 175

Tappan, Lewis, 90, 101, 129, 148; urges Hale to accept Liberty nomination, 92–93; and Liberty party, 93, 98–99, 103–104; and Free Soil party, 260

Tappan, Mason W., 156, 158–162, 176–180, 218–219, 234

Taylor, Zachary, 84, 111, 125, 135; Whig candidate, 94, 97, 104; on Compromise of *1850*, 125, 127, 132, 135; Conscience Whigs' objections to, 94, 259

Temperance movement, in N.H., 15–17

Ten Regiment Bill, 109–111

Test Act, in N.H., 158

Texas, annexation of, 47–51, 73–75, 83–84, 87; boundary dispute, 126, 132, 136

Thirteenth Amendment, 212–213

Thompson, George, 29

Thompson, Jacob, 174

Thoreau, Henry, 153, 183

Tilden, Samuel J., 100

Toombs, Robert, 107, 164

Trist, Nicholas, 109, 111–112

Trumbull, Lyman, 170, 186, 197, 216–217

Tuck, Amos, 80, 91, 107, 143, 146, 156, 178–179, 219–220, 274–275; and right of petition, 44–45; on annexation of Texas, 54; supports Hale's break from Democrats, 56, 60–62, 67, 71, 77, 81, 252; elected to Congress, 87, 256; on Liberty party, 90, 92

Tyler, John, 24, 26, 37; and annexation of Texas, 47, 49, 69

Underwood, Francis, 1

Upham, Nathaniel G., 18

Upshur, Abel P., 48, 53, 110

Van Buren, John, 97

Van Buren, Martin, 20, 21, 52, 57, 73, 149–150, 189, 260; and annexation of Texas, 47–48; Free Soil nomination, 95, 97–104; backs Pierce in *1852*, 145

Varney, John R., 224, 280

Wade, Benjamin, 164, 181, 186, 197, 223
Wakarusa War, 163
Walker, Lyman, 24
Walker, Robert J., 47
Washburne, Elihu, 173
Washington, D.C., 113–114; Hale's impressions of, 36–38; description of, in *1847*, 105–106; during Civil War, 193; *see also* District of Columbia
Washington Peace Conference, 188–189, 274–275
Webster, Daniel, 3, 8, 21, 47, 106, 125, 133, 135; views attacked by Hale, 130, 133; on Compromise of *1850*, 127–129, 130, 132, 264
Weed, Thurlow, 148
Weld, Theodore, 43
Welles, Gideon, 192, 231, 278; early relations with Hale, 193; quarrels with Hale, 197–207, 216, 218, 220–222
Wells, John S., 156, 179, 269
Westcott, James D., 116, 263
Wetmore, Nathaniel D., 69
Wetmore, Robert C., 69–71, 77
Whig party: *1840* campaign, 20–21; and right of petition, 43; and annexation of Texas, 47, 49–50; alliance with Independent Democrats in N.H., 59, 63–67, 86–87, 142–143; splits on slavery issue, 94–97; and Mexican War, 110–111; *1852* campaign, 144–146, 148–149

Whitman, Walt, 148
Whittier, John G., 46, 70, 97, 109; mobbed in Concord, N.H., 29; praises Hale's Texas stand, 64–65; celebrates Hale's triumph in verse, 78–80; and Liberty party, 89, 91–92, 258–259
Wigfall, Louis T., 186
Wiggins, John H., 34, 36
Wilyes, John, 111
Wilkins, Frederick (Shadrach), 140–142, 266
Willey, Austin, 90, 146–147
Williams, Jared, 78, 81, 155, 269
Wilmot, David, 85, 88, 106–107, 172
Wilmot Proviso, 88, 90–91, 112, 121, 127–130; 263
Wilson, Henry, 1, 147–148, 158, 169, 170, 172, 196, 203, 212, 273
Wilson, James, 87, 256
Winthrop, Robert C., 39, 49–50, 127
Wise, Henry, 36
Woodbury, John, 57, 62, 67–69, 75–78
Woodbury, Levi, 10, 25, 52, 56, 57, 82; befriends Hale, 37; denounces Hale's Texas stand, 54–55, 75
Woodman, Charles W., 19
Woodman, Jeremiah H., 8–9, 11
Woolsey, Theodore D., 105
Workingmen's party, 12
Wright, Silas, 90–92

Yale College, 105
Yancey, William L., 180
Young, Aaron, 217
Yulee, David L., 139